Ethical Speculations in Contemporary British Theatre

Ethical Speculations in Contemporary British Theatre

Edited by

Mireia Aragay

and

Enric Monforte

palgrave
macmillan

First published 2014 by
PALGRAVE MACMILLAN

Palgrave Macmillan in the UK is an imprint of Macmillan Publishers Limited,
registered in England, company number 785998, of Houndmills, Basingstoke,
Hampshire RG21 6XS.

Palgrave Macmillan in the US is a division of St Martin's Press LLC,
175 Fifth Avenue, New York, NY 10010.

Palgrave Macmillan is the global academic imprint of the above companies
and has companies and representatives throughout the world.

Palgrave® and Macmillan® are registered trademarks in the United States,
the United Kingdom, Europe and other countries.

ISBN 978–1–137–29756–3

This book is printed on paper suitable for recycling and made from fully
managed and sustained forest sources. Logging, pulping and manufacturing
processes are expected to conform to the environmental regulations of the
country of origin.

A catalogue record for this book is available from the British Library.

A catalog record for this book is available from the Library of Congress.

Typeset by MPS Limited, Chennai, India.

To our families

Contents

Foreword

Aleks Sierz

Like any other audience member, the Critic sets out for the theatre accompanied by mild anxiety. Will the tube and bus deliver him in good time? Is he in the mood for this slice of naturalism? Will he be able to do justice to the show within the slender word limit allocated to him? This time, he arrives early, lingers outside the theatre and dreams for a moment of lighting up a cigarette, although he has long since given up smoking. He greets his colleagues and participates in a few desultory conversations about the hot topics of the day. The bell rings, and the first-night audience troops in. At the interval, the Critic avoids the scrum at the bar, and tries to focus on his notes, which have been scribbled in the dark and are, in parts, barely legible. In his mind, he begins to frame the opening of his review. Then he returns for the second half. At the end, after the applause, in which the Critic politely joins in, he makes a rush for the exit, aided by the fact that he has an aisle seat and motivated by the deadline he has to meet. He rushes home, maybe hailing a cab outside the theatre. He bursts into his house, and boots up his computer. Then he gets to work.

Amid all of these kinds of quotidian concerns, where is our ethical sensibility most acutely engaged? The Critic has been part of a crowd watching a show, a public witnessing which is an innately political and ethical act. Wherever it comes from, our sense of ethics is a constant companion, which perhaps tugs hardest at our sleeve during moments of crisis. In *Hamlet*, the Prince of Denmark's soliloquy in Act Three, Scene 1 – arguably the most famous speech in all theatre history – is a good example. Hamlet starts off with one of the handful of fundamental questions: to be or not to be? Then he outlines some ethical choices: is it better to suffer 'the slings and arrows of outrageous fortune' or to take action to end such troubles? Should he kill the king, or kill himself? How much humiliation can a person take? In this scene, Hamlet shows how ethical reflections can sometimes 'make cowards of us all' (Shakespeare, 1994, pp. 239, 241). Perhaps. But, equally, ethical reasoning can be a spur to action.

The following chapters explore ethical questions in a variety of plays and contexts. The unique quality of theatre as a forum for the face-to-face interaction between whatever is happening on stage and the collective being of the audience is what makes ethics such a political concern.

We may muse in private on Hamlet's problems, but it is in public that we witness them in performance. The big questions of traditional ethics are: how do you define the good life? How should you behave to your fellow men and women? What does it mean to be true to yourself? In the postwar era, after the twin shocks of the Holocaust and the Atom Bomb, these questions have been clarified by a range of philosophers, among whom Emmanuel Levinas has been predominant, and the greatest inspiration. Yet the quest today is surely not to find definitive answers, but rather to explore better questions. Which reminds me of De Sade's haunting lines at the end of Peter Weiss's *Marat/Sade* (1964), which could easily be a manifesto for all intellectual adventures in ethics:

> Our play's chief aim has been to take to bits
> great propositions and their opposites
> see how they work then let them fight it out
> The point   Some light on our eternal doubt
> I have twisted and turned them every way
> and find no ending to our play [. . .]
> So for me the last word can never be spoken
> I am left with a question that is always open.

(1966, pp. 106–7)

This is an apt epigraph for this excellent book, which is edited by Mireia Aragay and Enric Monforte, members of Contemporary British Theatre Barcelona, a research group whose main field of inquiry is the great explosion of theatrical energy and creativity that has, since the mid-1990s, widened the parameters of British theatre (http://www.ub.edu/cbtbarcelona/). Based at the University of Barcelona, since the early 2000s the group has been engaged in a series of three-year research projects, the first of which, supported by the Spanish Ministry of Science and Education (BFF2002-00257), gave rise to the publication of *British Theatre of the 1990s: Interviews with Directors, Playwrights, Critics and Academics* (Palgrave Macmillan, 2007). The present volume emerges out of the group's second project, 'The representation of politics and the politics of representation in post-1990 British drama and theatre' (FFI2009-07598), funded by the Spanish Ministry of Science and Innovation, and it signals the group's shift from a focus on politics to a greater concern with ethics, which is confirmed in the title of the group's current project, 'Ethical issues in contemporary British theatre since 1989: globalization, theatricality, spectatorship' (FFI2012-31842), supported by the Spanish Ministry of Economy and Competitiveness. As the Critic hurries out to see another show, he remembers to slip his copy of this book into his pocket. Reading its chapters is a good way of sharpening his ethical sense.

London, May 2013

Works cited

Shakespeare, W. (1994) *Hamlet*, ed. G.R. Hibbard (Oxford: Oxford University Press).
Weiss, P. (1966) *The Persecution and Assassination of Marat as Performed by the Inmates of the Asylum of Charenton under the Direction of the Marquis de Sade* (London: Calder and Boyars).

Acknowledgements

Research towards this book was supported by the research projects 'The representation of politics and the politics of representation in post-1990 British drama and theatre' (FFI2009-07598), funded by the Spanish Ministry of Science and Innovation, and 'Ethical issues in contemporary British theatre since 1989: globalization, theatricality, spectatorship' (FFI2012-31842), funded by the Spanish Ministry of Economy and Competitiveness. We would like to extend our gratitude to Paula Kennedy, Ben Doyle, Sacha Lake and Peter Cary at Palgrave Macmillan for their generous care and unfailing commitment through the publication process of this book. Thanks also to the anonymous readers of the manuscript for their thoughtful, encouraging feedback. Our special gratitude goes to Pilar Zozaya, Emeritus Professor of English Literature and Theatre Studies at the University of Barcelona, who was the first to teach contemporary British theatre in the Department of English and German over 30 years ago, infected us with her passion for the subject, and has provided invaluable support, both moral and material, throughout the gestation of this volume. We are also very grateful to Aleks Sierz for his support and for taking the time to write the Foreword. Last but not least, we wish to thank our contributors for their immense generosity, intellectual rigour and enthusiasm for the subject. It has been a great pleasure working with them all.

Notes on Contributors

Vicky Angelaki is Lecturer in Drama at the University of Birmingham. Her research is internationalist in its scope, with a specialism in modern and contemporary British and European theatre, translation, adaptation, spectatorship and citizenship, aesthetics and politics, as well as performance, critical/cultural theories and philosophy, with a focus on phenomenology. Major publications include *The Plays of Martin Crimp: Making Theatre Strange* (2012) and *Contemporary British Theatre: Breaking New Ground* (2013).

Mireia Aragay is Senior Lecturer (accredited as Full Professor) in English Literature and Theatre Studies at the University of Barcelona, and Life Fellow of Clare Hall, University of Cambridge. Her research interests focus on Harold Pinter and contemporary British theatre, film adaptations of literary classics, Shakespeare and critical theory. She has edited *Books in Motion: Adaptation, Intertextuality, Authorship* (2005) and co-edited (with Hildegard Klein, Enric Monforte and Pilar Zozaya) *British Theatre of the 1990s: Interviews with Directors, Playwrights, Critics and Academics* (2007). She was Principal Investigator of 'The representation of politics and the politics of representation in post-1990 British drama and theatre', a three-year research project funded by the Spanish Ministry of Science and Innovation (FFI2009-07598) and is currently Principal Investigator of 'Ethical issues in contemporary British theatre since 1989: globalization, theatricality, spectatorship', funded by the Spanish Ministry of Economy and Competitiveness (FFI2012-31842).

Clara Escoda teaches drama and English literature at the University of Barcelona. She is the author of *Martin Crimp's Theatre: Collapse as Resistance to Late Capitalist Society* (2013). She has also published articles on Martin Crimp and the ethics of testimony and witnessing in *Ariel*, *New Theatre Quarterly* and *Platform*. She is a member of 'Ethical issues in contemporary British theatre since 1989: globalization, theatricality, spectatorship', a three-year research project funded by the Spanish Ministry of Economy and Competitiveness (FFI2012-31842).

Martin Middeke is Chair of English Literature at the University of Augsburg, and Visiting Professor of English at the University of Johannesburg. He is co-editor of *The Methuen Drama Guide to Contemporary*

Irish Playwrights (with Peter Paul Schnierer, 2010), *The Methuen Drama Guide to Contemporary British Playwrights* (with Peter Paul Schnierer and Aleks Sierz, 2011) and *The Methuen Drama Guide to Contemporary American Playwrights* (with Peter Paul Schnierer, Christopher Innes and Matthew C. Roudané, 2013), and of *The Literature of Melancholia: Early Modern to Postmodern* (with Christina Wald, 2011). He is co-editor of *Anglia: Journal of English Literature* and editor in chief of *JCDE: Journal of Contemporary Drama in English*. Forthcoming publications include *Theory Matters: The Place of Theory in Literary and Cultural Studies Today* and *The Methuen Drama Guide to Contemporary South African Drama*. He is a member of 'Ethical issues in contemporary British theatre since 1989: globalization, theatricality, spectatorship', a three-year research project funded by the Spanish Ministry of Economy and Competitiveness (FFI2012-31842).

Enric Monforte is Senior Lecturer in English Literature and Theatre Studies in the Department of English and German, University of Barcelona. He specializes in Caryl Churchill and contemporary British theatre, film studies and critical theory, with a special focus on gender and sexuality. He has published *Gender, Politics, Subjectivity: Reading Caryl Churchill* (2001) as well as studies on other contemporary British playwrights. He has co-edited (with Mireia Aragay, Hildegard Klein and Pilar Zozaya) *British Theatre of the 1990s: Interviews with Directors, Playwrights, Critics and Academics* (2007). He is a member of 'Ethical issues in contemporary British theatre since 1989: globalization, theatricality, spectatorship', a three-year research project funded by the Spanish Ministry of Economy and Competitiveness (FFI2012-31842).

Dan Rebellato is Professor of Contemporary Theatre at Royal Holloway, University of London, where he teaches theatre, philosophy and creative writing. He has published *1956 and All That* (1999), *Theatre & Globalization* (2009), *Contemporary European Theatre Directors* (co-edited with Maria Delgado, 2010), *Modern British Playwriting: 2000–2009: Voices, Documents, New Interpretations* (2013) and *The Suspect Culture Book* (co-edited with Graham Eatough, 2013), as well as numerous articles on contemporary theatre, playwriting, and theatre and philosophy. He is also a playwright and his plays and performance texts for stage and radio include *Whistleblower, Chekhov in Hell, Static, My Life Is a Series of People Saying Goodbye, Mile End, Beachy Head, Cavalry, Outright Terror Bold and Brilliant, Negative Signs of Progress* and *Theatremorphosis*.

Graham Saunders is Reader in Theatre Studies at the University of Reading. He is author of *'Love me or Kill me': Sarah Kane and the Theatre* *of Extremes* (2002), *Patrick Marber's Closer* (2008), and *About Kane: The Playwright and the Work* (2009) and co-editor of *Cool Britannia: Political Theatre in the 1990s* (with Rebecca D'Monté, 2008) and *Sarah Kane in Context* (with Laurens de Vos, 2010). He is Principal Investigator for the five-year AHRC-funded project '"Giving a Voice to the Nation": the Arts Council of Great Britain and the Development of Theatre and Performance in Britain 1945–1994' and co-investigator on the three-year AHRC-funded project 'Staging Beckett: The Impact of Productions of Samuel Beckett's Drama on Theatre Practice and Cultures in the United Kingdom and Ireland'. He has contributed articles to *Modern Drama*, *Journal of Beckett Studies*, *Contemporary Theatre Review*, *Theatre Research International*, *New Theatre Quarterly* and *Studies in Theatre and Performance*.

Christiane Schlote teaches drama and postcolonial literatures and cultures at the University of Zurich. She has published extensively on postcolonial and transnational literatures, British Asian theatre, post-colonial cityscapes, Anglophone Arab writing, war and commemoration and Latina/o American and Asian American culture. She is the author of *Bridging Cultures: Latino- und asiatisch-amerikanisches Theater in New York* (1997) and co-editor of *New Beginnings in Twentieth-Century Theatre and Drama* (with Peter Zenzinger, 2003) and *Constructing Media Reality: The New Documentarism* (with Eckart Voigts-Virchow, 2008). She is currently editing the manuscript for a book on transnationalism in British Asian and South Asian American drama and fiction and co-editing *Representations of War, Migration and Refugeehood: Interdisciplinary Perspectives* (with Daniel Rellstab) and a study on literature from the Middle East and its diasporas.

Hanna Scolnicov is Professor Emerita of Theatre Studies at Tel-Aviv University and Life Fellow of Clare Hall, University of Cambridge. She is the author of *Experiments in Stage Satire* (1987) and *Woman's Theatrical Space* (1994) and co-editor, with Peter Holland, of *The Play Out of Context: Transferring Plays from Culture to Culture* (1989) and *Reading Plays: Interpretation and Reception* (1991). Among her publications are over sixty essays, in English and Hebrew, on Elizabethan theatre, inter-textuality, Shakespeare, Stoppard and Pinter, among other topics. She has taught as Visiting Professor at universities in North Carolina, Rome, Beijing, Venice and Cagliari. Her book *The Experimental Plays of Harold Pinter* was published in 2012.

Aleks Sierz FRSA is Senior Research Fellow at Rose Bruford College, and author of *In-Yer-Face Theatre: British Drama Today* (2001), *The Theatre of*

Martin Crimp (2006), *John Osborne's Look Back in Anger* (2008), *Rewriting the Nation: British Theatre Today* (2011) and *Modern British Playwriting: The 1990s* (2012). He is editor of *The Methuen Drama Book of 21st Century British Plays* (2010) and co-editor of *The Methuen Drama Guide to Contemporary British Playwrights* (with Martin Middeke and Peter Paul Schnierer, 2011). He also works as a journalist, broadcaster, lecturer and theatre critic. He is a member of 'Ethical issues in contemporary British theatre since 1989: globalization, theatricality, spectatorship', a three-year research project funded by the Spanish Ministry of Economy and Competitiveness (FFI2012-31842).

Mark Taylor-Batty is Senior Lecturer in Theatre Studies at the Workshop Theatre, University of Leeds. He is co-author, with Juliette Taylor-Batty, of *Samuel Beckett's Waiting for Godot* (2008) and has authored two books on Harold Pinter's writings, *Writers and their Work: Harold Pinter* (2001) and *About Pinter* (2005). He is editor for Methuen Drama's new Engage series of books on theatre practitioners and movements, and co-editor of *Performing Ethos*, a journal that publishes work on matters of ethics and performance.

Clare Wallace is an Associate Professor in the Department of Anglophone Literatures and Cultures at Charles University, Prague and also teaches at the University of New York in Prague. She is author of *Suspect Cultures: Narrative, Identity & Citation in 1990s New Drama* (2006) and *The Theatre of David Greig* (2013), and has edited various other volumes including *Monologues: Theatre, Performance, Subjectivity* (2006) and *Stewart Parker Television Plays* (2008), and co-edited *Cosmotopia: Transnational Identities in the Work of David Greig* (with Anja Müller, 2011).

1
To Begin to Speculate: Theatre Studies, Ethics and Spectatorship

Mireia Aragay

In January 2011, *Small Hours*, written by Lucy Kirkwood and Ed Hime and directed by Katie Mitchell, was staged in the Michael Frayn downstairs studio space at the Hampstead Theatre. It is a solo piece, about one hour long, with very few spoken words, where an insomniac young woman (Sandy McDade in the Hampstead production) struggles through the small hours of the night – hoovering her sofa, playing CDs at full volume, watching late-night shopping channels, listening to music on headphones, trying to book a cinema ticket, phoning her partner, wrestling with the answer machine, attempting to dance – while her new-born baby cries disconsolately in another room. Although the woman does go out twice to see to the baby, and returns once with a dirty nappy, mostly her reaction is to drown the wailing in a cacophony of other sounds and noises. The Hampstead studio space was turned by designer Alex Eales into a living-room and spectators – 25 per performance only – were first asked to take off their shoes and then invited to take seats on the chairs, sofas, armchairs and benches arranged around the edges of the room in a row just one person deep. The effect on spectators of the installation-like set and seating arrangement has been discussed in terms of intimacy by Mitchell herself – you were certainly close enough to the woman at times 'to touch her, smell the perfume she sprays in the room and hear the tiny tap of plastic on wood as she puts the mascara down on her side table' (Mitchell, 2011) – and of complete sensory immersion on the *A Younger Theatre* website (Orr, 2011) and the *There Ought to Be Clowns* blog (2011). While active participation on the part of audience members was not encouraged at all, and in fact the woman never as much as acknowledged their presence, the show's impact was inseparable from the closely shared space between actress and audience, their co-presence in the small, windowless Hampstead studio-turned-living-room.

Small Hours raises a number of questions that have become central to recent discussions of the relationship between theatre and ethics. What is the function of theatre in a media-saturated culture like ours, where representations of violence, pain and vulnerability are almost automatically considered suspect as obscuring rather than enabling access to the realities of human suffering and precariousness? Does theatre, perhaps, occupy some kind of privileged cultural position in this connection, given the way in which it brings vulnerable human bodies together in one single space – its emphasis on co-presence, which was foregrounded in *Small Hours*? Does that guarantee theatre's potential for ethical solicitation, its capacity to transform spectators from (supposedly) passive voyeurs or consumers of images into actively engaged witnesses? Do experimental forms of theatre such as *Small Hours* offer a particular intensity in terms of audience address and ethical awakening? Crucially, what is the role of spectators in all this, given that the relationship with the audience constitutes the core of whichever ethical significance a theatre event may have?

In the case of *Small Hours*, such questions acquired a further twist given the institutional context in which the play was produced. When Edward Hall became Artistic Director of the Hampstead Theatre, he took a policy decision to use the downstairs studio as an experimental space for new plays. Critics were welcome to attend the show, but were not allowed to review it.[1] This circumstance stirred controversy, with some arguing that it was ethically questionable for a theatre to bar professional reviewers while the play was freely discussed on websites and blogs, not to mention Facebook or Twitter (Gardner, 2011; see also Sierz, 2011).[2] This turns *Small Hours* into an interesting case where the standard practice in theatre studies of focusing on the response of published reviewers is simply not possible, as all that remains as a record of the production are the reactions of 'ordinary' audience members on cyberspace – which brings to mind Helen Freshwater's insightful exploration of some of the reasons for the resistance on the part of theatre studies to engage with detailed observations of actual audience member's responses, instead of relying exclusively on the opinion of professional reviewers (2009, pp. 27–55). At the same time, the generally restricted possibilities of access to the production – as already noted, it played to audiences of 25 at a time, and was sold out both in the initial run (12 January–5 February 2011) and when it was extended – raised questions about how to assess the significance, ethical or otherwise, of a show that was only seen by a very tiny minority. How 'ordinary', after all, were the spectators who attended performances of *Small Hours*? Beginning to provide answers to such questions would require, as Freshwater suggests, extended and detailed research into real audiences; what is of interest in the present context is that, ultimately, the debate surrounding the Hampstead studio production of *Small Hours* brings us back once more to the question of spectatorship and spectator response, arguably the centrepiece around which questions of theatre and ethics hinge.

Comparatively speaking, the academic field of theatre studies has been a latecomer to what has come to be perceived as an 'ethical turn', the renewal of interest in ethical issues that has gathered force within the humanities in general and literary studies in particular since the mid- to late 1980s. The publication in 1983 of a pioneering special issue of *New Literary History* on 'Literature and/as Moral Philosophy' was followed by a spate of monographs and essay collections, not to mention scholarly articles, focusing on explorations of the interface of ethics with fiction and, to a lesser extent, poetry. To name only a few, J. Hillis Miller's *The Ethics of Reading* (1987), Adam Zachary Newton's *Narrative Ethics* (1995), Robert Eaglestone's *Ethical Criticism: Reading After Levinas* (1997), Andrew Gibson's *Postmodernity, Ethics and the Novel: From Leavis to Levinas* (1999), Jill Robbins's *Altered Reading: Levinas and Literature* (1999), Derek Attridge's *The Singularity of Literature* (2004b), and *The Ethical Component in Experimental British Fiction since the 1960s* (2007) and *Ethics and Trauma in Contemporary British Fiction* (2011), both jointly edited by Susana Onega and Jean-Michel Ganteau, collectively testify to the burgeoning of interest in the question of ethics and literature, as does the publication in 2004 of a special issue of *Poetics Today* on 'Literature and Ethics'.

In contrast, it is not until the late 2000s that a turn to ethics becomes apparent in theatre studies. In 2009, Nicholas Ridout was able to describe his 'Theatre &' monograph on *Theatre & Ethics* as the first to address 'the topic of theatre and ethics [. . .] directly in a single volume in English' (p. 71). The same year saw the publication of Helena Grehan's *Performance, Ethics and Spectatorship in a Global Age*. The collection *Ethical Encounters: Boundaries of Theatre, Performance and Philosophy*, edited by Daniel Meyer-Dinkgräfe and Daniel Watt, came out in 2010, which was also the year when the journal *Performing Ethos: An International Journal of Theatre and Performance* brought out its first issue, while *A Life of Ethics and Performance*, edited by John Matthews and David Torevell, was published in 2011.[3] This relative belatedness seems rather surprising, particularly perhaps given the fact that, as is apparent in some of the titles listed earlier, the resurgence of ethics has been informed by a turn to the work of Emmanuel Levinas, commonly agreed to have made a decisive contribution to reconfiguring the foundations of Western ethical philosophy in the wake of the experience of the Holocaust. In his 'Adieu' to Levinas, originally delivered upon the philosopher's death in Paris in 1995, Jacques Derrida leaves no doubt about the 'discreet but irreversible mutation' ultimately amounting to a 'historical shock wave' (1999, p. 12) brought about by Levinas's work – according to Derrida, it changed the course of philosophical reflection and reordered it according to 'another thought of ethics, another thought of the other, a thought that is newer than so many novelties because it is ordered according to the absolute anteriority of the face of the Other' (1999, p. 4).[4]

It is precisely the centrality of the Other to Levinas's pre-ontological ethical thought that makes it intuitively highly pertinent to the theatre situation, offering as it does the possibility of developing 'a model of performance as an ethical encounter, in which we come face to face with the other, in a recognition of our mutual vulnerability which encourages relationships based on openness, dialogue and respect for difference' (Ridout, 2009, p. 54). Similarly, Grehan is drawn to Levinas's philosophy because of its focus on the subject's responsibility for the Other – by engaging with Levinas's ideas, she writes, 'I wanted to try to understand and describe the responses of theatre spectators and also to think about what spectators might do with their responses once they leave the theatre' (2009, p. 6). And although Hans-Thies Lehmann mentions Levinas only once and almost in passing in *Postdramatic Theatre* (2006, p. 148), there seems little doubt that his 'aesthetic of response-ability', involving as it does an ethico-political '*mutual implication of actors and spectators in the theatrical production of images*' (2006, pp. 185–6; emphasis original), is informed by a Levinasian focus on the call of the Other, the 'interruption', as the foundation of the ethical relationship, as that which the subject has no option but to respond to and take responsibility for.[5]

Levinas's thought, thus, has an undoubted appeal for theatre studies, as it offers philosophical sustenance for a widely shared faith, as Freshwater puts it, in 'theatre's potential to be educative and empowering, to enable critical and ethical engagement, to awaken a sense of social responsibility, or to raise an audience's sense of its own political agency' (2009, p. 55). Theatre and performance may even appear, from a Levinasian perspective, as privileged cultural practices as regards the exploration of ethical issues since they seem to be based, almost literally, on co-presence, on the face-to-face encounter between embodied, vulnerable spectators and Others wherein the former are summoned to respond, to become actively engaged in an exemplary exercise of ethical 'response-ability'. Extending Shoshana Felman and Dori Laub's classic formulation of what is involved in the act of witnessing to encompass the theatre situation, spectators may be said to become 'double witnesses' (1992, p. 58), both to the theatre or performance piece as a mode of address inscribing within itself a 'you', an active receiver whose subjective change is enabled by his/her witnessing, and to their own process of subjective transformation. In the words of Peggy Phelan, whose work on performance is inflected by both Levinas's thought and Felman and Laub's explorations of witnessing, '[i]f Levinas is right, and the face-to-face encounter is the most crucial arena in which the ethical bond we share becomes manifest, then live theatre and performance might speak to philosophy with renewed vigor', as they turn spectators into witnesses of 'what [they] did not (and perhaps cannot) see' (2004, p. 577). It is thus that spectators enter the 'ethical frame' (Keefe, 2010).

Over the last few years, then, Levinas has inspired numerous groundbreaking explorations in theatre and ethics. However, two difficulties underlie the preceding brief presentation of the way in which the Levinasian reconfiguration of ethics has shaped recent work in theatre and performance studies. Firstly, and as has often been noted (see Eaglestone, 1997, pp. 98–128; Grehan, 2009, pp. 25–34; Ridout, 2009, pp. 55–6), given Levinas's profound suspicion of aesthetic representation, invoking his thought in order to discuss any form of art can never be a straightforward matter. Secondly, the assumption that spectators are passive and that therefore theatre's mission is to awaken them or make them active – one of the 'key concepts of ethical thought about theatre and performance' according to Ridout (2009, p. 59) – is problematic and has recently been interrogated, most cogently perhaps by Jacques Rancière. As will hopefully become apparent in what follows, the two difficulties are connected in important ways.

Levinas's suspicion of art and aesthetic representation is most forcefully articulated in his early work, up to and including *Totality and Infinity*, originally published in 1961. 'Reality and its Shadow', first published in 1948, is a key piece in this connection. In this essay, Levinas denounces the 'hypertrophy of art' (Levinas 1989b, p. 142), its being in his view overrated through its identification with transcendence, with the 'spiritual life' (1989b, p. 142) and the 'order of revelation' (1989b, p. 132). In fact, he argues, every act of artistic representation is a challenge to ethics and hence to transcendence, since it displaces the centrality of presence, of the face-to-face encounter with the Other that is the primeval foundation of ethics. Art, therefore, brings into the world 'obscurity' – it 'obscures being in images' (1989b, p. 142) – and 'irresponsibility' (1989b, p. 141) – '[t]he world to be built is replaced by [. . .] its shadow. [. . .] There is something wicked and egoist and cowardly in artistic enjoyment' (1989b, p. 142). Levinas pursues this line of thought in *Totality and Infinity*, where he insists that language can only be truly ethical and therefore aspire to transcendence if it is supported by the face, by the presence of the Other. Literature, as written language, is predicated on the absence of the face and hence, like all art, it is at best a plaything and at worst, an evasion from ethical responsibility. As Eaglestone aptly concludes, pinpointing the fundamental faultline in Levinas's thought about language, representation and art, '[l]anguage, in *Totality and Infinity*, seems to mean something other than language: it means presence, and not representation' (1997, p. 124).

As a way out of the conundrum and a means of recuperating Levinas for the study of ethics in theatre and performance, Ridout (2009, pp. 66–70) seems to rely on Levinas's insistence on the radical strangeness or unassimilability of the encounter with the face of the Other – it is 'the experience of something absolutely foreign, a pure "knowledge" or "experience", a traumatism of astonishment' (Levinas qtd. in Eaglestone, 1997, p. 121) – in order to argue, not unlike others before him, that the ethical force of an aesthetic production, its capacity to challenge the spectator's ethical framework, is not manifest at the level of theme, that is, of the representation of ethically charged characters or plots. Rather, it takes place at the level of form – when the form is truly 'absolutely foreign', it produces the Levinasian 'traumatism of astonishment' through placing spectators face-to-face with a radical alterity and singularity, an absolute otherness, which requires that they 'responsively/responsibly participat[e] in its co-creation' (Eskin, 2004, p. 567).[6] Formal innovation or experimentation thus becomes the cornerstone for the spectator's ethical engagement, the site from which 'a challenge from the place of the other' can truly be issued (Ridout, 2009, p. 68), and 'in Levinas' apparent condemnation of art and the artistic [as an obscuring of being in images] lies the very ground of its ethical potential' (Ridout, 2009, p. 69) – its potential, that is, to awaken the spectator's capacity for ethical reflection.

It is hardly surprising, in consequence, that many recent explorations of contemporary theatre and ethics have tended to privilege the most experimental kinds of performance, which are assumed to be capable of engaging audiences 'emotionally, viscerally and intellectually' (Grehan, 2009, p. 2) in a media-saturated world where we are, most of the time, cast in the role of passive spectators, immersed in what Guy Debord (1983) called 'the spectacle', consuming endlessly reproduced images – particularly of human-inflicted or endured suffering, pain or violence – that preclude our ethical response through being distanced from us (Lehmann, 2006, pp. 183–4). Thus Lehmann's 'namedropping' for postdramatic theatre includes, among many others, Goat Island, The Wooster Group, DV8 Physical Theatre, Forced Entertainment, La Fura dels Baus, Complicite or Socìetas Raffaello Sanzio (2006, p. 24); Grehan (2009) explores work by, again, Socìetas Raffaello Sanzio, as well as Australian Black Swan Theatre's *The Career Highlights of the MAMU* (2002), Ariane Mnouchkine's Théâtre du Soleil's *Le Dernier Caravansérail* (2003) and Ong Keng Sen's TheatreWorks' *Sandakan Threnody* (2004), among others; while Ridout's examples of work that makes 'the audience actively aware of their own participation in the event rather than a passive recipient of media saturation' (2009, p. 58) includes the performances of Lebanese artist Walid Raad, Marina Abramović's installations, Maria Donata D'Urso's dance performances and, again, Goat Island (2009, pp. 58–68). In contrast, Freshwater sets out in *Theatre & Audience* to question 'one of the most cherished orthodoxies in theatre studies' (2009, p. 3), namely the belief in an immanent connection between audience participation and ethical and political empowerment, as being based on a distrust or outright dismissal of the capacity of spectators to think for themselves. Ultimately, however, she also shows a preference for experimental performance work, albeit by companies like the London-based Blast Theory or recent work by Forced Entertainment, which show an awareness of the limitations of participation – where does participation end and coercion and manipulation begin? – and no longer seem 'frustrated with or suspicious of [audiences]' (Freshwater, 2009, p. 72). To borrow Ridout's Levinasian formulation, in the experimental work of all of these performers and companies 'presence matters' (2009, p. 64). It seems to be perceived as that which unlocks the impasse created by Levinas's suspicion of representation – and, simultaneously, disrupts the Debordian 'régime of the spectacle' – and can guarantee that 'the aesthetic will be a pathway towards the fully ethical' (Ridout, 2009, p. 65).

Thus, the emphasis on form, on aesthetic innovation, tends to privilege a very specialized type of theatre and performance, implicitly undervaluing less experimental work, which is assumed to sustain the alleged originary passivity of spectators. In 2004, Rancière's lecture 'The Emancipated Spectator', delivered at the Fifth Internationale Sommerakademie in Frankfurt, articulated the need to reassess the fundamental presupposition, both theoretical and political, which 'even in postmodern form, still underpin[s] the gist of the debate on theatre, performance and the spectator' – namely, the notion that 'being a spectator is a bad thing', the opposite of both knowing (ignorance) and acting (passivity) (Rancière, 2009, p. 2). To the assumption that spectators need to be mobilized, turned from passive voyeurs into active participants, Rancière opposes a radical critique of the presumed connection between seeing and passivity:

> Emancipation begins when we challenge the opposition between viewing and acting; [. . .]. The spectator also acts, [. . .]. She observes, selects, compares, interprets. She links what she sees to a host of other things that she has seen on other stages, in other kinds of place. [. . .] She participates in the performance by refashioning it in her own way – by drawing back, for example, from the vital energy that it is supposed to transmit in order to make it a pure image and associate this image with a story which she has read or dreamt, experienced or invented. They are thus both distant spectators and active interpreters of the spectacle offered to them. (2009, p. 13)[7]

For Rancière, then, the spectator is by definition always-already active, and there are as many ways of being active as there are spectators:

> The collective power shared by spectators does not stem from the fact that they are members of a collective body [. . .]. It is the power each of them has to translate what she perceives in her own way, to link it to the unique intellectual adventure that makes her similar to all the rest in as much as this adventure is not like any other. (2009, pp. 16–17)

To assume otherwise, to believe that the spectator is ignorant and passive and therefore needs to be 'taught' and 'mobilized', is to make an essentially undemocratic assumption about her inequality of intelligence (Rancière, 2009, p. 9). From this perspective, theatre's presumed privileged potential, in relation to other cultural practices – such as 'the telling of a story, the reading of a book, the gaze focused on an image' (p. 22) or, indeed, the spectator 'seated in front of a television' or a film (p. 16) – to transform 'representation into presence and passivity into activity' (p. 22) is radically deconstructed, as is, by implication, that of any particular kind of theatre or performance, experimental or otherwise. Ultimately, Rancière argues, demystifying the supposedly singular power of theatre may lead us to a sharper understanding of the ethical import and potentially transformative function of particular cultural interventions – and particular forms of theatre and performance. Rather than tend towards the construction of a normative aesthetics, explorations of theatre and ethics need to address the specific contexts in which theatre and performance events are produced and received, and be attentive to the diverse strategies of representation and, possibly, resistance which these contexts invite and necessitate. That is the spirit that animates the chapters that make up this collection.

Ethical speculations

Each of the chapters in this volume demonstrates a passionate engagement with the interface between ethics and theatre, but they should not be taken as constituting a unified body of writings providing a homogeneous approach. Each chapter exemplifies its author's 'unique intellectual adventure', in Rancière's terms (2009, p. 17); each has its own perspective and can be read independently, while at the same time it is modified through its encounter with the other essays in the collection. They all, however, manifest the post-Holocaust, post-Levinasian ethical universe we inhabit in that none assumes the existence of a fixed, normative ethical framework of 'trustworthy ethical rules [. . .] inherited from the past' (Bauman, 1993, p. 18). Rather, the essays are both written from and respond to a far more uncertain terrain, one made infinitely complex by the ethical crises represented by such key historical events as the Holocaust, the intensification of the processes of contemporary globalization after 1989, the events of 9/11 or the current economic crisis.

Three of the chapters that follow are centrally concerned with the Holocaust, which is of course fundamental to the Levinasian and post-Levinasian reconfiguration of ethics. Levinas's turn from Being, traditionally the touchstone of Western philosophy, to the Other amounts to a complete overhaul of the very foundations of European civilization and culture, of 'how Europeans had come to think about themselves and the world' (Ridout, 2009, p. 51), a framework that appeared untenable in the wake of the horrors of the Holocaust. As is well known, Levinas shares Theodor W. Adorno's and Max Horkheimer's seminal interpretation of the Holocaust, in *The Dialectic of Enlightenment* (1947), as the outcome of the very post-Enlightenment bureaucratic, technological and industrial processes that were supposed to bring about rational, efficient modes of organization, as well as progress and emancipation. In *Modernity and the Holocaust* (1989), Zygmunt Bauman extends that critique in order to argue that, as a product of Enlightenment-derived European modernity, the Holocaust is not a discrete event or an exclusively Jewish problem, but rather a 'window [. . .] through which one can catch a rare glimpse of things otherwise invisible' (1989, p. viii), an experience of horror that 'contains crucial information about the society of which we are members' (1989, p. xiv). In other words, Bauman is particularly concerned with the ethical conditions of possibility of Holocaust-like phenomena, which he sees as intrinsic to modernity itself and very much 'part of our life' still (1989, p. 84). Like Levinas, he argues that human beings have a pre-societal inclination to feel responsible for other human beings in their mutual vulnerability – a responsibility for the 'naked face', 'extreme exposure' and 'defencelessness' of the Other seen as the precondition for a truly ethical life (Levinas, 1989a, p. 83). The Holocaust revealed how, provided with the sophisticated tools of modern civilization, human beings can bring about a scale of brutality and destruction that would be inconceivable if their actions were guided by their natural impulse (Bauman, 1989, pp. 21–7; 1993, p. 125).

In the wake of Élisabeth Angel-Perez's claim, in *Voyages au bout du possible: Les théâtres du traumatisme de Samuel Beckett à Sarah Kane*, that 'contemporary British theatre compulsively dramatizes the problematic [. . .] of a post-Holocaust world' (2006, p. 12) even when it does not directly dramatize the Holocaust, Clara Escoda's 'Violence, Testimony and Ethics in Martin Crimp's *The Country* and *The City*' (Chapter 2 in this volume) reads the plays in the light of Bauman's compelling argument that the conditions that made the Holocaust possible are still part of our life in the present, decisively shaping personal relationships as they seek to render individuals *zoè* – docile biological bodies – instead of political bodies or *bios*, in Giorgio Agamben's terms. The plays are seen as instances of Crimp's ongoing concern with pushing the boundaries of theatrical realism in an attempt to articulate a dramaturgy of resistance that will position spectators as 'double witnesses', in Felman and Laub's terms, summoning their capacity for ethical reflection. According to Escoda, violence – Rebecca's in *The Country* – and, particularly, testimony – Corinne's in *The Country*, Chris's and, in a sense, Jenny's in *The City* – fulfil a vital role within the plays' poetics of resistance. She argues, ultimately, that in *The Country* both Rebecca and, particularly, Corinne come to represent Levinas's vision of subjectivity as inherently responsible, while *The City*, a 'bleaker play', ends in an 'image of paralysis' as the Girl cannot proceed beyond a certain bar on the piano.

Adorno's 1949 dictum, 'To write a poem after Auschwitz is barbaric', inaugurates an ongoing debate about the Holocaust as signalling an ethical crisis of representation.[8] The debate is intertwined with Felman and Laub's interpretation of the Holocaust as 'a radical historical *crisis of witnessing*, and as the unprecedented, inconceivable, historical occurrence of "an event without a witness" – an event eliminating its own witness' (1992, p. xvii; emphasis original) – an event that radically problematizes access to its atrocities. Hanna Scolnicov's and Mark Taylor-Batty's essays (Chapters 3 and 4) speak to each other across the fraught ethical terrain of the representability of the Holocaust, probably still the paradigmatic instance of the contemporary crisis of representation of trauma and violence. Read alongside each other, they are vivid demonstrations of Rancière's argument about the always-already ethically engaged spectator, who has 'the power [. . .] to translate what she perceives in her own way, to link it to the unique intellectual adventure that makes her similar to all the rest in as much as this adventure is not like any other' (2009, pp. 16–17). Where Scolnicov's 'Bearing Witness and Ethical Responsibility in Harold Pinter's *Ashes to Ashes*' argues that Pinter's 1996 play is about the Holocaust, 'the most serious ethical breakdown of the twentieth century', even if it never directly mentions it or makes any attempt to represent its atrocities, Taylor-Batty's 'How to Mourn: Kane, Pinter and Theatre as Monument to Loss in the 1990s' reads *Ashes to Ashes* as being centrally and self-reflexively concerned with the ongoing debate about the representability of the Holocaust, and connected from that point of view to a growing antagonism in the early- to mid-1990s in Britain 'between media representation and aesthetic/artistic representation of material with ethical implications', which Sarah Kane's *Blasted* (1995) was also a response to.

For Scolnicov, *Ashes to Ashes* resonates with the memories and testimonies of Holocaust survivors and second-degree witnesses, and focuses on questions of testimony and the ethical burden of memory rather than on documented events. The continuing presence of the Holocaust as an unfinished event is embodied in the play by Rebecca, most intensely in her final vision, through a window, of a woman whose baby is snatched from her before she herself is pushed onto a train – which, I would suggest, uncannily echoes Bauman's description of the Holocaust, quoted above, as a 'window' through which one can perceive that the conditions that made it possible are still with us. At the point where Rebecca crosses the frontier separating her from the Other – when her narrative suddenly shifts from the third to the first person and she 'becomes one' with the deported mother – her act of memory, Scolnicov claims, becomes an instance of *mémoire profonde*, where the past – the Holocaust – is re-enacted in the present, highlighting its continuing ethical import.

For Taylor-Batty, Ian's role as a tabloid journalist in *Blasted* thematizes Kane's concern that the manner in which atrocities are normally mediated fails to fully convey their horror and is 'driven by ideological discourses that are rendered invisible, subsumed into the means of representation'. Instead, Kane seeks to construct a theatrical aesthetic that will bring about what Antonin Artaud called a *retentissement*, a corporeal, physically transformative experience that will render spectators active witnesses rather than mere consumers. *Blasted*, deliberately frustrating any obvious connections with real-world events and complicating ethical choices on the part of spectators, becomes a monument to loss in Andreas Huyssen's terms, a mode of mourning that avoids sentimentality and transforms spectators into 'the testimony itself'. *Ashes to Ashes*, in many ways a response to *Blasted* according to Taylor-Batty, turns Rebecca herself into a monument to the Holocaust through her own experience of *retentissement*, her bodily transformation through a process of absorption of cultural memory. However, unlike Scolnicov, Taylor-Batty links Rebecca's 'memories' to the popular if contentious representations of the Holocaust articulated in the films *Sophie's Choice* (1982) and *Schindler's List* (1993), and argues that the key question the play poses is, how legitimate is it for Rebecca, who has clearly not experienced the Holocaust, to become a 'witness' to it through the absorption of mediated memories and images of it? The play's ultimate gesture of *retentissement* transposes Rebecca's dilemma onto the audience by placing them in an uncomfortable ethical space 'on an edge between empathy and objectivity'. *Ashes to Ashes* thus becomes a Holocaust monument that recognizes the event in its radical otherness, yet imprints some of its horror into the body of the spectator.

As noted earlier, Levinas's ambitious project, amounting to no less than 'an attempt to begin the work of philosophy all over again' (Ridout, 2011, p. 13) in the wake of the Holocaust, lies at the basis of the emergence of a poststructuralist relational ethics which, rather than articulating a set of predetermined codes and rules of conduct, grounds itself in the very experience or event of being open to the absolute, irreducible alterity of the Other. While such an emphasis on difference had a salutary impact in terms of deconstructing previously unchallenged narratives of knowledge and power and critically re-examining – indeed, deconstructing – their purported universal value, there is also a risk that the exclusive emphasis on difference and plurality, on the singularity of the event, may do away with any sense of collective action, particularly one based on 'a community that defines itself in terms of self-identity' (2011, p. 15). As Ridout perceptively puts it, '[w]hat has happened to politics in all these ethics?' (2011, p. 13). Can the poststructuralist ethics of alterity be seen as a form of politics, as its proponents contend, or is it rather part of a depoliticising, anti-universalist turn that has gained momentum in the wake of the crisis of the communist project around 1968 and its collapse after 1989 (2011, p. 15)?

Such a difficulty in dealing with the political is actually embedded in Levinas's own thought. There is a 'political impasse' at the basis of Levinas's overhaul of the foundation of ethics, for when it comes to social life the subject is never responsible only to one Other – 'As soon as there are three, the ethical relationship with the other becomes political' (Levinas and Kearney, 1986, p. 21). The subject, that is, is always-already immersed in the 'political world of the impersonal "third" – the world of government, institutions, tribunals, prisons, schools, committees, and so on' (p. 30), where the call of the Other inevitably comes from a plurality of others and it is necessary to negotiate, make decisions, choose alternatives. The question then is, on what basis are such decisions to be made? Levinas insists that 'the moral-political order [should never] relinquish its ethical foundation' (p. 30), and yet at the same time acknowledges that 'ethics cannot itself legislate for society or produce rules of conduct whereby society might be revolutionized or transformed' (p. 29). In other words, when navigating the hazardous crossing from an intersubjective, relational ethics based on the face-to-face encounter to the realm of politics, of community, Levinas acknowledges the predicament inherent to his ethical philosophy – namely, that it is hard to envisage how political decisions might be taken on the basis of a pre-ontological ethics defined as 'extreme exposure and sensitivity of one subjectivity to another' (p. 29) outside any geographical, social or, indeed, political context, and without recourse to any universal principle or rule.[9] Ultimately, while Levinas insists that 'to generalize the law for everyone else' is to exploit them and to disregard the infinite demand for our ethical 'watchfulness' (p. 31), he also contradictorily appeals to 'universal principles, locus of justice and objectivity' (qtd. in Popke, 2003, p. 305) in the face of the presence of the 'third party' – that is, in the 'world of citizens' (qtd. in Popke, 2003, p. 305), the domain of politics, which we can never 'completely escape' (Levinas and Kearney, 1986, p. 22).

For proponents of a radical poststructuralist ethics, Levinas's falling back on universal principles of rights and justice discloses an unsatisfactory dependence on the Cartesian/Kantian subject, whose autonomy and rationality enable him/her to make moral decisions – the bounded, sovereign subject of modern ethics whose coherence was constructed 'upon the specification and control of difference' (Popke, 2003, p. 302), precisely the kind of subject that Levinas's relational ethics of alterity set out to break away from. Arguing that 'when we can simply rely upon the application of rules and norms, our accountability to the other becomes elided in the universality of a politics and ethics based in the juridical norms of law and the state' (p. 306), poststructuralist ethics takes its cue from the later Derrida in pulling Levinas in the direction of articulating an ethics and a politics predicated on 'undecidability' – namely, the notion that the basis of our ethical and political responsibility is an unswerving commitment to the singularity of each situation and the particularity of the event of each decision, a clear-eyed awareness that there is no prior set of rules or universal principles that can guarantee its rightness or justness. It is in that sense that ethical decisions remain undecidable or incalculable in advance, and require a surrender of our autonomous sovereignty so that we may stay endlessly exposed to the always-already unprecedented call of the Other.[10]

Both Dan Rebellato's 'Two: Duologues and the Differend' (Chapter 5) and Martin Middeke's 'The Undecidable and the Event: Ethics of Unrest in Martin Crimp's *Attempts on Her Life* and debbie tucker green's *truth and reconciliation*' (Chapter 6) make an intervention into the disputed philosophical terrain delineated above. Rebellato's Kantian sympathies in moral philosophy and his objections to a (potentially) relativist ethics rooted exclusively in the singularity of the event are articulated in terms of an exploration of the prominence of the duologue or 'two-hander' in British theatre since the early 1990s, which he places in the context of the Bosnian and Rwandan genocides, both 'hard to explain in purely particularist terms'. By reference to a range of duologues written and produced over the last two decades, Rebellato disputes both Richard Rorty's anti-universalist claim that ethical obligation cannot be grounded in the 'metaphysical fiction' of a common 'human nature', and Jean-François Lyotard's equally anti-universalist contention that in the wake of the Holocaust, instead of sharing one common metalanguage or grand narrative, such as justice, we live in separate, incommensurable language games. This puts (universal) ethical judgement out of the question – all we can do is 'bear witness to the differend', the incompatibility between disparate language games. Claiming instead that 'universalism in ethics is a radical position, profoundly resistant to unfettered, aggressive, free-market capitalism', Rebellato sees duologues, with their focus on the 'fundamental ethical building block of human sociality' – relations between one self and another – as staging 'ethical relationships, asking whether we are [. . .] individuals or members of a common ethical community', however precarious. Through 'the felt experience of co-presence and mutual alienation', duologues affirm 'the desire and possibility of locating a common language (for which the theatre space often stands in) in which our rival ethical demands may be expressed' and summon spectators to ethical judgement, rather than positioning them to (im)passively 'bear witness to the differend'.[11] Similarly, Rebellato has argued elsewhere, in the context of a discussion of Alan Badiou's *Ethics: An Essay on the Understanding of Evil* (2001), that it is only on the basis of an 'infidelity to singularity', a transcendence of particulars, that ethical judgement can be articulated and become the basis for (collective) political action (Rebellato, 2006).

Badiou, together with Bauman, Derrida and Levinas, form the theoretical foundation of Middeke's positing that an 'ethics of unrest' defines contemporary drama, which entangles '(implicit) authors, texts and (implicit) readers/spectators in a complex, non-harmonizable, ultimately inconclusive network of dialogue and communication'. Drawing particularly on the Derridean concepts of singularity and undecidability and on Badiou's notions of Event, truth and Good/Evil, Middeke argues, in relation to Crimp's *Attempts on Her Life*, that both the absent 'protagonist' Anne (Anya/Annie/Anny/Annushka) and the rhetorical trope of repetition with a difference function as 'a medium of undecidability'. While the play constantly coaxes the reader/spectator to 'attempt' interpretation, it ultimately remains thoroughly enigmatic and heterogeneous as it ethically frustrates any 'normative moral stance' and projects 'undecidability onto the reader/spectator', asking them to endure 'competing interpretations without making any attempt at taking refuge in logocentric dichotomies'. tucker green's *truth and reconciliation*, Middeke argues, takes a different ethical route from *Attempts on Her Life*, even if aesthetically both disrupt traditional form. Unlike Crimp's play, tucker green's starts off from historically verifiable situations of conflict and violation of human rights – in South Africa, Rwanda, Bosnia, Zimbabwe and Northern Ireland – and it both unapologetically affirms the basis of moral/ethical experience in reality and 'is adamant in [its] analysis of why reconciliation or even forgiveness are respectively hard to accomplish and impossible' – an impossibility Middeke reads in terms of Badiou and Derrida. Like *Attempts on Her Life*, *truth and reconciliation* is characterized by an 'appeal structure' that projects undecidability onto the reader/spectator, 'setting in motion a complex, inconclusive, restless transformation process in the reception of the plays', which, Middeke concludes, qualifies the plays as Events in Badiou's sense of the term.

Clare Wallace's 'Playing with Proximity: Precarious Ethics on Stage in the New Millennium' (Chapter 7) opens a group of three chapters that share an emphasis on examining the ways in which spectators may be summoned to ethical judgement in contemporary British theatre, and what the nature of that ethical engagement may be. In its focus on how four contemporary British plays, Mark Ravenhill's *pool (no water)* (2006), Caryl Churchill's *Seven Jewish Children* (2009), Tim Crouch's *The Author* (2009) and David Greig's *Fragile* (2011), attempt to create 'moments of precarious connection', Wallace's piece links up with Rebellato's in its emphasis on the significance of relationality or, following Lehmann, spectatorial 'response-ability'. She warns, however, that the ethico-political 'efficacy of aesthetic relationality remains a point of contestation'. Drawing mainly on Judith Butler's post-Levinasian investigation into precariousness in 'Precarious Life' (2004, pp. 128–51), Wallace argues that the four plays under discussion, 'diverse as they are [. . .] reflect upon, reveal and generate senses of precarity' through their exploration of the relationships between representation, violence and proximity, while at the same time suggesting, not unlike Middeke, that they place spectators in 'radically uncomfortable', 'ethically undecidable' zones of ambivalence which, nevertheless, carry with them 'the imperative to respond'.

Vicky Angelaki's 'Witness or Accomplice? Unsafe Spectatorship in the Work of Anthony Neilson and Simon Stephens' (Chapter 8) sets out to 'probe the changing field of text-based [. . .] playwright-driven theatre'. Although Rancière is not directly mentioned, there does appear to be some resonance between Angelaki's approach and the Rancièrian refusal, noted above, to posit a normative aesthetics that sees formal experimentation as a privileged site for the production of an ethically transformative spectatorial experience. Both Neilson's *Relocated* and Stephens's *Three Kingdoms*, Angelaki claims, place the spectator on 'unsafe' ground – and again, Angelaki's notion of an 'alert', 'demanding', 'empowered', 'active', 'informed' spectator is akin to the Rancièrian always-already emancipated one. In the Royal Court Upstairs 2008 premiere production of the formally adventurous *Relocated*, whose content focuses on the abduction and abuse of children, the gauze through which spectators viewed the stage foregrounded the act of watching or seeing and brought about a 'sensory precariousness' in spectators that enveloped them in the play perceptually and affectively – that is, both corporeally and intellectually. This was the crux, Angelaki claims, of the production's ethical summons to spectators – namely, its highlighting of the fine line between failing to notice and becoming complicit. Similarly, by means of 'neo-expressionistic representational methods', the international 2011–12 co-production of *Three Kingdoms* directed by Sebastian Nübling took spectators on a nightmarish sensory journey through 'sexual exploitation, violence against women, the fragility of the individual in an increasingly globalized world'.[12] While refusing to provide any reassurance or resolution, the play positions spectators as 'a form of jury' – summons them, one might say, to the moment of decision. Specifically, Angelaki argues, Nübling's production interrogated its international spectators' 'degree of complicity' with the kind of globalization that, while enabling the potent 'cultural mosaic' at the basis of the production itself, also draws a veil over 'brutal truths'.

Enric Monforte's 'Witnessing, Sexualized Spectatorship and the (De) construction of Queer Identities in *Mother Clap's Molly House*, *The Pride* and *Cock*' (Chapter 9) draws on Felman and Laub's concept of 'double witnessing' and on Jenny Spencer's formulation of the notion of the 'racialized spectator' (2012) in order to argue that Mark Ravenhill's, Alexi Kaye Campbell's and Mike Bartlett's plays nudge spectators into 'sexualizing – and perhaps, inevitably, queering – their spectatorial positions', which may lead to 'acts of resubjectivization' and an active reexamination of dominant discourses on gender and sexuality. As Monforte points out, this amounts to following Rancière in taking for granted the spectator's always-already active position, an agency that entails a definite ethico-political potential. In *Mother Clap's Molly House*, Ravenhill's characteristic refusal to offer any moral comment on the action opens up a space for 'spectators to define their own ethico-political position' *vis-à-vis* the play's 'deconstruction of a commodified, bourgeois gay identity that replicates' heteronormative, homophobic, patriarchal schema. By alternating between two temporal moments, the London of 1958 and 2008, Campbell's *The Pride* articulates a strong critique of the hedonism that pervades significant sections of contemporary bourgeois gay/queer life and 'sexualizes' spectators at the level of confronting them with the effects of discourses on sexuality and gender on a few damaged queer lives. With spectators raked down towards the stage, 'in a witnessing position', Bartlett's *Cock* moves on from the deconstruction of (queer) sexual and gender identities to a satirical, mostly humorous querying of homonormativity. The three plays open up 'a dissident space where spectators – both gay and straight – can hopefully negotiate their own sexual identities' and perhaps construct more heterogeneous ones.

The last two chapters in the collection turn their attention to the ethics of institutions – war reporting and photography as represented in Stella Feehily's *O Go My Man* (2006), David Hare's *The Vertical Hour* (2008) and Vivienne Franzmann's *The Witness* (2012) in the case of Christiane Schlote's 'From Front Page to Front Stage: War Correspondents and Media Ethics in British Theatre' (Chapter 10) and theatre itself in

Graham Saunders's 'Kicking Tots and Revolutionary Trots: The English Stage Company Young People's Theatre Scheme 1969–70' (Chapter 11). Schlote's discussion of Feehily's, Hare's and Franzmann's plays shows that, while they all address the ethical dilemmas faced by war correspondents and photographers, their ethical range is limited by their reliance on '(partly stereotypical) notions and images of war journalists as propagated in the media and/or fictional representations', by their focus on the private sphere – which 'preclude[s] the war journalist characters from "performing" their professional identities' and 'obscures a wider perspective on global (media) ethics' – and by the absence of a thorough-going 'interrogation of the strategies and mechanisms of the dramatic representation of war reporting'. Schlote closes her chapter by highlighting the 'pressing ethical concerns' surrounding war reporting and war photography that are simply overlooked in the three plays, as much an ethical decision on the part of the playwrights as, for instance, the choices researchers make as to what to include in and exclude from their research (see Ajana, 2008, pp. 4–5).

Feehily's *O Go My Man*, Hare's *The Vertical Hour* and Franzmann's *The Witness* had their (British) premieres at the Royal Court Theatre, and it is precisely that particular theatrical institution that Saunders's chapter focuses on. Arguing as it does that the work of the Royal Court's Young People's Theatre Scheme in 1969–70 surreptitiously slipped the ethics and sensibility of the counterculture into the Royal Court, Saunders's contribution fittingly brings the collection to a close by linking up with some of the questions posed at the start of this introduction regarding the institutional potential of theatre for ethical solicitation. Drawing extensively on archival sources from the English Stage Company and the Arts Council of Great Britain, Saunders belies the generalized resistance on the part of theatre studies to engage in close observation of real spectatorial responses – discussed by Freshwater (2009, pp. 27–55), as noted earlier – by conducting minute analyses of actual audience members' responses to the 1969 'Violence in the Theatre' workshops, the student-devised 'Revolution' season in 1970 and the revival that same year of Ann Jellicoe's *The Sport of My Mad Mother* for schools – both those of 'ordinary' spectators (a designated audience of children and adolescents) and institutional observers (including the Arts Council, the press, the Department of Education, MPs and the Inner London Education Authority). All in all, Saunders concludes, the controversy stirred by the three productions 'demonstrates all too well the mechanisms by which moral panics can be generated' and foregrounds the nature of theatre as a site for ethical speculations.[13]

Notes

1. My thanks to Aleks Sierz for his help in clarifying this.
2. Lyn Gardner also wondered whether it was legitimate to charge audiences if the reason for *Small Hours* not 'going public' was that it was a developing work-in-progress (Gardner, 2011).
3. Other events confirm the comparatively recent turn to ethics in theatre studies: to name only a few, the 10th Conference of the European Society for the Study of English (ESSE) included a seminar on 'Ethics in Contemporary British Theatre', convened by Mireia Aragay, Enric Monforte and Hanna Scolnicov (Università degli Studi di Torino, 24–28 August 2010); the 20th Conference of the German Society for Contemporary Theatre and Drama in English (CDE) was devoted to 'Ethical Debates in Contemporary Theatre and Drama' (Johannes Gutenberg Universität Mainz, 2–5 June 2011); a debate on 'Performance and Ethics', conducted by Chris Megson, was held at the Barbican Theatre on 15 October 2011; and the seminar 'Representations of Political/Ethical Concerns in post-1989 British Theatre', convened by Mireia Aragay, Deniz Bozer and İbrahim Yerebakan, was held at the 11th Conference of the European Society for the Study of English (ESSE) at Boğaçizi University in Istanbul (4–8 September 2012).
4. Although, as noted by various commentators (Eaglestone, 1997, p. 1; Eskin, 2004, p. 558; Ganteau and Onega, 2011, p. 7), the ethical turn is sometimes perceived as a reaction against extreme poststructuralist positions, and in particular against deconstructive theory – especially in the wake of the 'Paul de Man controversy' in the late 1980s – there is a profound mutual implication between Derrida's and Levinas's thought which both Critchley (1999) and Eaglestone (1997, pp. 129–74) explore in depth.
5. Derrida recalls Levinas's 'anxiety of interruption' on the telephone, when 'he seemed at each moment to fear being cut off, to fear the silence or disappearance, the "without-response", of the other, to whom he called out and held on with an "*allo, allo*" between each sentence, sometimes even in mid-sentence' (1999, p. 9).
6. Derek Attridge's 'Ethical Modernism: Servants and Others in J.M. Coetzee's Early Fiction', included in the 'Literature and Ethics' special 2004 issue of *Poetics Today*, also argued that the force of the ethical in literature depends on aesthetic innovation, on the creation of 'foreign' forms that will actively engage the reader and make her respond aesthetically-ethically to the text's radical alterity (Attridge, 2004a).
7. As Rancière's use of the term 'spectacle' in this extract indicates, his critique includes a questioning of Debord's notion of the 'society of the spectacle', briefly mentioned above.
8. I quote Ruth Franklin's literal translation of Adorno's German phrasing, 'Nach Auschwitz ein Gedicht zu schreiben, ist barbarisch' (2011, p. 2). Her introduction to *A Thousand Darknesses: Lies and Truth in Holocaust Fiction* provides a nuanced, up-to-date overview of the debate about the representability of the Holocaust. See also Friedlander (1992), a key collection of essays on the subject.
9. Given the state of the world, one might be forgiven for wondering whether the ethical relation as Levinas describes it is entirely utopian and unrealistic (see Levinas and Kearney, 1986, pp. 32–3 in this connection).

10. Derrida's discussion of the ethics of undecidability appears in texts like *The Gift of Death* (1995), *The Politics of Friendship* (1997) and *Adieu to Emmanuel Levinas* (1999). In 'Nietzsche and the Machine: Interview with Jacques Derrida', Derrida describes undecidability as follows: 'However careful one is in the theoretical preparation of a decision, the instant of the decision, if there is to be a decision, must be heterogeneous to the accumulation of knowledge. Otherwise, there is no responsibility. In this sense not only must the person taking the decision not know everything [. . .] the decision, if there is to be one, must advance towards a future which is not known, which cannot be anticipated' (Derrida, 1994, p. 37). Critchley (1999) puts forward a powerful argument for the ethical dimension of Derrida's thought.

11. Since the early 1990s, the field of human geography has also responded to the impact of poststructuralist thought in diverse ways. In *Moral Geographies: Ethics in a World of Difference* (2000, p. 101), David Smith articulates a position not unlike Rebellato's, which also, incidentally, underlines the question of space: 'The stress on difference and particularity, while drawing attention to the specific needs of various groups of hitherto marginalized "others", dilutes the force of an argument from human sameness or similarity, which supports spatially extensive responsibility for people who are like ourselves in morally significant respects. [. . . T]he moral relativism (or nihilism) encouraged in some postmodern thinking is far from politically benign.'

12. The production, with an international cast, was first presented at Teater NO99 in Tallinn (Estonia) in September 2011, with subsequent openings at the Munich Kammerspiele in October 2011 and the Lyric Hammersmith in May 2012. The action of the play shifts between England, Estonia and Germany.

13. Research towards this chapter was conducted in the context of the project 'The representation of politics and the politics of representation in post-1990 British drama and theatre' (FFI2009-07598), funded by the Spanish Ministry of Science and Innovation.

Works cited

Adorno, T.W. and M. Horkheimer (1997) *The Dialectic of Enlightenment*, trans. J. Cumming (London: Verso).

Ajana, B. (2008) 'In Defence of Poststructuralist Ethics in Sociological Praxis: Derrida, Lévinas and Nancy', *Enquire*, 1 (1), pp. 1–8.

Angel-Perez, É. (2006) *Voyages au bout du possible: Les théâtres du traumatisme de Samuel Beckett à Sarah Kane* (Paris: Klincksieck).

Attridge, D. (2004a) 'Ethical Modernism: Servants and Others in J.M. Coetzee's Early Fiction', *Poetics Today*, 25 (4), pp. 653–71.

—— (2004b) *The Singularity of Literature* (London and New York: Routledge).

Badiou, A. (2001) *Ethics: An Essay on the Understanding of Evil* (London and New York: Verso).

Bauman, Z. (1989) *Modernity and the Holocaust* (Cambridge: Polity).

—— (1993) *Postmodern Ethics* (Oxford: Blackwell).

Butler, J. (2004) *Precarious Life: The Powers of Mourning and Violence* (London and New York: Verso).

Critchley, S. (1999) *The Ethics of Deconstruction: Derrida and Levinas*, 2nd edn (Edinburgh: Edinburgh University Press).

Debord, G. (1983) *Society of the Spectacle*, trans. F. Perlman et al., 2nd edn (Detroit: Black and Red).

Derrida, J. (1994) 'Nietzsche and the Machine: Interview with Jacques Derrida', by R. Beardsworth, *Journal of Nietzsche Studies*, 7, pp. 7–66.

—— (1995) *The Gift of Death*, trans. D. Wills (Chicago: University of Chicago Press).

—— (1997) *The Politics of Friendship*, trans. G. Collins (London and New York: Verso).

—— (1999) *Adieu to Emmanuel Levinas*, trans. P.-A. Brault and M. Naas (Stanford, CA: Stanford University Press).

Eaglestone, R. (1997) *Ethical Criticism: Reading after Levinas* (Edinburgh: Edinburgh University Press).

Eskin, M. (2004) 'Introduction: The Double "Turn" to Ethics and Literature?', *Poetics Today*, 25 (4), pp. 557–72.

Felman, S. and D. Laub (1992) *Testimony: Crises of Witnessing in Literature, Psychoanalysis, and History* (New York and London: Routledge).

Franklin, R. (2011) *A Thousand Darknesses: Lies and Truth in Holocaust Fiction* (Oxford: Oxford University Press).

Freshwater, H. (2009) *Theatre & Audience* (Basingstoke and New York: Palgrave Macmillan).

Friedlander, S. (1992) *Probing the Limits of Representation* (Cambridge, MA: Harvard University Press).

Ganteau, J.-M. and S. Onega (2011) 'Introduction' in S. Onega and J.-M. Ganteau (eds) *Ethics and Trauma in Contemporary British Fiction* (Amsterdam and New York: Rodopi), pp. 7–19.

Gardner, L. (2011) 'In the Age of Blogging, Can Shows Keep Critics at Bay?', *Guardian Theatre Blog*, 26 January, http://www.guardian.co.uk/stage/theatreblog/2011/jan/26/theatre-blogs-reviews-critics/ (accessed 28 January 2011).

Gibson, A. (1999) *Postmodernity, Ethics and the Novel: From Leavis to Levinas* (London and New York: Routledge).

Grehan, H. (2009) *Performance, Ethics and Spectatorship in a Global Age* (Basingstoke and New York: Palgrave Macmillan).

Hillis Miller, J. (1987) *The Ethics of Reading* (New York: Columbia University Press).

Keefe, J. (2010) 'A Spectatorial Dramaturgy, or the Spectator Enters the Ethical Frame', *Performing Ethos*, 1 (1), pp. 35–52.

Lehmann, H.-T. (2006) *Postdramatic Theatre*, trans. K. Jürs-Munby (London and New York: Routledge).

Levinas, E. (1969) *Totality and Infinity: An Essay on Exteriority*, trans. A. Lingis (Pittsburgh, PA: Duquesne University Press).

—— (1989a) 'Ethics as First Philosophy' in S. Hand (ed.) *The Levinas Reader* (Oxford: Blackwell), pp. 75–87.

—— (1989b) 'Reality and its Shadow' in S. Hand (ed.) *The Levinas Reader* (Oxford: Blackwell), pp. 130–43.

Levinas, E. and R. Kearney (1986) 'Dialogue with Emmanuel Levinas' in R.A. Cohen (ed.) *Face to Face with Levinas* (Albany: State University of New York Press), pp. 13–33.

Matthews, J. and D. Torevell (eds) (2011) *A Life of Ethics and Performance* (Newcastle: Cambridge Scholars Publishing).

Meyer-Dinkgräfe, D. and D. Watt (eds) (2010) *Ethical Encounters: Boundaries of Theatre, Performance and Philosophy* (Newcastle: Cambridge Scholars Publishing).

Mitchell, K. (2011) 'Welcome to my Front Room: Why I Love Directing in Small Spaces', *Guardian Theatre Blog*, 19 January, http://www.guardian.co.uk/stage/theatreblog/2011/jan/19/directing-small-spaces-katie-mitchell/ (accessed 21 February 2011).

Newton, A.Z. (1995) *Narrative Ethics* (Cambridge, MA: Harvard University Press).

Onega, S. and Ganteau, J.-M. (eds) (2007) *The Ethical Component in Experimental British Fiction since the 1960s* (Newcastle: Cambridge Scholars Publishing).

—— (eds) (2011) *Ethics and Trauma in Contemporary British Fiction* (Amsterdam and New York: Rodopi).

Orr, J. (2011) 'Review of *Small Hours*', *A Younger Theatre: Theatre through the Eyes of the Younger Generations*, http://www.ayoungertheatre.com/tag/lucy-kirkwood/ (accessed 21 February 2011).

Phelan, P. (2004) 'Marina Abramović: Witnessing Shadows', *Theatre Journal*, 56 (4), pp. 569–77.

Popke, E.J. (2003) 'Poststructuralist Ethics: Subjectivity, Responsibility and the Space of Community', *Progress in Human Geography*, 23 (3), pp. 298–316.

Rancière, J. (2009) *The Emancipated Spectator*, trans. G. Elliott (London and New York: Verso).

Rebellato, D. (2006) 'Doing Justice an Injustice', http://www.danrebellato.co.uk/doing-justice-an-injustice/ (accessed 18 June 2013).

Ridout, N. (2009) *Theatre & Ethics* (Basingstoke and New York: Palgrave Macmillan).

—— (2011) 'A Prologue' in J. Matthews and D. Torevell (eds) *A Life of Ethics and Performance* (Newcastle: Cambridge Scholars Publishing), pp. 7–17.

Robbins, J. (1999) *Altered Reading: Levinas and Literature* (Chicago: University of Chicago Press).

Sierz, A. (2011) 'Two Things I just don't Get', *Pirate Dog: Aleks Sierz's Blog*, http://sierz.blogspot.com/2011_01_01_archive.html/ (accessed 23 February 2011).

Smith, D. (2000) *Moral Geographies: Ethics in a World of Difference* (Edinburgh: Edinburgh University Press).

Spencer, J. (2012) 'Emancipated Spectatorship in Adrienne Kennedy's Plays', *Modern Drama*, 55 (1), pp. 19–39.

There Ought to Be Clowns (2011) 'Review of *Small Hours*', 18 January, http://oughttobeclowns.blogspot.com/2011/01/review-small-hours-hampstead-downstairs.html/ (accessed 23 February 2011).

Part I
(Post-)Holocaust Representations

2
Violence, Testimony and Ethics in Martin Crimp's *The Country* and *The City*

Clara Escoda

A post-Holocaust theatre

On 11 April 2000, Martin Crimp's *The Country* opened at the Royal Court Theatre Downstairs. On 1 March 2008, eight years after *The Country* and standing in close dialogue with it, *The City* premiered at Berlin's Schaubühne, shortly before opening at the Royal Court. Both *The Country* and *The City* have generally been seen as being conventional in form. Aleks Sierz, for instance, claims that, 'having pushed the boundaries of theatrical possibility to the limit with *Attempts on Her Life*, Crimp's next play, *The Country*, ostensibly [takes] a more traditional form' (2006, p. 60). In the same vein, Martin Middeke suggests that the play 'returns into the calmer, even if [. . .] more shallow waters of mainstream theatre' (2011, p. 92). Regarding *The City*, Vicky Angelaki points out that it 'retains a more conventional narrative structure than much of Crimp's theatre' (2012, p. 25). This chapter, in contrast, reads both *The Country* and *The City* as plays that set out, in Élisabeth Angel-Perez's potent formulation, to 'rethink the question of realism in the theatre' and push theatrical boundaries as Crimp seeks to find a language and a type of dramaturgy that may enable him to 'emerge out of the ethical and, therefore, aesthetic impasse' brought about by the Holocaust, which has 'plunged [contemporary art] into the so-called crisis of representation' (2006, p. 24).[1]

As Angel-Perez points out, for the most part English playwrights, and Crimp in particular, do not dramatize the Holocaust directly (2006, p. 213). However, 'perhaps more than any other type of theatre, contemporary British theatre compulsively dramatizes the problematic [. . .] of a post-Holocaust world' (p. 12) by recontextualizing the representational dialectic of a post-Holocaust theatre and actively searching for a post-Holocaust aesthetic (p. 214).[2] Crimp's *The Country* and *The City*, which Angel-Perez does not discuss, do not thematize the Holocaust;[3] rather, through a poetics of female violence and testimony, the plays articulate a dramaturgy of resistance that is arguably aimed at engaging spectators ethically in a reflection on the continuing presence within the current late capitalist world order of the seeds of totalitarianism and barbarism.[4] It is in this Baumian sense that both *The Country* and *The City* may be described as post-Holocaust plays – they resonate, that is, with Zygmunt Bauman's compelling argument in *Modernity and the Holocaust* (1989) that the conditions that made the Holocaust possible are still part of our life in the present.

In *The Country* Corinne and Richard, a forty-year-old London couple, 'move to the country in an attempt to save their marriage' (Angelaki, 2007, p. 9). Richard, a doctor, is soon revealed to be duplicitous both in the work and in the private spheres. The play begins as he brings home a twenty-five-year-old American woman, Rebecca, after she has taken an overdose of the drugs he illegally supplies her with. In Scene II, furthermore, a long telephone conversation between Richard and his colleague Morris makes clear that, in order to be with Rebecca and once again abusing his power, Richard has neglected an old patient who has just died. Morris agrees to cover up for him. As shall be seen, *The Country* can be understood as a metaphor of the West and its dissociation between economic growth and ethics. While Richard could be said to represent a 'progress' devoid of ethics, Corinne initiates a process of divesting herself of her husband's premises, becoming a more ethical subject at the end of the play than she was at the beginning. *The Country* is in fact the record of Corinne's transformation, which is presented for the audience to witness.

In *The City* Chris and Clair experience a marriage crisis which 'escalates when the husband is made redundant from his corporate job' (Angelaki, 2012, p. 24). In this case it is Clair, the female protagonist, an internationally recognized translator, who constructs herself as a subject of status. While Clair's career advances, Chris loses both his job and his self-confidence. At the same time, Clair is increasingly mesmerized by the life and personality of the author she is translating, Mohamed, who was tortured in prison; in Scene III the play even suggests she has been unfaithful to Chris with Mohamed while attending a conference. A Girl, representing one of the couple's two children, is not kept offstage as Richard and Corinne's children are in *The Country*, but appears in Scenes II and III. The fourth stage character is the couple's neighbour, Jenny, whose husband, a military doctor, is taking part in an unnamed war, and who comes to their house to complain that their children make too much noise in the garden. Finally, in Scene V Clair presents Chris with a diary Mohamed had given her, the diary he bought for his daughter when his sister-in-law took her away from him. Chris reads out loud the story Clair has written in it, and it appears that Mohamed, the Girl and Chris are just 'characters' (Crimp, 2008, p. 62), figments of her imagination. Through this metatheatrical ending, *The City* finds a metaphor to depict how the inner sense of security in Western societies has disappeared, and how 'everything can be abruptly taken away at any given time' (Angelaki, 2012, p. 28). The ending thus invites spectators to experience the crumbling of Chris's life and, beyond that, of any certainty, by foregrounding the very theatrical – that is, fictional – nature of the piece.

In his reflections on the Holocaust, Giorgio Agamben understands barbarism as the point where the market interests of late capitalism – capitalism in its deregulated, global form – filter down into the lives of individuals, thus rendering them *zoè* – mere biological, docile bodies – as opposed to political bodies or *bios* (2002, p. 156). In *The Country*, both Corinne and Rebecca are required to become *zoè*, docile bodies turned into conduits of ideology, for the sake of upholding Richard's and Morris's professional and economic status. Richard, in particular, attempts to exchange the women's silence regarding his duplicity both at home and at work for economic and other material compensations.[5] In this context, the play traces Rebecca's and Corinne's attempts to liberate themselves from Richard's subjection and his lies, especially through the act of violence Rebecca performs on Richard's body in Scene IV – when she stabs a pair of scissors into his hand – and through Corinne's delivery before Richard, in Scene V, of the testimonial account of her attempt to escape the previous night, whereby she enacts her final – albeit ambivalent – emotional separation from Richard. In *The Country*, female violence enacts a critique of the duplicity of the late capitalist, individualistic subject Richard represents, based as it is on a fundamental power abuse.

It is specifically through the poetics of testimony, however, that Crimp sets out to find a language capable of both encompassing the experience of barbarism and articulating a dramaturgy of resistance that will mobilize the spectators' ethical potential, their capacity to identify the seeds of barbarism in their own everyday context. While testimony is also present in both *Cruel and Tender* (2004) and *The Seagull* (2006) as a female mode of resistance, *The City* offers a revision of these plays – and particularly, as implied by the title, of *The Country* – regarding gender relations. In *The City* it is Clair, the female protagonist, who reproduces capitalist narratives of aggression and success that lead her to objectify her husband and, in Scene IV, it is Chris who passes on to their daughter the testimony of his wife's duplicity as well as of the growing emotional distance between them.

In their testimonial speech, both Corinne and Chris use a lyrical, inde-terminate, metaphorical language, expressing themselves 'through dark-ness and through fragmentation' and through 'cognitively dissonant' speech modes (Felman and Laub, 1992, p. 24). Corinne, for instance, refers to the series of stratified gender behaviours that separate her from her husband, as well as to the greed that characterizes both Richard and the late capitalist structures they both inhabit, in terms of a 'stone' (Crimp, 2005b, p. 364). In the same manner, Chris tells her daughter how Clair has built a successful work persona that has led her to discard her family by describing her as being followed by 'two enormous chest-nut leaves [. . .] right into the house' (Crimp, 2008, p. 46). This kind of defamiliarized language, in Theodor W. Adorno's terms, attempts to 'make those things be heard which ideology conceals' (2000, p. 214) in order to make social contradictions visible.[6] Adorno suggests that 'the subjective being that makes itself heard in lyric poetry is one which defines and expresses itself as something opposed to [. . .] the realm of objectivity. It has, so to speak, lost nature and seeks to recreate it [. . .] through descent into the subjective being itself' (pp. 215–16). Because the images Corinne and Chris use in order to refer to the sociopoliti-cal order their husband and wife embody are highly personal, specta-tors need to decode them by bringing to bear remnants of their own traumatic experiences of coercion, thus becoming 'double witnesses' (Felman and Laub, 1992, p. 58) – that is, witnesses to Corinne's and Chris's acts of testimony and to the presence of the seeds of barbarism in their own context. Through the poetics of testimony, that is, spectators are interpellated in their capacity for ethical responsiveness. Ultimately, it will be argued, both Rebecca's violent act in *The Country* and the dram-atization of testimony in both plays are part and parcel of a search for a new ethics grounded in subjectivity and the body. Through violence and testimony, spectators are impelled to move towards an ethical frame-work based on proximity and on what Emmanuel Levinas, in response to the post-Holocaust ethical impasse, metaphorically terms the space of the 'meeting' (1989, p. 69) or the 'face-to-face' encounter with the Other.

'It is only the flesh': Rebecca's moral imagination

Despite the apparently isolated life Richard and Corinne lead in the country, they inhabit what Sinkwan Cheng, drawing on Eric Hobsbawm, calls an 'age of extremes', in which 'it is not the shortage of goods' that is the problem, creating 'overabundance for a few, scarcity for the majority', but crucially the undemocratic 'politics of *entitlement'* (2004, p. 1; emphasis original) to these goods. In order to maintain certain privileges, the contemporary 'Empire' (Hardt and Negri, 2000, p. xii), made up of a global network of corporations and other powers, is engaged in 'cutthroat competition' (Cheng, 2004, p. 1) for the control of resources. This includes the continuous waging of wars abroad in the name of 'democracy' and 'freedom'. Thus, Corinne and Richard are part of a globalized world, which sees *'the rise of global capitalism operating under neoliberal policy conditions'* (Rebellato, 2009, p. 12; emphasis original).

Although the health service Richard works for as a doctor is not directly implicated in the control of the global economy as banks and corporations are, *The Country* explores the extent to which it is nonetheless imbued with the same type of neoliberal values that characterize more visible organisms of globalization, where human lives are valued in profitable or mercantilist terms. As noted, not only does Richard abuse his power as a doctor and sell Rebecca some drugs, but he also lets the old man die and asks Morris to cover up for him. In Scene IV, through Rebecca's act of violence, the play enacts a critique of the late capitalist male subject that hides his duplicity and power abuse behind a discursive display of 'reason'. The scene begins with Rebecca trying to force Richard to commit to her and to her presence in the house by asking him whether he has brought her home in order for her to be 'the maid' (Crimp, 2005b, p. 336). Richard diverts the conversation to his achievements as a doctor, and begins to talk about a baby he has successfully delivered. It is immediately after Richard's account of the birth that '[Rebecca] *grips his hand more tightly'* (p. 338), and suddenly and furiously stabs the pointed tip of a pair of tiny scissors into the palm of his hand:

- Don't hurt me.
- I'm not hurting you.
- I said: don't hurt me.
- What? Does that hurt?
- Yes. It hurts. Stop it. What is it?
- Really? Does that hurt?
- Yes.
  He pulls his hand out of her grip. The tiny scissors drop to the floor.
                                              (Crimp, 2005b, p. 339)

It is the dichotomy between how Richard constructs himself through the trust and authority others confer on him and how he behaves towards herself that triggers Rebecca's violent collapse. Through a carefully disembodied use of discourse, Richard constructs himself as a moral subject for Rebecca, albeit refusing to commit to her demands for honesty and empathy. Richard abstracts himself from reality, constructs his own narrative of success and, as Manuel Reyes Mate claims is characteristic of post-Enlightenment discourse, 'reduces the specific situation of inhumanity [which he imposes on both Corinne and Rebecca] to insignificance, to absence of importance and of meaning' (2003, p. 143).[7]

Precisely because Richard's remains a closed-off body – individualistic, unilateral, flaunting his success as a doctor while being unable to feel any empathy towards Rebecca – she is forced, so to speak, to become the Other of rational thought in order to remind Richard of the emotions and the real bodies he refuses to acknowledge. Richard embodies the Cartesian self inherited from the Renaissance and the Enlightenment (Burkitt, 1999, pp. 46–9), an exercise in domination whereby women and all those who are oppressed by such an instrumental use of reason are made to represent the body and irrationality. While Richard remains a closed-off body, Rebecca, who '*sucks* [his] *wound*' (Crimp, 2005b, p. 340) so that her mouth is besmeared with Richard's blood, evokes Mikhail Bakhtin's grotesque body, 'a body in the act of becoming [. . .] which ignores the impenetrable surface that closes and limits the body as a separate and completed phenomenon' (Bakhtin, 1995, pp. 226–7). Rebecca's body functions at this point as a representation of the 'openness' of the grotesque body, thus signalling her capacity for ethical commitment.

Rebecca's sudden outburst of violence thus unmasks Richard's totalitarian exercise of 'reason'; it literalizes the violence – Richard's – which had hitherto been latent and, because of its unexpected character, shakes the audience into becoming fully alert to the inequality of the relationship portrayed on stage. Although spectators cannot *experience* Richard's pain, they are summoned to imagine it, even project it onto their own flesh, and wonder whether they experience their bodies as autonomous, docile or in bondage in relation to other bodies. Rebecca's sudden, unexpected violent act destabilizes the conventional stage–audience separation and turns the spectators' attention to their own intersubjective spaces and relations, inviting them to imaginatively work towards a new ethics.

Not unlike Levinas, then, *The Country* seems to suggest that ethics should not lose sight of proximity and the body. In Scene IV, Rebecca both exemplifies and demands what Levinas envisioned as the 'I–Thou' relationship (Levinas, 1989, p. 73), which consists in 'confronting a being external to oneself, [. . .] one which is radically other, and in recognizing it as such' (p. 64). The ethics that emerges through the 'I–Thou' relationship is based on the radical equality between self and Other, where the self does not seek to master or appropriate the Other; it is an ethics that is realized in the intersubjective space of the 'meeting' (p. 69), that is, the face-to-face encounter with the Other.

When Rebecca sees Richard's contorted face after she has stabbed the scissors into his palm, she comments 'It's only the flesh' (Crimp, 2005b, p. 339), echoing the contempt for her suffering body – and that of his old patient – he had displayed earlier. Ironically, prompted by Rebecca's act of retribution, it is Richard himself who at this point acknowledges the utterly vulnerable, essentially dependent nature of individuals, when he says, 'There *is* only flesh' (p. 339; emphasis original). He thus redefines human beings as vulnerable, needy bodies. Through Rebecca's act of violence and its specific mode of interpellation of spectators, then, the play encodes a critique of the late capitalist (male) subject and alerts spectators as to the continuing presence of the seeds of violence and barbarism within late capitalist, 'civilized' relationships.

Collapsing boundaries: testimony and late capitalism

If Rebecca's act of violence in Scene IV points to the violence underlying the late capitalist, Cartesian male subject, Corinne's and Rebecca's repeated attempts to liberate themselves culminate at the end of the play, in Scene V, when Corinne passes on to Richard her testimony of her attempt to escape the night before. Corinne's testimonial speech partly draws on Rebecca's attempt, in Scene III, to pass on to Corinne her own testimony of the breakdown she experienced when she was with Richard the previous night. Using the lyrical, indeterminate language of testimony, both women refer to Richard's violence in terms of a 'stone' (Crimp, 2005b, pp. 316 and 364). As has been mentioned, through testimony, and like Rebecca in Scene III, Corinne seeks to divest herself of Richard's exploitative values and move on towards a new ethical framework.

What prompts Corinne to sever herself from Richard and to deliver her testimony of resistance is her sense of 'complicit[y]' (p. 362) with Richard's values. In Scene V, Sophie, the children's nanny, who remains like Morris an offstage presence throughout, phones Corinne to tell her Richard has left an inordinate amount of money in her money cup. Richard's motivation remains unspecified – he may have done so out of guilt, given Sophie's comparative poverty, or in order to obtain Sophie's silence regarding his duplicity.[8] The incident with Sophie brings the situation with the patient to Corinne's mind, and she tells Richard, in her first attempt to dissociate herself emotionally from him, that 'you left a man to die and Morris lied for you' (p. 359). It is when Corinne realizes that her life has been colonized by Richard's economic interests and duplicity that her act of testimony takes place, both as a means to denounce the erosion of the distinction between interpersonal and market relationships within late capitalist society, and in order to escape the docility Richard aims to impose on her.

Thus Corinne rejects Richard's suggestion that they should 'drive somewhere' (p. 359) and snaps at him that she has '*been* out' (p. 361; emphasis original) already – the previous night she 'went on a trip' (p. 361). She 'got into [her] car', 'twisted the mirror' and 'look[ed] at [herself]' (p. 361). She began to drive, then leapt across a ditch and began to follow a barren track that eventually ran out:

> – The track – that's right – gave out, and now there were just [. . .] clumps. [. . .] You should've seen me stepping the way a child steps from one clump to the next until I reached the stone. Well I say 'the stone', but the stone had arms, like a chair. So you could sit [. . .] within the stone. You could rest your arms along the arms of the stone, and from within the stone, look out at the land.
> *Pause.*
> – And how was the land?
> – Oh, the land was lovely. But the stone was cold. I don't think the sun had ever warmed it. I was afraid it would stick to my skin, like ice. And then Morris appeared. [. . .] He said, 'I've been following you for hours. Didn't you hear me calling you? You dropped this.'
> – Dropped what?
> – Well that's what I said. I said, 'Dropped what, Morris? Just what have I dropped?' 'Your watch, of course,' he said. And he dangled it in front of my face from its golden strap, so I could see all its tiny works. I said, 'I'm afraid you're mistaken. It's very beautiful, but it's not mine. It's very delicate, but it isn't mine.' Which is when I noticed – and this will amuse you – that the stone had started to devour my heart.
> *Pause.*
> – Oh really?
> – [. . .] I said to Morris, 'Morris. Help me. This stone is devouring my heart.' [. . .] He said, 'Are you afraid?' I said, 'Well yes, Morry,

of course I'm afraid. I don't seem able to move and this stone is devouring my heart. When I get up from this stone, what if my heart has gone? What if I have to spend the rest of my life simulating love?'

(Crimp, 2005b, pp. 364–6)

As in Rebecca's testimony in Scene III, here the stone becomes a metaphor for the hard core of late capitalist individualism Richard embodies, which infuses Corinne's life with violence. It is the cluster of lies and self-interest which has characterized Richard's relationship with her. The stone Corinne finds is clearly the same stone Rebecca reaches just before she collapses. Like Rebecca's stone, which she also claims was 'cold' yet had 'arms, like a chair' (Crimp, 2005b, pp. 316–17), the stone Corinne comes to is both cold and alluring, its 'arms' offering rest and comfort (p. 364). The stone, like the current 'empire' (p. 316) or world order, is both comfortable and violent. Not only does it offer wealth and privileges to some while withholding them from others, but it also oppresses those, such as Corinne, who appear to benefit from the material abundance it offers. Richard himself is both comfortable and scary – he provides Corinne with rest and material ease, yet is violent to others and seeks to subjectify Corinne herself as utterly docile, as *zoè*.[9]

Corinne's testimony is ultimately prompted by what late capitalism defines as 'progress', or rather the dichotomy between 'progress' and absence of ethics – the unbearable tension between material comfort, the sacrifices it demands, and the hidden, suppressed violence it implies. As she recounts her breakdown, Corinne mentions having dropped Rebecca's watch, which Morris subsequently found and attempted to give back to her.[10] Thus, while Corinne symbolically places the continuum of 'progress' in suspension, Morris seeks to remind her of the 'watch', that is, the imperatives of family and property, gripping her shoulders in order to 'establish a certain authority' (p. 365).

The coldness of the stone, then, represents the extent to which late capitalist market forces shape interpersonal relationships and the violence they bring about – both active, in the form of coercion, and reactive, in the form of rebellion on the part of those who feel victimized. Corinne thinks the sun had never 'warmed' (p. 365) the stone – that is, it is not humane enough. Rebecca's stabbing of the scissors into Richard's palm in Scene IV is a warning that the 'stony' subjectivity produced by the cold, ultimately undemocratic late capitalist system engenders violence as its victims attempt to impose limits on it.

Path of discovery: testimony and the ethics of spectatorship

As has been noted, early on in her testimony Corinne recalls driving until the road stopped, leaping across the ditch and beginning to climb a promontory so barren that there was nothing human to be found:

> – (quietly) I didn't want to go back to the car, not now I had discovered the track. It wasn't at all what I'd imagined, [. . .] it was [. . .] broad, and littered with shale. [. . .] It made a noise as I walked, a kind of clatter. And that's when I realised, as I slithered and clattered my way along the shale, that there was nothing human. Well *I* was there, obviously. *I* was human, but nothing else was. I looked out for human things. [. . .] I thought I might see a needle or a piece of brick. I longed – you know – to see something human like a needle, or a piece of brick mixed with the shale. Or to hear – even to hear something human other than myself. Other than my feet. Other than my heart. A plane. Or children screaming. Only there was nothing. Not even a track now. Because the track – just like the road – stopped. Or it [. . .] what did it do? [. . .] it 'gave out'.
>
> (Crimp, 2005b, p. 364; emphasis original)

The barren land is a sign of the sterility of Corinne and Richard's relationship and of Richard's violence, but the apocalyptic landscape, read against the play's historical context, suggests a global, not just a personal, *cul-de-sac*. The images of barrenness strongly intimate that following the road of the 'stone' can only lead to a no-man's-land of sterility – a post-Holocaust landscape. The Holocaust, as noted earlier, was the result of the implementation of the Enlightenment ideas Richard embodies – progress based on instrumental rationality and '*categorial*' reason (Bauman, 2008, p. 87; emphasis original) – to the point of paroxysm. According to Bauman, the singularity of genocides is that of being '*categorial murders*' (ibid.; emphasis original); that is, in genocides, individuals are exterminated because of their belonging to a specific category. During the Holocaust, Bauman clarifies, it became irrelevant 'how old or young, strong or weak, genial or malevolent the victims were' (ibid.) since, in genocide,

> the prospective targets of violence are unilaterally defined and denied a right to response. The victims' conduct or the qualities of the condemned category's individual members are irrelevant to their preordained fate. The sufficient proof of the capital offense, of

the charge from which there is no appeal, is the fact of having been accused. (Bauman, 2008, p. 82)

Richard classifies individuals according to the profit he can extract from them; he objectifies them and places his patients and the women in his life into different categories of importance within his own mental map. At work, his instrumental rationality leads to the death of the old patient. At home, it makes the women feel victims of a totalitarian type of violence, which prompts them to deliver their testimony to one another and to spectators. Ultimately, through Corinne's testimony, her life, which has become sterile through Richard's categorial-instrumental rationality, resonates with the ethical rupture the Holocaust signified. As mentioned earlier, there is a sense that time stops during Corinne's escapade, which is conveyed by her losing sight of any signs of civilization as well as by her accidentally dropping Rebecca's watch. Only the wind can be heard – as she puts it at the beginning of her testimony, 'everything flapped' (Crimp, 2005b, p. 363). By 'stopping time', Corinne's excursion, which leads her to understand the furthest reaches of Richard's unethical deployment of power, metaphorically evokes the sense of paralysis history underwent with the Holocaust.

The play's poetics of testimony – Corinne's defamiliarized, highly metaphorical use of language – require that spectators become active listeners, partaking, as Shoshana Felman and Dori Laub phrase it, 'of the struggle of the victim with the memories and residues of his or her traumatic past. [. . .] The listener, therefore, has to be at the same time a witness to the trauma witness and a witness to himself' (1992, p. 58). Spectators, that is, are impelled to become double witnesses, both to Corinne and to themselves, by allowing Corinne's testimonial language to resonate with their own, possibly fragmented, memories of experiences of coercion. The play's ending is open – whether Corinne finally leaves Richard or succumbs to him is left unspecified – but in positioning spectators as double witnesses, Corinne's testimonial speech articulates the ethical desire that *they* may activate their own potential for resistance.[11] According to Adorno, it is only if the audience can *experience* the contradictions dramatized on stage – not just listen to or discursively comprehend them – that art can produce resistance: '[p]olitical messages will be filtrated through false consciousness and dismissed. Rather, social contradictions need to be *experienced*' (O'Connor in Adorno, 2000, p. 240; emphasis added). In *The Country*, the defamiliarized, highly poetic language of testimony demands that spectators become aware of their own experience of contemporary forms of oppression and take on the ethical burden of their own testimony.

The crisis of late capitalism in *The City*

The social and ethical *malaise* of late capitalism Crimp relentlessly explores from *Dealing with Clair* (1988) through *The Treatment* (1993) to *The Country*, *Cruel and Tender* and *The Seagull* comes to its ultimate expression in *The City*, which dramatizes the 2008 financial crisis and how 'the inner sense of security in Western societies has disappeared [and] trust in the Western lifestyle has vanished' (Shaubühne 2008). As noted earlier, *The City* can be considered to be a rewriting of *The Country* and an exercise in self-questioning, since here it is Clair, a woman, who reproduces the dominant capitalist narratives of individualism and aggression while Chris, who stands at a further remove from power, can to some extent perceive its contradictions and has a more ambivalent relation to it. *The City* thus stands in dialogue with *The Country* in that it continues to show how it is the *position* individuals occupy within the late capitalist system that accounts for their behaviour and subjectivity.

Crimp's denunciation of late capitalism culminates in Scene IV, when Chris passes on to his daughter his testimony of Clair's pursuit of status. The Girl thinks Clair is still at the conference, yet it turns out she came back earlier, perhaps in a drunken stupor, and is now sleeping. By means of a parable-like language, as if it was a children's bedtime story, Chris tells the Girl about her mother's bizarre behaviour and the confusion this has brought about in the family:

> Chris (*begins very soft and fast*) Listen, sweetheart, there's something you ought to know: Mummy came home last night – she came home from Lisbon in the middle of the night – well – like it says in a book – 'unexpectedly' – and went straight to bed. She's here now – yes – that's right – in the house – but I've left her asleep because she was so tired. (*Laughs.*) You should've seen her. She was so worn out that she didn't even go into your room, she didn't even have the strength (she said) to push the hair back behind your ear and kiss you, the way she normally does. Not because she was unhappy – you're not to think that Mummy was unhappy – because – well – in fact she was laughing. That's how I knew she was home. I heard Mummy laughing out in the street – and there she

was – under the street-lamp – sharing a joke – something about crocodiles – with the taxi driver out in the street. (*Laughs.*) Oh, it was windy! You should've seen all the leaves swirling round the shiny black taxi under the orange light. And when she came through the front door – still laughing, by the way – guess what: two enormous chestnut leaves followed her right into the house. (*Laughs.*) I said 'Well this is a surprise: I didn't expect you back till the middle of next week!'

(Crimp, 2008, pp. 46–7)

Thus Chris intimates to the Girl that Clair's obsession with profit margins and financial success has overtaken ethics, yet he spares her the need of trying to actually understand the violence of the economic order Clair represents. While in *The Country* it is Corinne who is driven to the point of collapse by capitalism's dark underside, in *The City* it is Chris, a man, who, as it were, borrows Corinne's language to denounce the violence of the economic order. Through such parable-like, metaphoric language, he attempts to recover a linear narrative both for himself and his daughter that will bridge the rupture created by the late capitalist order, manifested by the entrance, into the couple's relationship, of the market economy values of disposability and aggression.

Chris's ability to sense his society's contradictions does not prevent him from devising an aggressive work persona and, desperate to live up to social expectations, take a job as a butcher's assistant that isolates him from his family due to its long hours. As Angelaki puts it, 'the mistake of Crimp's characters in [*The City*] is that they allow work and profit to become the driving force, sacrificing pieces of their individuality' (2012, p. 44). However, Jenny and the Girl do introduce interstices of contestation to the dominant late capitalist ideology. In order to connect both characters, Crimp dresses them in a nurse's uniform, and in Scene V has them appear in pink jeans and high heels, 'colouring' them, as it were, for the spectators to recognize. In Scene II, when Jenny comes to Chris and Clair's house to complain about the children's noise, she delivers an intense monologue about the war her husband is involved in, thus bringing into their life the dark side of the economic order they seek to profit from. As she puts it,

what they're doing now, in the secret war, is they're attacking a city – pulverising it, in fact – yes – turning this city [. . .] into a fine grey dust.[. . .] So the boys – what the boys have to do is they have to go in and kill the people clinging on to life. [. . .] And the last thing the baby sees as its mother uses her finger to slip its mouth off her nipple is a serrated kitchen knife – and I have my husband's word for this – a small knife with a stainless serrated blade being used to cut the soldier's heart out – d'you see? (*Slight pause.*) I said: d'you see?

(Crimp, 2008, p. 24)

Jenny thus becomes a nagging presence that questions the world of the family, revealing it as a mere 'picture of happiness' (Crimp, 2005a, p. 10). She also unveils the fake stability and security adults devise for their children, which offers them no real future and 'lock[s]' them instead in the 'playroom' (Crimp, 2008, p. 25) of material abundance. On her part the Girl, at the end of the play, refuses to move in the direction of the system, offering an image of paralysis. *The City* closes with her trying to play the piano yet getting stuck and being unable to get '*beyond bar 4*' (p. 64). Just as she could not 'get [her] arm in the right place' (p. 45) the way Chris was holding her coat in Scene III, she cannot strike the right notes in the world adults have created. The play thus ends in an image of personal collapse.

Ethics, proximity and the body

Both *The Country* and *The City* dramatize the effects of late capitalism on character and intimate relationships. *The City*, a bleaker play than *The Country*, shows how late capitalism hardens women like Clair into acceptance, and deprives people like Chris of the agency and voice to effect any meaningful, progressive change, as they are merely left with the possibility to 'cling on to life' (p. 23) or survive on the margins of the system. In *The City*, in short, the characters themselves are not able to find alternatives to late capitalism. It rather seems that the whole inexhaustible 'city' or subjectivity inside individuals, as Clair puts it in her diary, has been thoroughly eroded, attesting to the loss of individuality and ethics in contemporary society.[12]

The Country, in contrast, shows a reconfiguration of ethics taking place within the self – within Corinne – in an 'inner horizon' of values (Smith, 1999, p. 32). Both Rebecca and Corinne come to represent Levinas's vision of subjectivity as inherently responsible. Levinas calls that essential responsibility of the subject an 'anarchic responsibility' that does not stem from external regulations, but is the 'system of an immemorial freedom that is even older than being, or decisions, or deeds' (1989, p. 84). Such a pre-ontological responsibility is distorted by hierarchical, depersonalized social and economic structures (Bauman,

1989, p. 183) that favour 'greed', as Rebecca puts it in Scene III (Crimp, 2005b, p. 329), and by social structures which are not built on equality, on what Levinas calls the space of the 'meeting' (1989, p. 69) or the face-to-face encounter with the Other.[13]

Notes

1. For want of a published English text, Angel-Perez's translation is mine. From now on, my translations of non-English texts will be indicated by providing the quotation in the source language in a footnote. In French, Angel-Perez's lines read, '[Il s'agira donc de] repenser la question du réalisme au théâtre [. . .]. [L'enjeu qui s'impose aux dramaturges contemporains est de trouver un nouveau langage de théâtre] qui permette de sortir de l'impasse éthique et, de là, esthétique, qui frappe l'art contemporain et l'a plongé depuis quelques décennies dans ce qu'il est maintenant convenu d'appeler la crise de la représentation.'
2. '[. . .] peut-être plus qu'aucun autre, le théâtre anglais contemporain rebrasse compulsivement les problématiques [. . .] de l'après-Auschwitz'.
3. Angel-Perez devotes one last brief chapter to Crimp (2006: 197–215), where she examines *Attempts on Her Life* (1997) and *Cruel and Tender* (2004).
4. Late capitalism designates a phase of expansion of capitalism itself, generally considered to have decisively intensified following the fall of the Berlin Wall in 1989. In the wake of the dissolution of the Communist bloc, Keynesian capitalism was swiftly replaced with *laissez-faire*, neoliberal, corporate-led policies aimed at making economic structures more flexible and delocalized.
5. For a different approach to *The Country* and to the characters of Richard and Morris in particular, see Peter Buse's 'Solicitations téléphoniques: *La Campagne* de Martin Crimp' (2007). Buse also locates *The Country* explicitly within the field of ethics – 'the strength and interest of Crimp's play [lies] in the treatment of language and the field of ethical reflection' (2007, p. 156; 'la force et l'intérêt de la pièce de Crimp se situent ailleurs: dans le traitement du langage et dans la reflexion éthique') – but takes a Lacanian perspective that sees *The Country* as being about Richard's attempt to 'free himself from a series of contradictory orders which emanate from an alienating moral conscience' (2007, p. 165; '[Richard] tente de se dépêtrer de tout un réseau d'ordres contradictories émanant d'une conscience morale aliénante'), represented particularly by Morris.
6. Angelaki's 'Subtractive Forms and Composite Contents: Martin Crimp's *Fewer Emergencies*' (2008) offers a detailed analysis of the techniques of defamiliarization Crimp employs in the triptych *Fewer Emergencies*, drawing in this case on Viktor Shklovsky's, Bertolt Brecht's and Terry Eagleton's reflections on the political significance of alienation in performance.
7. '[La idea ilustrada de la humanidad hace] abstracción de la realidad y, por tanto, reduc[e] a insignificancia, a carencia de significado, la situación concreta de inhumanidad.'
8. Crimp suggests Richard gives Sophie too much money out of guilt when he says, '[Richard and Corinne] are not people who've inherited their

middle-class status – they've climbed out to it – which is why they are ill at ease with it' (qtd. in Sierz, 2006, p. 105).

9. In Toni Casares's 2005 production of the play for Sala Beckett, Barcelona, while delivering her testimony Corinne suddenly poured the water from the jug Richard had brought her at the start of the scene on her face and body, drenching her clothes – a gesture that functioned as a visual sign of her desire to free herself from her complicity with Richard's values, as well as from the role of victim Richard imposes on her.

10. Sierz sees Morris's discovery of Rebecca's watch as ambiguous, possibly a suggestion that Richard is still seeing Rebecca (2006, p. 59).

11. Middeke claims that the play 'ends in a Beckettian fashion as a cul-de-sac situation of paralysis' (2011, p. 93) where neither Corinne nor Richard make any gesture of approach or of final rupture, while the '*phone continues to ring*' (Crimp, 2005b, p. 366).

12. As Angelaki notes (2012, p. 33), *The City* resonates strongly with Crimp's reading of Richard Sennett's *The Corrosion of Character: The Personal Consequences of Work in the New Capitalism* (1998).

13. Research towards this chapter was conducted in the context of the research project 'The representation of politics and the politics of representation in post-1990 British drama and theatre' (FFI2009-07598), funded by the Spanish Ministry of Science and Innovation. I would like to thank Mireia Aragay and Enric Monforte for their invaluable comments. An early version of this chapter, focusing only on *The Country*, was presented at the conference 'The Viewing of Politics and the Politics of Viewing: Theatre Challenges in the Age of Globalized Communities' held at Aristotle University, Thessaloniki (Greece) on 18–20 April 2013.

Works cited

Adorno, T.W. (2000) *The Adorno Reader*, ed. B. O'Connor (Oxford: Blackwell).

Agamben, G. (2002) *Remnants of Auschwitz: The Witness and the Archive*, trans. D. Heller-Roazen (New York: Zone Books).

Angelaki, V. (2007) 'Performing Phenomenology: The Theatre of Martin Crimp' in D. Watt and D. Meyer-Dinkgräfe (eds) *Theatres of Thought: Theatre, Performance and Philosophy* (Newcastle: Cambridge Scholars Publishing), pp. 6–12.

—— (2008) 'Subtractive Forms and Composite Contents: Martin Crimp's *Fewer Emergencies*' in E. Redling and P.P. Schnierer (eds) *Non-Standard Forms of Contemporary Drama and Theatre* (Trier: Wissenschaftlicher Verlag Trier), pp. 31–46.

—— (2012) *The Plays of Martin Crimp: Making Theatre Strange* (Basingstoke and New York: Palgrave Macmillan).

Angel-Perez, É. (2006) *Voyages au bout du possible: Les théâtres du traumatisme de Samuel Beckett à Sarah Kane* (Paris: Klincksieck).

Bakhtin, M. (1995) *Bakhtinian Thought: An Introductory Reader*, ed. S. Dentith (New York and London: Routledge).

Bauman, Z. (1989) *Modernity and the Holocaust* (Cambridge: Polity).

—— (2008) *Does Ethics Have a Chance in a World of Consumers?* (Cambridge, MA and London: Harvard University Press).

Burkitt, I. (1999) *Bodies of Thought: Embodiment, Identity and Modernity* (London and New Delhi: Sage).

Buse, P. (2007) 'Sollicitations téléphoniques: *La Campagne* de Martin Crimp' in É. Angel-Perez and N. Boireau (eds) *Le théâtre anglais contemporain* (Paris: Klincksieck), pp. 153–68.

Cheng, S. (2004) 'Introduction: Law, Justice, and Power in the Global Age' in S. Cheng (ed.) *Law, Justice and Power: Between Reason and Will* (Stanford, CA: Stanford University Press), pp. 1–22.

Crimp, M. (2000) *Plays One (Dealing with Clair, Play with Repeats, Getting Attention, The Treatment)* (London: Faber).

—— (2004) *Cruel and Tender: After Sophocles's Trachiniae* (London: Faber).

—— (2005a) *Fewer Emergencies* (London: Faber).

—— (2005b) *Plays Two (No One Sees the Video, The Misanthrope, Attempts on Her Life, The Country)* (London: Faber).

—— (2006) *The Seagull: In a Version by Martin Crimp* (London: Faber).

—— (2008) *The City* (London: Faber).

Felman, S. and D. Laub (1992) *Testimony: Crises of Witnessing in Literature, Psychoanalysis, and History* (New York and London: Routledge).

Hardt, M. and A. Negri (2000) *Empire* (Cambridge, MA and London: Harvard University Press).

Hobsbawm, E. (1994) *The Age of Extremes: The Short Twentieth Century (1914–1991)* (London: Abacus).

Levinas, E. (1989) *The Levinas Reader*, ed. S. Hand (Oxford: Blackwell).

Middeke, M. (2011) 'Martin Crimp' in M. Middeke, P.P. Schnierer and A. Sierz (eds) *The Methuen Drama Guide to Contemporary British Playwrights* (London: Methuen), pp. 82–102.

Rebellato, D. (2009) *Theatre & Globalization* (Basingstoke and New York: Palgrave Macmillan).

Reyes Mate, M. (2003) *Memoria de Auschwitz: actualidad moral y política* (Madrid: Trotta).

Schaubühne (2008) 'Premieres & Repertoire: *The City* and *The Cut*', http://www.schaubuehne.de/en_EN/program/repertoire/253249/ (accessed 15 March 2013).

Sennett, R. (1998) *The Corrosion of Character: The Personal Consequences of Work in the New Capitalism* (New York: W.W. Norton).

Sierz, A. (2006) *The Theatre of Martin Crimp* (London: Methuen).

Smith, D. (1999) *Zygmunt Bauman: Prophet of Postmodernity* (Oxford and Malden: Polity).

3

Bearing Witness and Ethical Responsibility in Harold Pinter's *Ashes to Ashes*

Hanna Scolnicov

Ashes to Ashes (1996) stands out among Pinter's plays for in it he dares to address, although obliquely, the most serious ethical breakdown of the twentieth century, the Holocaust. The play engages with the ethical enormity of an actual historical event, though not with its historical dimension. Indeed, for Pinter the reality of the event lies in our memory of it, in the particular place it occupies in our consciousness, not in any meticulously described facts.

Pinter's early plays do not address ethical questions directly, but the behaviour of the characters provokes a moral reaction from the reader and spectator. In *The Homecoming* (1965) the question of morality is ironized when Max praises his dead wife, 'She taught [those boys] all the morality they know, I'm telling you. Every single bit of the moral code they live by – was taught to them by their mother' (pp. 45–6). This commendation is undermined by what we hear and see for ourselves in the play. *The Homecoming* is a play that slaps us in the face, forcing us to reflect on the (im)morality of the characters without offering any inbuilt ethical framework. We are faced with incest and prostitution and the complete breakdown of family relations without any sense of shame or hurt, as though all these were perfectly natural. Ruth negotiates the terms of her employment as prostitute with the family as if it were an ordinary business proposition. Her husband Teddy accepts the new situation and returns alone to his children in America without protest. Neither of them expresses any moral doubts and the effect is to force us to bring our own morality to bear on the action of the play. If we are shocked, we must ask ourselves why we are shocked, what it is that makes us feel uncomfortable or even outraged. Pinter purposely oversteps the boundaries of propriety when Lenny asks his father, 'That night [. . .] you know [. . .] the night you got me [. . .] that night with

Mum, what was it like?' (Pinter, 1965, p. 36). We feel immediately that he is breaking the taboo about sexual relations between parents and asking something that we usually repress. Pinter thus makes us examine the boundaries of our moral behaviour. Are the old boundaries still in place? Do we want to move them?

A similar effect is created by *Betrayal* (1978), a play that examines our reaction to what used to be considered a sin. In the sophisticated, Western, secular, upper-middle-class *milieu* depicted in the play, sexual betrayal seems to be an accepted norm, and we are called upon to ponder whether we are prepared to accept such a change in our moral beliefs. Clearly the burden of moral judgement is here shoved in the direction of the beholder and depends on his or her beliefs, and the reaction will differ wildly between viewers according to their cultural backgrounds. The playwright set out to shock us by refraining from providing any frame of reference, leaving us to judge the behaviour of his characters in view of our own moral standards and forcing us to review those standards in the light of contemporary life.[1]

In some of the so-called 'political plays' that preceded *Ashes to Ashes*, especially *One for the Road* (1984), *Mountain Language* (1988) and *Party Time* (1991), Pinter tackled the inhumanity of torture, taking up the contemporary concern with human rights, abstracting it from any particular political context and articulating a universal, humanist protest against that evil. These plays address the ethical question of torture forcefully, without actually showing it. The torture remains in the theatrical space without, although we are made keenly aware of its taking place there and then and can see its effects. Thus, in *One for the Road*, Victor first enters walking slowly, visibly bruised and with his clothes torn. At the end of the play, he is revealed sitting and tidily dressed, but something has been done to his tongue, so that he cannot speak clearly. The strongest impact is created by a subtle shift in tenses, when the torturer's statement about Victor and Gila's seven-year-old son, 'He's a little prick', is replaced by his final words in the play, 'He was a little prick' (Pinter, 1984, pp. 22, 24). In *Mountain Language*, we join the women's visit to their imprisoned dissident men. Speaking the 'mountain language' is forbidden by the ruling regime, but once this arbitrary restriction is lifted, the old mother, who can speak no other language, has lost her power of speech. The haunting images of the hooded man and the old woman whose hand has been mauled by one of the guard dogs are the closest we get to viewing the torture. And at the very end of *Party Time*, the appearance of the thinly dressed Jimmy in the doorway, coming out of the intense light and into the darkened living room, allows us to hear from him about his suffering in prison. His sister attempts to find out throughout the party 'what's happened to Jimmy?', a question that is deemed inappropriate and impolite by the rest of the characters (Pinter, 1991, p. 4; cf. pp. 17, 25). The whole play thus draws attention to the reality outside the party held to celebrate the well-being of a society that relies on repression and denial of wrongdoing.

Mother, child, and the breach of ethics

But nowhere did Pinter tackle the breach of ethics at its very core as he did in *Ashes to Ashes*. In this play, he went beyond politically motivated torture by placing at its centre the most touching, universal image of the bundled baby torn from its mother's arms on the railway platform, soon to be murdered. This is the most devastating Nazi image, which we know from the evidence given by numerous survivors, including some at the Eichmann trial. At the same time, the image also has wider cultural resonances. In Shakespeare's *Macbeth*, in order to prove her own fortitude to her husband, Lady Macbeth evokes the tender image of herself as the mother nursing her smiling baby only to demonstrate her own ruthlessness and callous ability to murder the child. The Christian iconography of Madonna with child and, especially, the *Madonna lactans* – the mother breast-feeding her baby – is a poignant expression of humanity, its common denominator. The haunting image of the bereaved mother holding on to her dead child also appears on the left-hand side of Picasso's *Guernica*.

Thus snatching the baby from its protective mother is highlighted by Pinter as an icon of cruelty, with the wrapping up of the baby into a bundle accentuating its helplessness and vulnerability. As noted, the bundle appears in countless Holocaust survivor stories. Thus, for example, the French Gentile Auschwitz survivor Charlotte Delbo remembers a woman with the bundle in her story 'Voices'. Standing at roll call, in freezing cold, a Gypsy woman holds a bundle of rags, 'in the crook of her arm, the way a baby is held, the baby's head against its mother's breast' (Delbo, 1995b, p. 83). The following day, the woman is clubbed to death by a female guard and the bundle of rags, her dead baby, is thrown into the garbage heap.[2] Pinter, if he indeed used this passage as an artistic source, preserved the shawl in which the Gypsy woman had wrapped the baby as well as the haunting image of the bundle held under the arm and the gesture of checking the baby's breathing. He pared down what was already a stark story, so as to highlight the core image of the Holocaust mother. The realization that he could equally have gleaned these materials from any other number of sources only strengthens the totally abstracted image he formed.

Indeed, another instance of the bundle appears in the testimony of Bessie K., which, again, may or may not have been one of Pinter's sources:

> [Bessie K.] was a young wife with an infant in 1942 at the time of a selection for work from the Kovno ghetto. Children were of course excluded, but she wrapped her baby in her coat as if it were a bundle and tried to sneak it by the Germans. Unfortunately the baby cried out, and they seized it. 'And this was the last time I had the bundle with me.' [. . .] She cannot remember details of the subsequent train ride, though the consequences of that awful moment are etched on her memory. (qtd. in Langer 1991, p. 49; see also Merritt 2000)[3]

Bessie's husband, Jacob K., explains why this can never be forgotten:

> We perceive life as a precious thing. And then Bessie gives birth to a child and the German takes away the child and kills it. What are we, superhuman, to just brush it aside and say to the world, 'Thank you for liberating us?' And that's all, we wash the hands clean like nothing happened? [. . .] I can't make peace with that. (qtd. in Langer 1991, p. 52)

The magnitude of the crime is such that the victim cannot come to terms with it – in other words, the murder of the baby cannot be accommodated within any ethical discourse.

The ethical burden of memory

In a private communication to Michael Billington, the critic and author of the monumental biography of the playwright, Pinter himself referred specifically, in connection with *Ashes to Ashes*, to the Nazi murders of babies as an image triggered by his reading of Gitta Sereny's *Albert Speer: His Battle with Truth* (1995):

> One of the central images of the play came from Pinter's choice of holiday reading in Barbados: Gitta Sereny's biography of Albert Speer who was Hitler's favourite architect, Minister for Armaments and Munitions from 1942, and virtually the Führer's second-in-command. [. . .] 'I was very struck by the fact that Speer organized and was responsible for the slave-labour factories in Nazi Germany. Yet he was also,

in some ways, a very civilized man and was horrified by what he saw when he visited the factories. That image stayed with me. Also, the fact that these places had no lavatories and that there were these primitive privies. [. . .] Reading the book also triggered lots of other associations. I've always been haunted by the image of the Nazis picking up babies on bayonet-spikes and throwing them out of windows.' (Billington, 1996, pp. 374–5)

However, as Billington himself notes in 'Staging Speer', his review of David Edgar's play *Albert Speer* (2000), Speer's name is never even mentioned in *Ashes to Ashes* and Pinter seems never to have declared publicly that the play was based on Sereny's biography. It is only Billington who revealed that Sereny's book had served as a source and inspiration for Pinter's play.[4] This revelation is quite different from Pinter's own admission, in a note prefixed to *A Kind of Alaska* (1982), that he used Oliver Sachs's *Awakenings* (1973) as a source, a reference that directs the reader to view the play as an exploration of some of the psychic cases treated by the famous neurologist. In his review of Edgar's play, Billington (2000) stresses Pinter's use in *Ashes to Ashes* of 'the horrific image of an underground labour camp in the Harz mountains' and his oblique interest in Speer's late-life love affair with a young German woman, both putatively drawn from Sereny's book. His remarks, both in the Pinter biography and in the review of Edgar's play, do offer important clues to the significance of a number of passages in *Ashes to Ashes*, but the emphasis on a single source, Sereny's magisterial biography of Speer, has deflected critical attention from the central, thematic interest of the play around the puzzling figure of the Nazi lover.[5] A close reading of the play will show the centrality of the questions of testimony, the reliability of memory and ethical responsibility with which the play is concerned.

A comparison of *Ashes to Ashes* with Edgar's *Albert Speer* may help elucidate what is unique about Pinter's play. Edgar's play announces beneath its title that it is '[b]ased on the book *Albert Speer: His Battle with Truth* by Gitta Sereny' and employs a large cast of 56, even though Edgar claims that he found it necessary 'to conflate characters' (2000, p. ix). Following in Sereny's footsteps, Edgar is interested in retelling her story in the dramatic medium and exploring the truth of Speer's self-fashioning. Pinter's austere minimalism is accentuated by this comparison, as are also his very different ethical concerns. For his chamber play, Pinter needs no more than two non-historical characters, Rebecca and Devlin, who are only characterized as being in their forties. He has no use for the figure of Speer, confining himself to some oblique allusions, which are examined below.

In his review of Edgar's play, Billington (2000) sets out to probe 'what's the best way to represent the evils of Nazism'. Pinter's play is mentioned as an example of an imaginative treatment of historical material in contrast to *Nuremberg*, the documentary verbatim reproduction of the Nuremberg Trials compiled by Richard Norton-Taylor and staged at the Tricycle Theatre in 1996. Billington sees Edgar's *Albert Speer* as an attempt to combine the two opposite approaches, albeit with limited success.[6] *Nuremberg* and *Albert Speer* were intended to raise the spectators' ethical indignation at the Nazi leaders' refusal to accept responsibility, their denial of knowledge and their complicity in the 'final solution' to the Jewish problem. Unlike these plays, *Ashes to Ashes* does not set out to investigate the character of a particular Nazi leader. Neither is it a play about one or more of the victims, although it is a play about the Holocaust. Rather than attempt to represent the atrocities of the Shoah, Pinter deals with its memory. Rebecca experiences the Shoah as a surrealist hallucination in which she becomes implicated. She describes scenes that take on the appearance of private screenings of a surrealist film, which her partner Devlin has not been admitted to and only she can see. Like Devlin, the spectator can only hear Rebecca's report of her vision, but not see it.

Already in his so-called political plays, Pinter managed to convey the dreadfulness of torture and other forms of political oppression without actually showing them on stage. In those earlier plays, he dealt with what was happening at the present dramatic moment, with the torture taking place in the theatrical space without, in an adjacent room or in the street below. In *Ashes to Ashes* he is dealing with the past, with the memory of the Shoah rather than with the Shoah itself, with its deep imprint on the mind rather than with its documented events. In this respect, *Ashes to Ashes* differs from all the plays Pinter had written previously – it deals with the ethical burden of memory, of bearing witness, of living with the haunting memory. Unlike the torture that takes place somewhere outside the entrance door in *Party Time*, here it is the memories of the Holocaust that are viewed through the window and even these are recounted as having taken place elsewhere and in the past, albeit the near past – not here and now.

The Shoah does indeed appear to be uppermost in Rebecca's mind, but as she is in her forties and the play takes place 'Now' (initial stage direction) – that is, in the present time of the original performance, 1996 – she was clearly born after the Second World War and can have no first-hand knowledge of the Holocaust.[7] This raises the question of the epistemological status of Rebecca's narrated memories and visions. As she herself insists that 'Nothing has ever happened to me' (Pinter, 1996, p. 41), a plausible conclusion is that what she remembers is taken from our collective memory of the Holocaust, from what we have picked up by listening to survivors' testimonies, watching documentaries, reading books and so on.[8] Shoshana Felman has described the filmmaker Claude Lanzmann and the historian Raul Hilberg, who worked with Lanzmann on the film *Shoah*, as second-degree witnesses, 'witnesses of witnesses, witnesses of the testimonies' (Felman and Laub, 1992, p. 21). Lanzmann himself has questioned the notion that the Holocaust was an historical event of limited duration – 'When does the Holocaust really end? Did it end the last day of the war? Did it end with the creation of the State of Israel? No. It still goes on. These events are of such magnitude, of such scope that they have never stopped developing their consequences' (qtd. in Felman and Laub, 1992, p. 242). Following Lanzmann's line of thought, Felman and Laub view the Holocaust 'not as an event encapsulated in the past, but as a history which is essentially *not over*, a history whose repercussions are not simply omnipresent (whether consciously or not) in all our cultural activities, but whose traumatic consequences are still actively *evolving* [. . .] in today's political, historical, cultural and artistic scene' (Felman and Laub 1992, p. xiv; emphasis original). Arguably, Pinter's ascetic, minimalist play engages precisely with these evolving consequences, with the manner in which the Holocaust continues to be with us, infecting our ethical thinking, intervening in our most intimate relationships, in our everyday thoughts and actions. Pinter shows that you do not need to be a survivor in order to be deeply disturbed by Holocaust memories.

Felman and Laub highlight the paradoxical nature of the Holocaust 'as a radical historical *crisis of witnessing*, and as the unprecedented, inconceivable, historical occurrence of "an event without a witness" – as eliminating its own witness' (Felman and Laub, 1992, p. xvii; emphasis original). Because the Nazis attempted to exterminate the Jewish people, most of the potential witnesses were eliminated, so that establishing what actually happened becomes very difficult. That is why assembling the evidence at the trials of the Nazi murderers and their collaborators still proves so problematic. The various projects of recording and archiving the testimonies of the dwindling number of survivors are essential, especially as many of the victims who survived were too traumatized to tell their story until many years had gone by. The victimizers, on the other hand, by and large chose to deny their personal involvement and even knowledge of the terrible crimes, so that establishing the truth through testimony has become a major issue. This problem is exacerbated by the prominent Holocaust deniers. Thus the Holocaust is the case *par excellence* that links ethics to testimony, to the gathering of first-hand evidence about what happened. Rebecca's Holocaust memories have baffled many readers and spectators of the play because, as noted above, given her young age they cannot possibly be based on her own experience. Growing up in England, Pinter himself had no direct memories of the Shoah, but as a sensitive intellectual and a Jew, as a second-degree witness, he found the way to express his own, indirect response to the horrors through Rebecca's surrealist nightmare visions.

The year before the play was written marked the publication of a book that perhaps throws some oblique light on Pinter's presentation of memory in this play, Binjamin Wilkomirski's moving, but fraudulent, memoir, *Fragments: Memories of a Wartime Childhood* (English translation, 1996). The Swiss journalist Daniel Ganzfried was the first to uncover the hoax; then historian Stefan Maechler researched Wilkomirski's background and showed conclusively that he was not Jewish and had never been in the concentration camps – his real name was Bruno Grosjean and his life-story was quite different from the moving tale of his supposed childhood memories (Maechler, 2001). And yet, if seen as a manifestation of extreme self-identification with the fate of Holocaust survivors and understood as a psychological quirk, Wilkomirski's book may offer an interesting real-life analogue to Rebecca's identification with the victims.[9] Pinter wrote his play in 1996, so possibly too early to have heard of the scandal surrounding Wilkomirski. But even with no knowledge of that affair, Pinter clearly understood the imaginative force of taking upon oneself the ethical responsibility of bearing witness.

At a public interview held in Barcelona in 1996, in response to Mireia Aragay's question whether the play was about Nazism, Pinter answered in the negative, but qualified his answer – 'It *is* about the images of Nazi Germany; I don't think anyone can ever get that out of their mind. The Holocaust is probably the worst thing that ever happened because it was so calculated, deliberate and precise and so fully documented by the people who actually did it' (Pinter, 1998, p. 65; emphasis original). He added his political rebuke of countries that call themselves democracies but support repressive and tyrannical regimes. It should be noted that, here as elsewhere, the contemporary political dimension lies completely outside the perimeter of the play itself and belongs to Pinter's public pronouncements. The views he voiced in interviews and in the public media have given rise to interpretations of *Ashes to Ashes* as a play that deals with genocide in general. However, not only is the play full of references to the Holocaust but, as just noted, Pinter was quite specific about the play being 'about the images of Nazi Germany'. Charles Grimes has observed that '[t]he play is at odds with its author' (2005, pp. 211–12), an observation that can perhaps be understood as the gap between Pinter the playwright and Pinter the political activist.

Surreal images of the Holocaust

The familiar images of the Holocaust stare us in the face in *Ashes to Ashes*, starting with the overpowering image of the ashes invoked by the title, reminding us primarily of the crematoria and of the Anglican burial service.[10] In the play itself, the first, veiled evocation of the Shoah appears in Rebecca's response to being questioned by Devlin about her former lover's job – 'I think it had something to do with a travel agency. I think he was some kind of courier. No. No, he wasn't. That was only a part-time job. I mean that was only part of the job in the agency. He was quite high up, you see. He had a lot of responsibilities' (Pinter, 1996, p. 19). Rebecca is very hesitant when answering Devlin's simple, factual question, which raises the question of why it is so difficult for her to give a straight answer. When pressed by Devlin about the travel agency, she states that, '[h]e was a guide, you see. A guide', as though this would explain it all. The mystified Devlin then asks her, '[a] tourist guide?', a question she leaves unanswered (p. 21).

To remove the mystifying veil from Rebecca's words, we must recall that in German a guide, including a tourist guide, is a *Führer*. The word not only served as Hitler's title, but also formed part of rank definitions such as *Sturmbannführer* in the SA, or *Obergruppenführer* in the SS. When he was appointed Minister for Armaments and Munitions, Albert Speer was granted the rank of *Oberstgruppenführer*. Among his ministerial charges, he was responsible for transportation, primarily the railway system. Hence the travel agency, the responsibilities and the high-up position in Rebecca's account of her lover's job. The repeated insistence on the role of the guide – the tourist guide, the guide connected with the travel agency and, later in the play, the guides that ushered the people into the sea – points to the special significance of the word, without, however, divulging its hidden German referent.[11] But because Rebecca hedges her answers, skirting unseen obstacles, her words become weighted with meaning.

This initial, tentative reading turns into certainty when Rebecca suddenly implicates the guide in the Nazi atrocities – 'He did work for a travel agency. He was a guide. He used to go to the local railway station and walk down the platform and tear all the babies from the arms of their screaming mothers' (Pinter, 1996, p. 27). This is the first appearance in the play of the Nazi image of tearing a baby from its mother's arms, and it erupts quite unexpectedly from the renewed discussion of the lover's occupation. The image is sketched lightly, a mere generalized outline, but its effect is shattering, evoking the endless stories of the train transports of Jews arriving at the extermination camps and the cruelty of the camp guards, especially to babies. Without so much as mentioning them, the reality of the camps suddenly invades the here and now, the English room in 1996, exploding the tranquillity and serenity of the English surroundings. Similarly, Rebecca's account of her visit to 'a kind of factory' that 'wasn't the usual kind of factory' (p. 23) raises the spectre of the Nazi labour camps. As noted by Billington (2000), this strange factory, with its workers who doffed their caps to salute Rebecca's lover, its dampness, the absence of suitable clothing for the workers and the lack of a bathroom are all indebted to Speer's own description of his inspection of the labour camp in the Harz mountains. In short, the mother refusing to let go of her dead bundle, the trains, the forced labour, the double life of the cruel camp commanders as lovers or family men, and so on, are not just generalized signifiers – we *know* what the signifieds are.[12]

The most painful reference to the baby occurs in the final, closing movement of the play (Pinter, 1996, pp. 71–85). Towards the end of Rebecca's vision through a window at the top of a very tall building, she suddenly sees a woman carrying a baby in her arms. Rebecca stays close to the curtains, looking down at the icy street on a star-lit night. The insistence on the window, on watching the scene from above and on the curtains that can shut off the view – all this indicates the separateness, the line of demarcation that cuts off the viewer form the scene taking place outdoors, below. But Rebecca does not close the curtains, because she wants to continue watching what the woman is doing. She sees her kissing her baby and observes that the baby was a girl. After kissing the baby, the woman listens to its heartbeat, indicating that the baby is alive. Then comes the startling change, with '*I* held her to me. She was breathing. Her heart was beating' (p. 73; emphasis added). A transition is effected through the deft change of pronouns from 'she' to 'I', a shift from the observed woman to Rebecca's own speaking voice. No longer standing behind the high-up window, shielded by the curtains, Rebecca now enters the previously detached scene and identifies with the mother, linking herself physically and maternally to the baby girl.

The eerie echo that punctuates her words adds pathos to the emotionally charged, surrealistic experience. Here Pinter uses a totally unrealistic effect that reinforces the other surreal elements in the play. The echo joins the carefully designed visual effect, indicated in the stage directions, of the light in the room darkening, while the lamps burn bright. The scene captures some of the riddling mystery expressed by Paul Delvaux's *L'Écho* (1943), a painting that depicts a naked woman walking along a deserted road lined with classical buildings, under a shining moon. Her figure is repeated three times along the road, in receding scale, creating a visual echo, and the silence contained within the image is contrasted with its aural title. Delvaux's nocturnal scene is bathed in a mysterious light. Like the suppressed echo of the painting, Pinter's echo is unsettling, expanding the impact of the series of words that are echoed – 'bundle', 'train', 'baby'. Rebecca's final words, 'I don't know of any baby', are followed by a *'[l]ong silence'* and *'[b]lackout'* (Pinter, 1996, p. 85). Having crossed the frontier that separated her from the nightmare vision of the Holocaust, Rebecca re-enacts in her mind the steps of the trauma – the deportation in the trains, the snatching of the babies, the mother's desperate attempt to save her baby by carrying it under her arm as though it were a mere bundle of clothes, and the baby's crying which gives away the attempt to conceal it. The effect on her of having had to give up the baby is so devastating that, after the train trip to 'this place' (p. 81), presumably a concentration camp, when she meets a woman who inquires about the baby, she denies having had a baby.[13] Thus Pinter manages to distil the Shoah experience and provide its experiential aspect without ever recounting or recording any actual or particular episode. He is not interested in the documentation of the Nazi crimes, but in their continued presence in our consciousness, in the intimate sense of the desecration of our most cherished values.

By its very nature, the echo is a disembodied voice, an automatic reflection, but one that is a natural effect, often experienced while walking through a natural landscape. The voice that has left the person that emitted it is replicated and expanded and points to the lack of an interlocutor, thus creating a sense of the speaker's loneliness, the lack of a responsive partner. Trapped in time, this particular echo will continue to reverberate after the *'[l]ong silence'* that ends the play. The haunting words and Rebecca's enigmatic experiences will rattle spectators, making them ponder the nature of her surrealistic narratives and the meaning of the play as a whole. The echoes of the past are all that remains of the cataclysmic events. It is these echoes that Pinter is out to capture in this play, rather than the past events that created them and that can only be approached through memories, through the recorded testimonies of survivors.

'Profound memory' as ethical responsibility

In a number of his early plays, Pinter pursued the many questions concerning the nature of memory – its unreliability, primarily, but also its role in both life and art. Drama unfolds within a given theatrical space at the present moment, but the past is also present, now, in the *present*, in the form of memory. The evasiveness of memory and its deliberate manipulation and fabrication are themes Pinter treated widely throughout his career. As stated above, the so-called 'political plays' – *One for the Road*, *Mountain Language* and *Party Time* – broke away from the earlier, more light-hearted concern with love and betrayal, moving into the unambiguous grim reality of torture. This was a radical change that spelled ethical engagement. The earlier investigation of the poetics of theatre was superseded by a humanist commitment, a sense of outrage and an overriding wish to bring about change in the world through its representation. Following these plays, Pinter's inquiry into the nature of memory took on a new turn, focusing on the collective, and verifiable, memories of the Holocaust. In *Ashes to Ashes*, Pinter found a way to engage with the Shoah without so much as mentioning it, evoking its horrors without documenting them. His procedure is especially striking when set against the contemporary background of documentary and verbatim theatre.

Pinter's reliance on particular testimonies was for him a new technique, which may have developed in the wake of gathering evidence about the infringement of the human rights of dissidents in Turkey. But in his resulting plays, *One for the Road* and *Mountain Language*, Pinter did not represent the oppression of the Kurds. Rather, he distilled the testimonies, giving artistic shape to the general structure of brutal repression. In *Ashes to Ashes*, Pinter distanced himself from the historical event, approaching the Holocaust at second remove, through its memory. As already noted, the protagonist of the play is too young to have experienced the Holocaust at first hand, so that what she remembers are vicarious experiences, which she visualizes as hallucinations.

The memory of the past is what sets Devlin and Rebecca apart in the present. Devlin tries to ferret out Rebecca's secret, and she is willing to answer his questions and talk about her past liaison. He tries to reach her by enacting the lover's typical sexual handling of her, but he cannot share her memory of the Holocaust, despite her telling him about it.

This constitutes her inner world, the world of a sensitive person whose life has been marred by the knowledge of what has happened. Her later entrance into the surrealistic dream, her acceptance of the fate of the woman whose baby was snatched and murdered, even the guilt feelings of the mother that bring her to deny having had such a baby – all these are expressions of her deep empathy, of her identification with the eye-witnesses, of taking upon herself the responsibility. Witnessing here is no longer an objective fact, but an ethical assumption of moral responsibility. The witness reports are no longer external reports, but become internal, personal experiences.

The gulf that separates Devlin from Rebecca is the ethical question, whether it is possible *not* to see the Holocaust through the window. Can one forget, rather than can one remember? Is it possible *not* to be constantly aware of the horrors? Can one escape the 'mental elephantiasis' that is spreading and suffocating Rebecca 'in a voluminous sea of gravy'? (Pinter, 1996, p. 51). Is it possible *not* to assume personal responsibility for having handed over the bundle? Can one ignore the corpse-like figure sitting in front of us in the cinema, who never laughs? (p. 65). The siren of the passing police car is similarly a reminder of the atrocity; it cannot be ignored (p. 29). The Holocaust has poisoned Rebecca's life, even though she is not its direct victim.

Rebecca's memories take on two forms: her recollections of her lover, prompted by Devlin's inquiring about him; and her two spontaneously recounted visions through the windows of the house in Dorset, looking out at the garden (p. 47), and from the room at the top of a tall building in the middle of town (p. 71). The first type of recollection has a more realistic appearance, while the latter is largely hallucinatory. At the end of the play, the two types of memories blend, as Rebecca seems to enter the framed hallucination, overstepping the borderline between recollection and reverie. Rebecca's two kinds of remembrance of the past can be conceptualized with the help of an incisive distinction made by Delbo between two kinds of memory, *mémoire ordinaire* and *mémoire profonde* (Langer, 1995b, p. 13; see also Delbo, 1985, p. 13; Langer, 1991, p. 5). The first kind views the past from the perspective of the present, as something that took place then, but is now over. The second re-enacts the past *in* the present. In a piece titled 'One day', part of her Auschwitz memories, Delbo is simultaneously sitting in the Parisian café, 'writing this text', and standing in the snow for hours at roll call, benumbed and freezing, watching the crazed and the dying (Delbo, 1968, pp. 26, 29). There can be little doubt as to which of the two presents possesses a stronger reality. As Delbo 'sees' Auschwitz in Paris, so too Rebecca sees visions of the Holocaust in Dorset. Pinter's double exposure, the English room in the present and the view of the Holocaust through the window, can perhaps best be understood in relation to Delbo's distinction between common and deep memory.

Rebecca's surrealist Holocaust visions through the window demonstrate that, for her, the accounts of the atrocities have become profound memories, which cannot be put aside. Whether Pinter was familiar with Delbo's writings or not, his approach to the question of memory was quite close to hers, as can be seen from his statement that, 'I'm talking about us and our conception of our past and our history, and what it does to us in the present' (Pinter, 1998, p. 66). In *Ashes to Ashes*, Pinter shows that, for us too, the memories of the Holocaust have become profound memories, and we too can never lay them to rest. Pinter's pronouncement contradicts Grimes's assertion that in *Ashes to Ashes* 'Pinter is no longer dramatizing the persistence of the past in the present; memory now can no longer sustain the presence, the presentness, of the past' (2005, p. 216). *Ashes to Ashes* is a play about the Holocaust – though not directly. The word is never once mentioned and there is no reference to Jews, Nazis or concentration camps. Instead, it is a play about the place of the Holocaust in our present consciousness, about the ethical role it plays in our memory.

Notes

1. For a fuller discussion of Pinter's treatment of betrayal, see Scolnicov, 1997.
2. I already pointed to the interesting parallels in the treatment of Holocaust themes between Pinter and Delbo in Scolnicov, 2001. Élisabeth Angel-Perez (2009) picks up my suggestion of the parallels with Delbo, but then takes it as an established fact that Delbo served as Pinter's direct source.
3. Geoffrey Hartman's report of the contents of this testimony can be found at http://writing.upenn.edu/wh/archival/documents/karlan/hartman.php.
4. However, Katherine H. Burkman bases her entire reading of the play on the idea that Devlin and Rebecca are a 'metaphor' for Speer (1999b, pp. 86, 89).
5. For a wider discussion of the impact of Sereny's book on Pinter, see Scolnicov, 2012, pp. 160–1. In a later book, Sereny recounts her visit to Bochum in 1998, on the invitation of the Bochum Schauspielhaus, which was then rehearsing *Ashes to Ashes*. She was invited 'to talk to them about how Pinter had started to write this play "after reading your book"' (2001, p. 286). Sereny writes that until then she was not aware of having written something that contributed to Pinter's play. She wrongly assumed that they were interested in the figure of Franz Stangl, commandant of Treblinka, about whom she had written another book, *Into that Darkness* (1974). On meeting Pinter shortly before leaving for Bochum, he corrected her supposition, told her it was Speer he had been interested in and sent her Billington's *The Life and*

Work of Harold Pinter. In any case, Sereny's initial misunderstanding of her contribution and her subsequent brief dismissal of her part in the conception of the play show that she, for one, did not regard her book as a source for the play and underline the simple fact that, although the play may have been instigated by the book, it is not at all a play about Speer.

6. Janelle Reinelt and Gerald Hewitt (2011) also refer to the blending of 'fact and fiction' in Edgar's 'grand epic play on Brechtian principles' (p. 194) and compare it with the 'strict verbatim version of *Nuremberg*' (p. 191).

7. Martin Regal (1997, p. 99) develops this argument convincingly.

8. In a similar vein, Susan Hollis Merritt regards Rebecca's memory as vicarious experience and as an example of 'cultural memory (in a Jungian sense)' (2008, p. 147).

9. Sereny writes of Wilkomirski that he was 'a human being who, out of a need I suspect of sharing the suffering, attempted to adopt the identity of the suffering child' (2001, p. 165).

10. The title also echoes that of Lawrence Langer's anthology of Holocaust writings, *Art from the Ashes* (1995a). Pinter may have come across this impressive volume, or perhaps Langer's is only yet another use of this overwhelming image.

11. Piotr Kuhiwczak (2001) deals with the problem of English translations of Holocaust memoirs that disregard the specific meanings of words in the original languages used by the victims.

12. In her review of the 1999 New York production, Burkman asserts that Rebecca's lover was 'an SS officer who took babies from mothers at train stations and who took her on a tour of a factory that has many signs of being a slave-labor one'. She argues forcefully that '[t]o feel the Holocaust in one's bones as one's inheritance is what the play is all about' (1999a, p. 155). On his part, Mark Taylor-Batty seems to argue that the Englishness of the setting points to the possibility that the atrocities 'could happen in modern-day Britain' (2001, p. 56). In the absence of any support from the play itself, the juxtaposition of Holocaust memories with contemporary life in England calls for a different, non-realistic interpretation that will make sense of having these two totally disparate worlds side by side.

13. Mireia Aragay sees Rebecca as imaginatively identifying with the woman whose baby was torn away by the soldiers, but at the same time, paradoxically, resigning human responsibility, allowing babies to be brutally torn away from mothers, 'handing over the bundle' (2009, p. 292).

Works cited

Angel-Perez, É. (2009) '*Ashes to Ashes*, Pinter's Dibbuks' in B. Gauthier (ed.) *Viva Pinter: Harold Pinter's Spirit of Resistance* (Bern: Peter Lang), pp. 139–60.

Aragay, M. (2009) 'Pinter, Politics and Postmodernism' in P. Raby (ed.) *The Cambridge Companion to Harold Pinter*, 2nd edn (Cambridge: Cambridge University Press), pp. 283–96.

Billington, M. (1996) *The Life and Work of Harold Pinter* (London: Faber).

—— (2000) 'Staging Speer', *Guardian*, 31 May, http://www.guardian.co.uk/culture/2000/may/31/artsfeatures/ (accessed 2 May 2013).

Burkman, K.H. (1999a) '*Ashes to Ashes* in New York', *The Pinter Review: Collected Essays 1997 and 1998*, pp. 154–5.

—— (1999b) 'Harold Pinter's *Ashes to Ashes*: Rebecca and Devlin as Albert Speer', *The Pinter Review: Collected Essays 1997 and 1998*, pp. 86–96.

Delbo, C. (1968) *None of Us Will Return*, trans. J. Githens (New York: Grove Press).

—— (1985) *La mémoire et les jours* (Paris: Berg International).

—— (1995a) *Auschwitz and After* (New Haven, CT: Yale University Press).

—— (1995b) 'Voices' in L.L. Langer (ed.) *Art from the Ashes: A Holocaust Anthology* (Oxford and New York: Oxford University Press), pp. 77–94.

Edgar, D. (2000) *Albert Speer* (London: Nick Hern).

Felman, S. and D. Laub (1992) *Testimony: Crises of Witnessing in Literature, Psychoanalysis, and History* (New York and London: Routledge).

Grimes, C. (2005) *Harold Pinter's Politics: A Silence beyond Echo* (Madison, NJ: Fairleigh Dickinson University Press).

Kuhiwczak, P. (2001) 'How do We Read the Holocaust Memoirs?' in J. Parker and T. Mathews (eds) *Tradition, Translation, Trauma: The Classic and the Modern* (Oxford: Oxford University Press), pp. 283–97.

Langer, L.L. (1991) *Holocaust Testimonies: The Ruins of Memory* (New Haven, CT: Yale University Press).

—— (ed.) (1995a) *Art from the Ashes: A Holocaust Anthology* (Oxford and New York: Oxford University Press).

—— (1995b) 'Introduction' in C. Delbo, *Auschwitz and After*, trans. R.C. Lamont (New Haven, CT and London: Yale University Press), pp. ix–xviii.

Lanzmann, C. (1985) *Shoah* (Historia/Les Films Aleph/Ministère de la Culture de la République Française).

Maechler, S. (2001) *The Wilkomirski Affair* (New York: Schocken Books).

Merritt, S.H. (2000) 'Harold Pinter's *Ashes to Ashes*: Political/Personal Echoes of the Holocaust', *The Pinter Review: Collected Essays 1999 and 2000*, pp. 73–84.

—— (2008) '(Anti-)Global Pinter', *The Pinter Review: Nobel Prize/Europe Theatre Prize Volume, 2005–2008*, pp. 140–67.

Norton-Taylor, R. (1997) *Nuremberg* (London: Nick Hern).

Pinter, H. (1965) *The Homecoming* (London: Methuen).

—— (1978) *Complete Works Three (The Homecoming, Tea Party, The Basement, Landscape, Silence, Night, et al.)* (New York: Grove Press).

—— (1981) *Complete Works Four (Old Times, No Man's Land, Betrayal, Monologue, Family Voices)* (New York: Grove Press).

—— (1982) *Other Places (Family Voices, Victoria Station, A Kind of Alaska)* (London: Methuen).

—— (1984) *One for the Road* (London: Methuen).

—— (1988) *Mountain Language* (New York: Grove Press).

—— (1991) *Party Time* (London: Faber).

—— (1996) *Ashes to Ashes* (London: Faber).

—— (1998) 'Writing, Politics and *Ashes to Ashes*', interview by M. Aragay and R. Simó, in *Various Voices: Prose, Poetry, Politics 1948–1998* (London: Faber), pp. 58–70.

Regal, M. (1997) '"You can only end once": Time in *Ashes to Ashes*', *Cycnos*, 14 (1), pp. 99–104.

Reinelt, J. and G. Hewitt (2011) *The Political Theatre of David Edgar* (Cambridge: Cambridge University Press).

Sachs, O. (1973) *Awakenings* (London: Duckworth).

Scolnicov, H. (1997) 'Pinter's Game of Betrayal', *Cycnos*, 14 (1), pp. 1–9.

—— (2001) '*Ashes to Ashes*: Pinter's Holocaust Play', *Cycnos*, 18 (1), pp. 15–24.

—— (2012) *The Experimental Plays of Harold Pinter* (Newark: University of Delaware Press).

Sereny, G. (1974) *Into that Darkness* (New York: Albert A. Knopf).

—— (1995) *Albert Speer: His Battle with Truth* (New York: Albert A. Knopf).

—— (2001) *The Healing Wound: Experiences and Reflections on Germany, 1938–2001* (New York and London: W.W. Norton).

Taylor-Batty, M. (2001) *Harold Pinter* (Tavistock: Northcote House/British Council).

Wilkomirski, B. (1996) *Fragments: Memories of a Wartime Childhood*, trans. C. Brown Janeway (New York: Schocken Books). Orig. publ. in 1995 as *Bruchstücke: Aus einer Kindheit 1939–1948* (Frankfurt Am Main: Suhrkamp Verlag).

4
How to Mourn: Kane, Pinter and Theatre as Monument to Loss in the 1990s

Mark Taylor-Batty

The 1990s and the aestheticization of authenticity

To that generation of people entering early adulthood at the turn of decade from the 1980s to the 1990s, there was a palpable sense of change in the world, a sense that decades of atrophying cold war were thawing around them, and that the political paradigms of the 1960s, 1970s and 1980s – and by consequence the cultural paradigms that had been sustained by or in opposition to these – might give way to exciting new opportunities. If we were to identify a key event that participated in generating this sense of renewal, then we might first consider the fall of the Berlin Wall in November 1989, an act that resonated on the plane of symbolic value across Europe. The face of this change was often brutal, with, for example, images of the executed bodies of Romanian tyrant Nicolae Ceaușescu and his wife Elena presented in news bulletins on Christmas Day 1989. Nelson Mandela's release in February 1990 continued the momentum of this sense of a new era, partially later manifested in British politics by the resignation of Margaret Thatcher in November 1990.

In October 1990, a few weeks before Thatcher's reluctant withdrawal from politics, something of a television phenomenon began in the UK, with the broadcast on BBC2 of David Lynch and Mark Frost's *Twin Peaks*. The airing of the first programme on 23 October attracted 8.15 million viewers, a historical high for a BBC2 Tuesday evening 9pm slot. The drama series, infused with surreal narrative strategies and imagery, applied and redesigned tropes of horror and detective genres within a predominantly aesthetically-motivated frame. If there was something of a cultural threshold forming in the UK, then the impact of this US show participated in that renewal from the platform of its own medium.

One of the primary images from *Twin Peaks* was of the corpse of Laura Palmer, wrapped in plastic, recovered from a river. This, along with grim forensic scenes such as the removal of evidence from beneath fingernails, was a first manifestation of a concern in popular television to represent death with regard to its social impact and the representation of the corpse: prolonged attention to the affects of mourning within a family and community of friends had never before received such screen time in popular entertainment. Certainly, the show stands to be accused of aestheticizing these issues as its ethical motor was much more monochrome than its aesthetic ambitions. Nonetheless, a corpse became a central character of sorts in the manner in which, by deliberate juxtaposition, the family portrait of Laura Palmer would form the sole imagery of (most of) the programme's end credit sequences. UK television series such as *Prime Suspect* (1991–2006) and *Cracker* (1993–95) made this attitude to death, and the bodily 'testimony' of the corpse, a fundamental aspect of their syntax of expression, and as such issues of authentic representation of death and its impact upon the living became part of the fabric of popular programming in the 1990s. A relationship was thereby established between the ambition of entertainment (and attracting audiences), and the ethical resonances of death and mourning. Against such contexts, this article sets out to examine how Sarah Kane sought to wield the potential of live performance to address tensions in representations of trauma and death, and to reflect on how she might have exerted an influence on Harold Pinter's concern for cognate issues. In doing so, it considers the axis between impact and affect on the one hand, and entertainment on the other, and the place of ethical judgement in relation to such issues.

On 15 May 1991, Steve Lamacq, a journalist for the *New Musical Express*, went to Norwich to interview a relatively new band with as yet no album contract, The Manic Street Preachers. Part of the soundscape of Kane's early twenties, she later added the job of 'a roadie' for this band to the fictional biography of her pseudonym Marie Kelvedon, to whom she attributed her play *Crave* in 1997 (Kane, 1998, p. v). Once the interview was over, guitarist Richey Edwards invited Lamacq backstage and sought to demonstrate that he and his band had integrity by carving the characters '4REAL' into his forearm with a razor blade. As an abridged statement of authenticity, this piece of writing was subsequently lauded by admirers of the band's work as a prime example of just what it purported to be: an ultimate statement of integrity mapped onto the band's claimed aesthetic objectives. Notably, it is the first public instance of an act of self harm being equated, in contemporary popular culture, with integrity and authentic expression. This event participated in something of a codification of self harm and the troubled mind in 1990s British culture as a stamp of individuality, of an anti-establishment stance, and as an index of genuine experience that would find articulation in the plays of Sarah Kane and qualify the celebrity of artists such as Sinéad O'Connor and Tracey Emin, and later Pete Doherty and Amy Winehouse. Recognition of the personal tragic flaw as an emblem of authenticity and integrity became part of the understanding that bound admirers to some cultural figures, and this was sealed significantly by, for example, the suicide of Kurt Cobain in April 1994 and the disappearance of Richey Edwards in February 1995.[1] This discourse, though, further troubles the boundaries (established by new paradigms of representations of death and mourning) between authentic experience, its representation and its (adopted or encoded) value as cultural currency for the attraction of a public.

Cutting skin and perforating the body was not new in art, of course, though they were to become a common element of the syntax of body art and extreme performance art in the 1990s, with artists such as Franko B, Ron Athey and Orlan applying it specifically to offer audiences challenging experiences that might speak to issues of gender construction, sexuality and identity formation more generally. International artists such as these were championed by a growing industry of performance art in the UK in that decade, which found itself embraced and adopted by the academy, as universities and new 'post-92' universities, especially, founded and developed arts centres in tandem with employing performers in roles as tutors and facilitators for students. While the growing prominence of body and performance art that involved forms of bloodletting contribute to a general shift in the aesthetic vocabulary of the decade to incorporate the corporeal and its experience in suffering, they (mostly) stand apart from acts of deliberate self harm as a frustrated form of self-expression which might subsequently inform or be incorporated into aesthetic objects such as Emin's *My Bed* (1999) or Kane's *4:48 Psychosis* (2000). A concern to explore human experience through a focus on the vulnerabilities of the body was to become a central motif in much 1990s theatre and performance. Mark Ravenhill declared that 'the highest form of reality is found in physical pain' (qtd. in Tabert and Carr, 1998, 71; my translation) and one might consider new theatrical work such as his and Kane's as representing a challenge to the poststructuralist de-materialization of bodily experience into textual fragments, taking place within a British cultural shift towards a new concern for the 'authentic' as located and manifested precisely within bodily experience.[2]

Retentissement and *divertissement*: war, the media and *Blasted*

Before considering how Kane addressed representations of atrocity and the boundaries between the experience and the appeal(s) of the authentic, one further context that informed the cultural environment of her years as a maturing artist might be considered. The growing political crisis in the Persian Gulf in 1990 developed into a significant sociopolitical event in early 1991, which would put something of a halt to any optimistic perspective arising from an awareness of an environment of political renewal. On 4 January 1991, prior to the outbreak of hostilities, Jean Baudrillard published an article, 'La Guerre du Golfe n'aura pas eu lieu' ('The Gulf War Will not Take Place'), in the French national newspaper *Libération*.³ Paul Patton's 1995 translation of the article's title simplifies the future perfect tense ('will not have taken place') to a straightforward future tense ('will not take place'), perhaps in recognition of the retrospective position of the translated text to the 'future' war, or simply to apply a less complicated construction. This now commonly accepted English title to Baudrillard's first Gulf War essay unfortunately misrepresents the intended irony of projecting forward to the media and political representations of an event yet to occur.

Baudrillard's choice of title for his article, though, might not just have been a cynical statement of challenge against the seemingly inevitable, but must also have been a deliberate reference to Jean Giraudoux's 1935 play *La guerre de Troie n'aura pas lieu*. This reference would have been made in part so that Baudrillard might ally himself with Giraudoux's pacifist objectives in locating an argument against war within an iconic piece of European narrative that concludes – as is well known – in a decade of war. In part, also, he must have wished to mobilize the theatricalization of message. In Giraudoux's play, a peace treaty brokered by Hector with Ulysse is rendered unworkable by the misrepresentation of the poet Demokos who, slain by Hector, claims he dies at Greek hands. The wielding of dissimulation as a diplomatic stratagem, and the elevation of symbolic value over lived experience as a crucial aspect of diplomatic discourse, must have had obvious attraction to Baudrillard: 'We are all hostages of media intoxication, induced to believe in the war [. . .] and confined to the simulacrum of war as though confined to quarters. We are already all strategic hostages in situ; our site is the screen on which we are virtually bombarded day by day, even while serving as exchange value' (Baudrillard, 1995, p. 25). Baudrillard might be accused of rendering the 'Western' viewer as victim here, ironically bypassing the prioritized access to human suffering he wishes to indicate is deliberately circumvented in the construction of ideological artefacts for us to consume. Nonetheless, his argument that our cultural discourses had been invaded by managed representation that controlled and designed our sense of access to real events was to inform a growing reliance on irony and cynicism in the kinds of cultural activities I address in this chapter.

The US-led aerial bombardment of Iraq began a fortnight after *Libération* published Baudrillard's first Gulf War article, and the ground campaign lasted from 23 to 28 February 1991. While our popular cultural vocabulary was demonstrably shifting to find space for the contemplation of death, murder, incest and discourses of authenticity in relation to the representation of such realities via bodily materiality and pain, the reporting that surrounded the Gulf War, by contrast, managed to displace any access to the authentic articulation of the experience of the victims of war. Oxymorons such as 'clean war' or 'friendly fire' became ready components of the reporting of the events in the Gulf, embellished by videogame-like footage of cross-hair accurate destruction of non-civilian military targets, employing the visual vocabulary of entertainment forms to inform news viewers of military successes. The 'cosmetically treated spectre of death, and its even more deceptive televisual subterfuge' (Baudrillard, 1995, p. 28) in our daily consumption of the Gulf War acted as a cynical oppositional correlative to a growing cultural vocabulary of frankness, authenticity and an embrace of the interface between suffering and identity, whilst also fuelling that vocabulary. This accelerated and exacerbated an antagonistic relationship between media and aesthetic/artistic representation of material with ethical implications, an oppositional condition that could only be augmented and further nuanced by the onset of the Bosnian War in April 1992.

Sarah Kane was studying drama at the University of Bristol during the decade shift. She had begun as a fresher there a couple of months before the fall of the Berlin Wall and the release of Mandela. During her second year, Margaret Thatcher resigned and the Gulf War exploded at the time of her twentieth birthday. She graduated with a first class honours in the summer of 1992, before immediately going on to an MA course in playwriting at the University of Birmingham over the 1992–93 academic year. Kane wrote what was to become the first two scenes of *Blasted* as part of her final presentation towards her MA in 1993, and these were first performed on 3 June that year as part of a weekend series of workshopped rehearsed readings of her cohort's output. These scenes were being drafted and compiled, then, during a period when the daily newspapers and television news bulletins were populated with an unending series of images and information about the war in Bosnia-Herzegovina, especially the sieges of Srebrenica (1992–93) and Sarajevo (1992–95). Kane herself testified to how her consciousness of the events of the war in Bosnia informed the early drafts of *Blasted*: 'At some point during the first couple of weeks of writing I switched on the television. Srebrenica was under siege. An old woman was looking into the camera, crying. She said, "Please, please, somebody help us. Somebody do something." I knew nobody was going to do a thing' (qtd. in Sierz, 2001, pp. 100–1). Her first impulse, she recalled, was to jettison the scene in a hotel room she had written between Cate and Ian, a scene in which a terminally ill middle-aged man abuses and rapes a naive, much younger, former girlfriend – 'do I abandon my play [. . .] in order to move on to a subject I thought was more pressing?' (qtd. in Sierz, 2001, p. 101), she asked herself. A moral concern arising from an emotional connection with a woman's plight 900 miles away temporarily interrupted her artistic impulses. Instead of rejecting what she had written to focus on what she felt was more compelling material, she came to the position that the two issues were conjoined morally, and so connected two pieces of writing with an explosion in that hotel room, bringing war and metaphor brutally, suddenly and confusingly into a previously naturalistic theatrical discourse.

Aleks Sierz argues that Kane made an association between Ian's racist attitudes and sexual violence and the war in Bosnia, which she articulated as 'one is the seed and one is the tree' (qtd. in Sierz, 2001, p. 101), and that this represents a straightforward rationalization of her position as a writer. The logic here is important in considering the dramatic representation of atrocity and the experience it offers an audience, but while the seed/tree analogy offers insight into Kane's desire to structure an ethical response, it does not clarify how that might operate theatrically. Whilst issues of authenticity and realism have of course always contributed to concerns about making art, the 1990s generation of writers of British theatre, including Kane, arguably addressed the issue from an experience inflected by an extended period of awareness of media representations of atrocity.

Kane addresses the media directly in *Blasted* by having her seemingly irredeemable character Ian work as a freelance tabloid hack, with two sequences in the first and second half of the play acting as something of a bridge between the play's two halves. Within fifteen minutes of the play's start, Ian answers the hotel room phone to dictate his copy for a story about the murder of a local teenage girl, one of a number of victims of a serial killer in New Zealand. His necessary utterance of the punctuation and paragraph sections causes an estrangement of the text as heard, emphasizing its content and foregrounding its intended status as a textual item divorced from the actuality it represents. Ian embellishes the basic story with an unnecessary description of the victim as 'a beautiful redhead with dreams of becoming a model' (Kane, 2001, p. 12) which exemplifies the discourses of tabloid newspapers that regularly promote and trade off a sexualized representation of young women, whilst simultaneously (and seemingly unproblematically) adopting a stern moralistic angle on crime informed by that same take on gender. Such tabloid outrage was also directed at those (including, of course, Kane herself) who would address such attitudes by representing the violent or socially irresponsible outcomes of discourses of sexualized youth.[4] In the second half of the play, upon learning that Ian is a journalist, the soldier appeals to him to testify to his existence, and thereby his experience as both a victim and a perpetrator of atrocity – 'Tell them you saw me' (Kane, 2001, p. 48), he instructs Ian (paraphrasing Vladimir to the boy in Samuel Beckett's *Waiting for Godot*), maintaining that a journalist's job is '[p]roving it happened' (p. 47). Ian, though, offers a different definition of a journalist's duty, one that first suggests the distancing from reality of fictionalized accounts – 'I write [. . .] stories' – and then clarifies that a story has to be 'personal', indicating that there needs to be a distinct form of appeal (for readers) to a story for it to be newsworthy. And yet the list of examples he offers matches precisely the list of crimes the soldier has confessed to – 'Shootings and rapes and kids getting fiddled' (p. 48).

The play would remain recognizable if Ian's background as a journalist was removed. There is even something mildly contrived about this aspect of his character; his answering the phone in the first scene is at odds with his objective to isolate and protect himself from perceived threat, and the role of a journalist as a passive commentator contrasts with the active interventionist role as 'soldier' he purports to maintain for some unnamed, nationalistic organization. But Kane's decision to mark him thus is central to a theme she wants to address at the core of her contemplation of atrocity. She is concerned not just that atrocity happens and – as with her response to the woman in Srebrenica – that it happens with a lack of appropriate response to hinder its promulgation, but that the manner in which it is mediated for us fails fully to either address or communicate the horror of such experience. Moreover, war and atrocity are often mediated in such a way that leaves little room for moral ambivalence, through representations that might effectively be driven by ideological discourses that are rendered invisible, subsumed into the means of representation. There is a concern, then, in *Blasted* to provide a theatrical experience that might elicit an ethical empathic response in its audience, without directing or governing that ethical response. Kane's ambition in rendering her response to the Bosnian War into artistic material, then, meets the demand Baudrillard set himself in defence of his Gulf War writings – 'it is not a question of being for or against the war. It is a question of being for or against *the reality of war*' (Baudrillard, 1995, p. 9; emphasis original).

In contemplating the realities of war in her play, Kane constructs a theatrical aesthetic similar to that of Edward Bond, who sought to rend asunder a spectator's ideological positions through initiating a process of self-interrogation and promoting creative, imaginative thought processes. She extends this aesthetic, going beyond the use of Bondian 'aggro-affects' which might seek 'to make the audience question what they normally accept' (Bond, 1995, p. 32) by implicating spectators into making an emotional, judgemental response on violence as symptomatic of societal failure, instead piling on 'aggro-affects' in such number and speed that an audience must defer judgement and experience their immediate, visceral responses to the images and testimonies of atrocity. Graham Saunders suggests that Kane sought to craft the sort of immediate experience a spectator at a football match or a Jesus and Mary Chain concert might enjoy (Saunders, 2002, pp. 15 and 17) and quotes the *Guardian* interview where she argued that 'performance is visceral. It puts you in direct physical contact with thought and feeling' (qtd. in Saunders, 2002, p. 15).

This ambition of theatre's 'direct physical contact' with its audience is clearly reminiscent of the Artaudian objective of activating a *retentisse-ment* (resonance, reverberation) in an audience. Now, the coupling of Kane's achievements with Antonin Artaud's aspirations is all too often predicated upon the usual misunderstandings of his concept of a 'theatre of cruelty' being fundamentally about bombarding an audience with horrific images, sounds and scenarios. Artaud was nonetheless clear that his 'cruelty' was a demand placed on both artist and audience as a means of transforming both, through their co-corporeal experience of theatre. He argued that art commonly 'deprived a gesture of its resonance inside the organism' but that through concentrated theatrical strategies (including horror) the resonance of the gesture could oblige the organism – the body of the spectator – 'to adopt attitudes in harmony with that gesture' (Artaud, 1973, p. 125; my translation).[5]

In direct opposition to Artaud's *retentissement* we might place *divertissement* – which translates as 'entertainment', but also as 'distraction', diversion away from something – as a common ambition of commercial theatre. Of course, maintaining an opposition between an ambition to entertain or have some other impact is common in drawing distinctions between or within forms of art, but Artaud's argument for art that imposes or offers a *retentissement*, a physically transformative power, is distinct from, for example, the argument that art might be socially relevant. Notably, a concept of communication that might transform its recipient is also precisely that which Kane activates in the conversation between the soldier and Ian in their discussion on the function of journalism. Here, she employs an argument of accessing authentic experience ('Proving it happened') as correlated to achieving a *retentissement* in the recipient of a news item, rendering consumers of news as witness to that experience rather than simply consumers of it. This is in contrast with the *divertissement* of Ian's approach, which equates journalism with entertainment, diverting those who consume it from actual experience by subsuming that experience within attractive, digestible narrative.

By way of partial example, consider the reporting of the deaths of Admira Ismić and Boško Brkić, a young couple who were both shot dead upon crossing a bridge in a 'no man's land' area between military factions in Sarajevo on 19 May 1993. The two, both twenty-five years of age, were of different ethnic origins, as was not untypical of young Sarajevan couples – one a Bosnian Serb and the other a Bosniak.[6] Brkić received a mortal shot to the head, while his girlfriend Ismić did not die immediately but remained alive for a quarter of an hour after being shot, embracing Brkić's dead body as life left her own. The image of their intertwined corpses spread across the international news media and was cast as something of a symbol for the fracturing of Yugoslavian society. In 1994, their plight became the subject of a documentary entitled *Romeo and Juliet in Sarajevo*, written and directed by John Zaritsky, in which the image of their bodies and the course of events that led to their deaths was described as 'one picture and one story that seemed for a moment to break through the fatigue of horror' (Zaritsky, 1994). That statement acknowledges a condition of assumed weariness in news recipients with the persistent stream of disturbing information from the former Yugoslavia, and with the manner in which this one story and its associated key image could serve as a syphon for understanding the conflict. Here we have an example of how 'the personal' is used as a catalyst for conveying news, folded into a ready-made tragic narrative available to all. While well-meaningly conveying a detail of the everyday brutality of the siege of Sarajevo, the reductive formula it articulates and encourages fails to activate a full communication of the horror of such deaths; rather, it diverts the pathos from that event towards a broader notion of loss, and though this does not amount to the *divertissement* (entertainment) of the titillation Ian promotes in his journalism, it does manifest the *divertissement* (distraction) of news media strategies that seek to reduce real experience in ways that make it communicable through recognizable tropes.

Blasted, then, might be seen not just to be condemning the failures and weaknesses of news reporting of human tragedies such as the Bosnian War, but seeking to fulfil the role of communicating a horror that the media does not or cannot convey, or simply elides through finding narrative conduits for the material that, in effect, direct and replace our responses. In *Writing History, Writing Trauma*, Dominick LaCapra considers how art can offer 'a discursive analogue of mourning':

> empathy should rather be understood in terms of an affective rela-
> tion, rapport or bond with the other recognized and respected as
> other. It may be further related to the affirmation of otherness within
> the self – otherness that is not purely and discretely other. This affir-
> mation applies to the imbrication of the past in the present as well
> as to one's interaction with particular others, including the dead,
> who may exert possessive force in the present and require modes of
> understanding which combine cognition and critical analysis with
> more complex responses, including, when appropriate, a discursive
> analogue of mourning as a mode of working through a relation to
> historical losses. (2000, pp. 212–13)

Kane's achievement with *Blasted* can be considered as something of a cultural monument which might activate such a mode of mourning in its audience, one divorced from any immediate object of mourning and thereby avoiding the sentimental. Her drama seeks to erase the alterity of the real and the simulated, through the visceral experience of being immersed in the play; her 'aggro-affects' do not jolt us into immediate introspection, but their accumulation cause us to lose any anchor in social referentiality whilst subject to them. As such, the play inspires our sorrow, without facilitating the attachment of that sorrow to any object outside ourselves. Even our pity for the characters is steadily troubled, and the play deliberately frustrates any sense that the war referred to belongs in the real world that we know and shall return to. Similarly, the play incites moral outrage, but activates ethical double binds in which empathy and revulsion are entangled – both Ian and the soldier merit our disgust, but also incite our sympathy. Certainly, after the performance we can begin to examine the emotional rubble and construct ideological responses to what we have experienced that do very much belong in the real world, in terms of gender or global issues of social fragility in the face of conflict, but the in-theatre experience itself is an aesthetic, experiential monument to mourning, an implacable stripping of any culturally sustained denial that such suffering and trauma happens, is wrought by humans upon humans, and is ironically held at arms' length from ethical consciousness by the very means of reporting it.

The word 'monument' is applied to the play here with reference to Andreas Huyssen's writing on cultural memory and amnesia, and the tension between a monument as a trigger to cultural memory or as a physical testimony to forgetting. In a culture in which access to objective truth about atrocities that we ourselves do not experience is impossible, and where we risk being trapped and defined by the implications of hyperreal events and reductively narrativized media representations, a natural gravitation towards irony and cynicism as the syntax of aesthetic commentary or representation is irrepressible. Kane avoids this by not attempting to address any objective truth of a real-world event. She instead presents the material quality of an object, a monument, through visceral experience – we become the testimony itself, 'a substitute site of mourning and remembrance' (Huyssen, 1995, p. 258) through the potent resonance of the imagery she employs. Huyssen's writing about the failure and potential value of monuments as a medium of remembrance and proliferation of knowledge centred predominantly on the Holocaust. He articulated his concern over the growth and proliferation of a Holocaust trope in the 1980s and early 1990s as a cultural tendency which contaminated and extended reference to the Holocaust beyond its original reference point, so that 'the original trauma is often reenacted and exploited in literary and cinematic representations in ways that can also be deeply offensive' (p. 256).

Ashes to Ashes and theatre as monument to loss

Harold Pinter's *Ashes to Ashes*, written and first performed in 1996, can be considered in many ways as a direct response to Kane's play, and concerns itself with the cultural saturation of Holocaust tropes in the mid-1990s and the managed distance between a comfortable middle-class British existence and the reality of atrocity. The character of Rebecca repeatedly recounts memories of children being taken out of the arms of mothers on railway stations, of factories of obedient but poorly treated workers and of refugees being herded into the sea to drown. In my article 'What Remains? *Ashes to Ashes*, Popular Culture, Memory and Atrocity' (2009), I discuss how Pinter here mobilizes examples of arguably contentious representations of the Holocaust, such as *Sophie's Choice* (Alan J. Pakula, 1982) or *Schindler's List* (Steven Spielberg, 1993), in order to suggest that cultural memory is absorbed, internalized and personalized by various routes, including populist art. In this way, Pinter makes Rebecca something of a monument to the Holocaust in the manner in which I above argue that an audience is transformed through their experience of *Blasted*'s deployment of *retentissement* to collapse *divertissement*.

However, in representing aspects of the Holocaust in his play, Pinter activates a moral enquiry into whether one has the right to discuss or represent atrocities. In this way, *Ashes to Ashes* might be viewed as positioned in direct dialogue with Kane's play and extending its vocabulary to embrace and address the quandary of artistic representations of the Holocaust. Pinter was certainly aware of and engaged with *Blasted* in 1995, and he championed and corresponded with Kane from then until the end of her life. In a public statement in support of the play, he defended it as a play that confronted 'something actual and true and ugly and painful' and contrasted its horror with that of Quentin Tarantino's 'truly demeaning' and 'just for fun' cinematic brutality which he argued 'undermines the spirit and the intelligence' (qtd. in Sexton, 1995, p. 12), thereby activating the kind of *retentissement/divertissement* opposition argued for above. Elsewhere in this volume, Hanna Scolnicov clarifies how Pinter's *Ashes to Ashes* 'deals with the ethical burden of memory, of bearing witness, of living with the haunting memory' of the Holocaust which 'continues to be with us, infecting our ethical thinking, intervening in our most intimate relationships, in our everyday thoughts and actions'. I seek here to extend her attention to the cultural ubiquity of the Holocaust, and consider how Pinter teases out the seemingly inherent conflict between representation and commentary within aesthetic treatment of acts of atrocity.

Ashes to Ashes is a play with just two characters, husband and wife, engaged in a lengthy and difficult discussion that incorporates remembrances of instances of atrocity. During his interrogation of his wife, Devlin, a university professor who insists rigidly on the attainability of and respect for objective truth,[7] demands that Rebecca disassociate herself from the horrors she claims to recall:

Devlin   A little while ago you made [. . .] shall we say [. . .] you made a somewhat oblique reference to your bloke [. . .] your

lover? [. . .] and babies and mothers, etc. And platforms.
I inferred from this that you were talking about some kind
of atrocity. Now let me ask you this. What authority do
you think you yourself possess which would give you the
right to discuss such an atrocity?

Rebecca I have no such authority. Nothing has ever happened to
me. Nothing ever happened to any of my friends. I have
never suffered. Nor have my friends.

(Pinter, 1998, p. 413)

Pinter is addressing both the ethics of representation, as foregrounded
by Kane, and also the cultural processes by which memories of human
abomination are necessarily kept alive – if Rebecca has not experienced
the things she recounts, where do her recollections originate? Devlin's
question is pointed and deliberate, and one cannot avoid noting that
the author must essentially be asking himself the same question, and
by extension asking the question of his art. Pinter tackles this via some
unambiguous positions. He has Rebecca utterly deny the possibility of
her association with the experiences she nevertheless recounts and, as
if to nail that point, he offers an extra-dramatic textual note to indicate
that his play is taking place in contemporary Britain (or, rather, 1996 at
the earliest) by noting 'Time: Now' at the head of the published script,
immediately after giving the ages of Devlin and Rebecca as 'in their forties'. The implication is clear; the play's characters have not experienced
the events of the Holocaust that the play nonetheless establishes as being
key to Rebecca's psychological crisis. At the centre of his enquiry about
fictionalization of atrocity, then, Pinter gives his suffering lead character
a series of false memories, fictions of atrocity seemingly formed from
other cultural narratives of the Holocaust, including popular film.

It is not the fact that the images Rebecca recounts might reflect her
memories of certain films that is crucial here; these are not explicit
enough to elicit the suspicion of direct referencing from the audience.
As she narrates these recollections, though, we may process them
through recognition of the tropes activated, and even our own associations with the kinds of films that make use of such tropes. In this way,
as Varun Begley states, *Ashes to Ashes* was able to 'critique [its] own
conditions of possibility' (2005, p. 17) and address the key concern long
articulated by people such as Elie Wiesel, namely, that to represent the
Holocaust in art is to risk falsifying the memories of the lost victims of
that catastrophic event. Rebecca may serve primarily to acknowledge a
broad palette of access to Holocaust discourse via its mediation in film

and other cultural forms, and secondarily as a means by which (following Kane) to demonstrate how human-engineered atrocity 'must, impossibly, be "thought" as an event that challenges and denies the assumptions that we can comprehend and interpret experience through language or in any other way' (Grimes, 2005, p. 212). Pinter offers art as a solution to the kind of 'personal' representations of horror that journalistic necessity might often resort to in totemistic place of the kind of direct testimony that the soldier in Kane's *Blasted* craves. He also obliquely extends Kane's critique of the 'personal' in journalism to artistic representations of atrocity – any activation of our recognition of the train platform scene from *Sophie's Choice* or the factory or *Kristallnacht* sections of *Schindler's List* causes a discomfort in us, as we are bound to empathize with Rebecca, whose suffering is manifest before us, whilst that empathy is compromised by our awareness that these cannot be (and are confessed as not being) her memories. The lacuna between our awareness of atrocity and our own (lack of) experience of it is made manifest in our response to that paradoxical lacuna in Rebecca, and this associates itself with the shortcomings of major cultural artefacts that seek to address the Holocaust through a 'personal' aesthetic that necessarily reduces and funnels our empathic attachment to atrocity through emotional association with individual characters' experiences, whether fictional or fictionalized versions of real people (Sophie Zawistowski, Oskar Schindler, Itzhak Stern).

Rebecca is a character that has been rendered a monument to twentieth-century genocide through a process of absorption of cultural memory, and contains and suffers the impossibility of maintaining and sustaining memories that are not hers, or ours, but which must be remembered. She is afflicted by the permanent *retentissements* of her awareness. Her reference to her own disquiet at police sirens fading into the distance is perhaps indicative of the permanent agitation of her suffering, and her expressed desire to want to possess that sound, and not let it reach others (Pinter, 1998, p. 408), suggests a consolation in suffering in the place of, as monument to, the suffering of others. At the end of the play Pinter employs a shift in stage discourse that characterizes a number of his late plays, where a single voice addresses the audience as though from within a hermetically sealed dramatic locus beyond the locale of the rest of the play – *Party Time* (1991), *Moonlight* (1993) and *Celebration* (2000) all share this feature, often associated with death. The technique draws an audience's attention in on Rebecca, aided by a reduced lighting plot that focuses on her and marginalizes Devlin (who no longer speaks). This heightened attention is further augmented by the introduction of an echo to Rebecca's words, as she recounts one last time an event where a woman had a child taken from her arms at a railway station. To add further to our concentration on this narrative, Rebecca switches her recollection from the third to the first person, and 'becomes' the person who first had her baby taken away, only then to deny ever having had a baby in the play's final words. The poignancy is at its most extreme here, when this denial chimes in to counter the earlier one of ever having been victim of atrocity. Rebecca's suffering is authentic within the context of our dramatic encounter of her, our investment in her as tragic figure is uncompromised, and her denial at the end becomes the denial of a survivor, the narrative of erasure of the trauma victim.

Yet Rebecca remains the impossible victim of the Holocaust. This is Pinter's gesture of *retentissement*; a difficult, irresolvable pathos, stamping Rebecca's dilemma into an audience, to be subject to attempted resolution only once the play closes. A character who is and is not a victim, and who, in being a victim, necessarily denies the source of her victimhood, is an exemplary facet of Pinter's stated approach to truth in art when, in his Nobel acceptance speech, he described how 'truths challenge each other, recoil from each other, reflect each other, ignore each other, tease each other, are blind to each other' (Pinter, 2005). Pinter's dialogue with *Blasted*, if such a process might be envisaged, involves a movement away from his usual approach to political playwriting, which involved structuring the consequences of reactionary politics through images of threatened and fractured families set in unnamed countries that manifest British features (*One for the Road* (1984), *Mountain Language* (1988), *Party Time* (1991)). Instead, like *Blasted*, *Ashes to Ashes* locates its impossible events – Rebecca's memories – within a more openly British context where they cannot belong. The mismatch between activity and perceived location no longer serves to indicate a commentary of British implication in atrocity, but to embed an uncertainty that is key to the articulation of an ethical concern. As with the soldier occupying a Leeds luxury hotel, Rebecca's false (and yet authentic) memories permit the creation of a pathetic space in the spectator that bridges empathy and objectivity. In this way, Pinter approaches Huyssen's prescription for a compelling Holocaust monument:

> Post-Holocaust generations can only approach that core by mimetic approximations, a mnemonic strategy which recognizes the event in its otherness and beyond identification or therapeutic empathy, but which physically innervates some of the horror and the pain in a slow and persistent labor of remembrance. [. . .] The ultimate success of a Holocaust monument would be to trigger such a mimetic approximation. (Huyssen, 1995, p. 259)

Artaud's ambition of inserting affective *retentissements*, via horror and association, into the body of the spectator and thus transforming him or her, matches well a process that Huyssen describes as one that 'physically innervates some of the horror and the pain in a slow and persistent labor'. Applying this concept of monument to the construction of dramatic events and the manipulation of theatrical discourse to bring about a transformative experience for audiences, it is possible to consider an ideological application of *retentissement* that engages spectators in contemplating ethical issues relating to real-world conflicts by activating sites of mourning, acts of remembrance. Kane and Pinter, with *Blasted* and *Ashes to Ashes*, achieve ethical engagement deliberately without overtly relating the action of their plays to contemporary political events. Separating the aesthetic experience of sorrow and horror from an object of sorrow or horror outside the theatre facilitates a free association and application of the achieved mourning to contemporary events, without channelling such a response through the kinds of narrative of 'personal' associations commonly employed in journalistic prose or the conventional story-telling through identifying with blighted characters of popular entertainment.

Notes

1. Edwards's car was found abandoned at the Severn View service station, near the notorious suicide spot of the Severn bridge. He was not pronounced 'presumed dead' until 2008.
2. In the original German, Ravenhill's words read: 'Im körperlichen Schmerz manifestiert sich ein Höchstmaßan Realität'.
3. Following the publication in *Libération* on 4 January 1991 of 'La Guerre du Golfe n'aura pas eu lieu', Baudrillard went on to publish two other pieces in that newspaper as the conflict in the Persian Gulf unfolded. Published on 6 February and 29 March 1991, these were respectively entitled 'La Guerre du Golfe a-t-elle vraiment lieu?' and 'La Guerre du Golfe n'a pas eu lieu' (translated by Paul Patton as 'The Gulf War: Is it Really Taking Place?' and 'The Gulf War did not Take Place'). All three articles were published collectively in English in 1995 under that last title.
4. The reaction of some of the tabloid press to the 'Paedogeddon!' episode of the Channel 4 comedy series *Brass Eye* broadcast on 26 July 2001 was typical of this contradictory behaviour. The *Daily Mail* (27 July 2001) ran an image of princesses Eugenie and Beatrice (11 and 13 years old) wearing bikinis in the same edition that decried using paedophilia as a subject for comedy as 'unspeakably sick', and *The Daily Star* (28 July 2001) printed an image of the 15-year-old singer Charlotte Church to emphasise her breast size (describing her as 'chest swell') directly juxtaposed against an article describing the *Brass Eye* episode as a 'sick show'. All quotations from Ferguson (2001).
5. Original text: 'à prendre des attitudes conformes au geste qui est fait'.

6. Bosniaks were commonly, and inadequately, referred to as 'Bosnian Muslims' in media reporting of the Bosnian War. The term differentiates from 'Bosnian' (inhabitant of Bosnia) and indicates an ethnic Slavic group determined by a historic connection to the territories of Bosnia and Herzegovina alongside a traditional adherence to Islam. Such religious adherence may or may not be active in current members of that group.

7. In the text, Devlin refers to having lived 'a life of scholarship' (Pinter, 1998, p. 415). In a fax dated 16 July 1997 to Gianni Quaranta (stage designer of the Italian premiere of the play), Pinter explained, 'I believe that Devlin is a professor at a university' (Pinter, 1997).

Works cited

Artaud, A. (1973) *Le théâtre et son double* (Paris: Flammarion).

Baudrillard, J. (1995) *The Gulf War did not Take Place*, trans. P. Patton (Bloomington: Indiana University Press).

Begley, V. (2005) *Harold Pinter and the Twilight of Modernism* (Toronto: University of Toronto Press).

Bond, E. (1995) *Letters I*, ed. I. Stuart (London: Routledge).

Ferguson, E. (2001) 'Why Chris Morris had to make *Brass Eye*', *Observer*, 5 August, http://www.guardian.co.uk/uk/2001/aug/05/news.film (accessed 3 January 2012).

Grimes, C. (2005) *Harold Pinter's Politics: A Silence Beyond Echo* (Cranbury: Associated University Presses).

Huyssen, A. (1995) *Twilight Memories: Marking Time in a Culture of Amnesia* (New York and London: Routledge).

Kane, S. (1998) *Crave* (London: Methuen).

—— (2001) *Complete Plays (Blasted, Phaedra's Love, Cleansed, Crave, 4.48 Psychosis, Skin)* (London: Methuen).

LaCapra, D. (2000) *Writing History, Writing Trauma* (Baltimore, MD: Johns Hopkins University Press).

Pinter, H. (1997) 'Fax to Gianni Quaranta', 16 July, Pinter Archive, British Library, Add MS 88880/6/15.

—— (1998) *Plays Four (Betrayal, Monologue, Family Voices, A Kind of Alaska, Victoria Station, Precisely, One for the Road, Mountain Language, The New World Order, Party Time, Moonlight, Ashes to Ashes)* (London: Faber).

—— (2005) *Art, Truth and Politics*, http://www.nobelprize.org/nobel_prizes/literature/laureates/2005/pinter-lecture-e.html (accessed 4 January 2012).

Saunders, G. (2002) *'Love Me Or Kill Me': Sarah Kane and the Theatre of Extremes* (Manchester: Manchester University Press).

Sexton, D. (1995) 'Life in the Old Dog Yet', *Daily Telegraph*, 16 March, p. 12.

Sierz, A. (2001) *In-Yer-Face Theatre: British Drama Today* (London: Faber).

Tabert, N. and M. Carr (eds) (1998) *Playspotting: Die Londoner Theaterszene der 90er* (Reinbek: Rowohlt Taschenbuch Verlag).

Taylor-Batty, M. (2009) 'What Remains? *Ashes to Ashes*, Popular Culture, Memory and Atrocity' in C. Owens (ed.) *Pinter etc.* (Newcastle: Cambridge Scholars Publishing), pp. 99–116.

Zaritsky, J. (1994) *Romeo and Juliet in Sarajevo*, http://www.pbs.org/wgbh/pages/frontline/programs/transcripts/1217.html (accessed 3 January 2012).

Part II
Theoretical Speculations

5
Two: Duologues and the Differend

Dan Rebellato

In April 2011, three major new plays opened in London. Jon Fosse's *I Am the Wind*, directed by Patrice Chéreau, began a European tour at the Young Vic. It was a riddling, cryptic fable about two young men cast adrift on a raft on a perilous sea, one of them appearing eventually to drown. At the Southwark Playhouse, in a production directed by David Mercatali, Philip Ridley's *Tender Napalm* pitted a man and a woman against each other on a bare stage, telling athletic tales of bravery on a fantasy island, torn apart by numerous nameless catastrophes. Meanwhile, at the Royal Court, Simon Stephens's *Wastwater* was a nervous, alienated triptych of scenes: the young man saying a long goodbye to a middle-aged woman, a couple meeting in a hotel room for sex, and a man apparently attempting to arrange to buy a child through an intermediary. These three plays by major authors – two British, one Norwegian – opened in prominent new writing theatres in the same month.[1] Something else they all had in common was that they are all told exclusively through duologues (or 'two-handers'). In none of these plays are there ever more than two people on the stage.

And these are by no means unusual examples in the theatre of the last two decades. Let us recall Kay Adshead's *Bones* (2006), Howard Barker's *The Twelfth Battle of Isonzo* (2001), Mike Bartlett's *Contractions* (2008), Richard Bean's *The Mentalists* (2002), Edward Bond's *The Children* (2000), Leo Butler's *The Early Bird* (2006) and *Faces in the Crowd* (2008), Jim Cartwright's *I Licked a Slag's Deodorant* (1996), Caryl Churchill's *A Number* (2002) and *Drunk Enough to Say I Love You?* (2006), Tim Crouch's *ENGLAND* (2007), Fiona Evans's *Scarborough* (2007), Brian Friel's *Afterplay* (2002), David Greig's *Being Norwegian* (2003), *Ramallah* (2004), *Midsummer* (2008) and *Kyoto* (2009), David Hare's *The Breath of Life* (2002), Zinnie Harris's *Nightingale and Chase* (2001), David Harrower's

Blackbird (2005), Robert Holman's *Jonah and Otto* (2008), Charlotte Jones's *Airswimming* (1997), Marie Jones's *Stones in His Pockets* (1996), Dennis Kelly's *Debris* (2003) and *After the End* (2005), Ayub Khan-Din's *Notes on Falling Leaves* (2004), Bryony Lavery's *Stockholm* (2007), Liz Lochhead's *Quelques Fleurs* (1991), Duncan Macmillan's *Lungs* (2011), Owen McCafferty's *Mojo-Mickybo* (2003) and *Days of Wine and Roses* (2005), Chloe Moss's *This Wide Night* (2008), Gregory Motton's *The World's Biggest Diamond* (2005), Rona Munro's *The Basement Flat* (2009), Anthony Neilson's *The Censor* (1997) and *Stitching* (2002), Nick Payne's *Constellations* (2012), Harold Pinter's *Ashes to Ashes* (1996), Rebecca Prichard's *Yard Gal* (1998), Mark Ravenhill's *Product* (2005) and *Over There* (2009), Philip Ridley's *Fairytaleheart* (1998) and *Vincent River* (2000), Enda Walsh's *Disco Pigs* (1996) and *The Small Things* (2005). This is by no means an exhaustive list.

Even if the casts feature more than two characters, several other plays are constructed, like *Wastwater*, entirely in duologues. Sarah Kane's *Blasted* (1995) has three characters that are never on stage at the same time; the same is true of Martin Crimp's *The Country* (2000). Simon Stephens's *Country Music* (2004) has four characters but there are never more than two characters on stage together, only the central character meeting the other three – a structure repeated in Mark Ravenhill's *The Cut* (2006). David Eldridge's *Under the Blue Sky* (2000) comprises three scenes, each of them a duologue. David Hare's *The Blue Room* (1998) is a tag-game of two-handers. Apart from two brief moments, Caryl Churchill's *Far Away* (2000) is written entirely in two-handers. Indeed, over her fifty-year career, Churchill has repeatedly shown herself the keenest barometer of how dramaturgical form must be remade to respond to contemporary culture, so when we reflect that in the 2000s she wrote virtually nothing that was not in duologue form, it will encourage us to ask what it is in the two-hander that seems so appropriate for capturing the world around us.

This is not to suggest that the two-hander was invented in the 1990s; there have, of course, been plays for two people before that: *The Zoo Story* (1959), *The Dumb Waiter* (1960) or *A Life in the Theatre* (1977) are hardly obscure. The Chorus aside, many Greek tragedies are built around two-handers, and playwrights through history have recognized the power of stripping a play bare to place a two-person confrontation or relationship at the centre of the action, whether that be between Hamlet and Gertrude, Nora and Helmer, or Vladimir and Estragon. The last example reminds us that on the popular stage, in music hall and cabaret, the double act has a long comic pedigree. Nonetheless, in this chapter I shall argue that the two-hander has become one of the most distinctive forms of the last twenty years. Its value for playwrights is that it enables us to focus very directly on some key questions about the nature of our ethical obligations to one another and what that tells us about the nature of judgement and of our selves.

The return to ethics

The same period in academic life has seen a 'return to ethics'. An earlier generation, under the influence of Nietzsche via Foucault, had somewhat sidestepped ethics, presenting it as a historically local phenomenon. This move was supported by certain Marxists who accepted at face value Marx's insistence that 'communists do not preach *morality* at all' (Marx and Engels, 1976, p. 247; emphasis original).[2] Ethics, or moral philosophy, was criticized for its 'universalizing' tendencies; that is, asserting universal moral principles showed a violent disregard for cultural difference and more often than not was an ideological strategy to assert particular (Western, patriarchal, bourgeois) principles under the guise of enlightened universalism. A certain kind of relativism was a powerful corrective for thinking through the radical potential of the particular and local. As such, rather than ethics, *politics* was felt to be a more honest location for thinking through the assertion of particular rights. (We might even consider the title of the very book you are holding: thirty years ago it would have been virtually inconceivable to publish a collection of essays on ethical speculations in contemporary British theatre.) However, in the late 1980s, an ethical turn passed across the face of the humanities (see Garber, Hanssen and Walkowitz, 2000; Davis and Womack 2001).

There are many reasons why, in the 1990s, we might have seen a shift away from a stance of pure scepticism towards moral philosophy. For one thing, it became clear, in theoretical terms, that the circles of ethics and politics overlap but are not fully concentric. It is possible to speak meaningfully of the ethics of politics – and indeed the politics of ethics – which suggests two different areas coming into dialogue, rather than one masquerading as the other. Second, in the 1990s the world saw the resurgence of genocidal acts – in Bosnia and Rwanda – which were hard to explain in purely particularist terms. It seemed perhaps that what was taking place was not just wrong in Srebrenica and Nyange but wrong everywhere. It was also uncomfortable to note that a certain kind of relativism was adopted by some Western governments as a reason not to intervene, thus allowing these genocides to proceed (Conversi, 1996).

These events helped revive an ethical discourse of 'human rights' and of 'crimes against humanity' – both somewhat universalizing concepts, but they captured the force of the wrongs committed in a way that other concepts seemed not to. However, this return to ethics has been a complex and contradictory process. The period has by no means seen a wholesale re-adoption of the language of ethical universals; instead, we have seen a serious attempt to reconcile ethical discourse with the anti-universalism that had been so important in the 1970s and 1980s. Key figures include Richard Rorty and Jean-François Lyotard and I shall return to their work later.

Could there be a connection between the near-simultaneous reappearance of ethical thinking and the rise to prominence of the duologue?[3] I do not imagine that the connection is one of direct influence; rather, I suggest that the return to ethics in academic life and the prominence of the duologue are both responding to the same social conditions, and yet their attitudes towards the force and foundations of ethical judgement are widely divergent.

The moral obligations between us, the bonds that tie us together in ethical relationships, are not empirically observable as such – they can only be thought or felt. The duologue is a means to foreground, particularly sharply, a fundamental ethical building block of human sociality, the relation between two people, exploring both their separateness and intimacy, their rivalry and mutual dependence – the dynamics of our mutuality. And often duologues do this by seeming to make tangible that primal mutuality, playing with visibility and invisibility as if aiming either to make visible those unseen ethical bonds or else to underline their absence, daring us to feel what it would be like if there were no ethical connections between us at all.

Intimacy and alienation

Two (wonderfully-titled) plays, at either end of the historical period under discussion, will illustrate this point: Jim Cartwright's *I Licked a Slag's Deodorant* from 1996 and the more recent *it felt empty when the heart went at first but it is alright now*, written by Lucy Kirkwood and first performed in 2009. Both of these plays, through their subject matter and their formal devices, explore the separateness of two people and their urge for intimacy and often do so through the interplay of particularity and universality, visibility and invisibility.

Cartwright's play has two characters, Man and Slag, the boundaries between whom are immediately permeable. Why is he 'Man' and she

'Slag'? Are they identifying themselves in these ways or are they presented as seen by each other? She – a contemptible object of desire – and he – just another punter. The results are ambiguous. The naming may betoken a *reduction* to a depersonalized alienation, but it may also suggest an *augmentation*, a transcendence of individuality to a kind of universality, where the Man may stand for Everyman (and perhaps Slag for Everyslag).

The play begins with the moment of perverse intimacy signalled by its title. Man, having just had sex with Slag, and left alone in her room, licks her deodorant. It is an act both intimate and distanced; sensuous and fetishistic. As the play develops we discover that the woman has run off with his money. Later he spots her in a nightclub; this encounter leads them back to the bedroom whereupon she steals his money once again. Towards the end of the play they meet again and Slag appears to reconcile with him but probably to rob him for a third time. Instead they lapse into a quasi-relationship, she still turning tricks, he under the bed occasionally taking licks at her deodorant.

The play is a story of alienation and rejection, but also an affirmation of the need for intimacy. Boldly, the two characters never actually speak to each other. This is not dialogue as such. In the first act, they do not even occupy the same diegetic spaces and tell their sides of the story in each other's absence. In the second act, Cartwright allows them to share spaces, but even here it is purely physical juxtaposition, physical proximity standing in for a desired personal intimacy. It is a startling effect in performance, reminiscent of James Macdonald's Royal Court production of Martin Crimp's *Fewer Emergencies* (2005) where the characters appeared to occupy the same imagined space but they never made eye contact with each other, something you did not notice at first but which built up a gnawing sense of emotional sterility and thwarted human contact.

This sense of alienation is echoed throughout: the play is filled with images of abject body horror, other people's bodies described as objects. Slag describes having sex with her dealer for drugs: he 'has a horrible cock, bluey and knobbly, like the shiny joint of a chicken leg bone, like a jabbing, jabbing elbow' (Cartwright, 1996, p. 6). But the characters are alienated from themselves too: the woman admits that she never gives her real name and when she offers to reveal it, she realizes she has forgotten it. Man relates his own numbed feelings to the lingering effect of his mother's death: 'I touched her', he says, '[s]he was cold. I still have the chill in my finger' (p. 7). The chill seems to have spread right through him as the play begins, his yearning for contact finding an outlet only in a stolen moment, licking a Slag's deodorant. These motifs establish a tension between the absence and presence of the characters to each other. The absence of contact between them represents a deep mutual alienation and yet this is haunted by a countervailing theatrical force, embodied in the actors' skilful co-presence and mutual regard. The characters may not be there for each other, but the actors are.[4]

A similar play with visibility and invisibility takes place in Kirkwood's *it felt empty when the heart went at first but it is alright now*, which follows another sex worker, an Eastern European prostitute called Dijana. The play is not chronological but we build up a picture of this young woman's life, tricked into prostitution and perhaps escaping from it at the end. It is largely a monologue though she is surrounded by invisible others. In the first act, a client enters. The text indicates that he is invisible, though we see money thrown down on the bed, and the mattress sags where he sits on it. And then we see, grotesquely, comically, the sex act itself, with Dijana pushed and pulled about by the punter like a doll (Kirkwood, 2009, pp. 15–17).

Unsurprisingly, Dijana's experience as a trafficked sex worker gives her a horror at intimacy and being touched. We see that in dozens of ways. As the play begins, a bird has flown into her room and she has killed it. Towards the end of the first scene, she picks it up, takes it to the bin and the directions tell us she is disgusted at 'the feel of feathers on her skin' (p. 14). Even her child, another invisible other, to whom she talks many times in the play, becomes a source of terrifying intimacy that she tries neurotically to reject at one point, suddenly screaming:

Go away
GO AWAY PLEASE
I SAID GO AWAY I AM SORRY OKAY I AM SO SORRY BUT YOU CAN'T BE HERE ALL THE TIME I am so tired just
looking at me GO AWAY [. . .] I CAN'T SEE YOU!

(Kirkwood, 2009, p. 26)

It is very striking that it is the invisibility of her child that revolts Dijana, as the play conjures a range of invisible others who exploit her, abuse her, use her for their own purposes. The one visible presence on the stage, Gloria, an African woman that she meets while in police custody, tries to give her a hug but Dijana rejects her in a panic, biting her cheek (p. 34). This action takes place in the dark so it is not visible, and it is unclear whether Gloria is trying to comfort or assault her, the moment expressing the play's profound ambivalence about the possibility of positive human contact.

At one precious moment, Dijana describes an experience taking drugs and dancing in a club. In this fleeting memory, the barriers flung up by her history of exploitation and abuse fall away, 'like your skin prickles with happy', she says, 'and you melt to other bodies and your blood go fast and slow and normal I don't like strangers touch me but tonight I like their sweat on me legs pushes on mine' (p. 38). It recalls a similar epiphany in Mark Ravenhill's *Shopping and Fucking* (1996) when Robbie describes the revelation he had after taking a load of ecstasy tablets and seeing what the rest of the play seems not to see, the radical connectedness of the entire world. Drug-induced though these moments may be, they punch a hole through alienated, atomized lives portrayed elsewhere.

The two-hander form provides an opportunity for intense scrutiny of relations between self and other. Theatrically, duologues are haunted by two extremes: one is absolute connectedness, absolute absorption of one in another. Bryony Lavery's *Stockholm* shows an idyllic relationship falling into crisis. The transition from happiness to jealousy is partly indicated by a third character – though played by the two onstage characters – called 'Us', a malevolent demon living under the stairs, perhaps representing the threat to the self generated by their unbridled togetherness. Robert Holman's *Jonah and Otto* centres on an older and a younger man, who meet by chance. The young man taunts and baits the older man demanding money; he insists on their moral separateness – 'The thing is', Jonah tells the old man, 'I only care about myself, to be honest with you' (Holman, 2008, p. 41). But the two keep meeting and at the end of the first half, Otto falls asleep and slowly, carefully, Jonah swaps clothes with the old man, their identities seeming to mingle and merge. Both *The Censor* and *Stitching* by Anthony Neilson are two-handers that end with one character giving in to the desires of another in an act of extreme taboo submission, while it is at least possible that *I Am the Wind*'s two characters are really aspects of one personality.

At the other extreme is the terror of sheer disconnectedness. On stage this thought is provoked by theatre's materiality. We are shown two people. What if that is all there is? What if there are no bonds that tie us together, what if we were truly, morally alone? This effect is heightened in plays like Ridley's *Tender Napalm*, which dispenses completely with location. These are two people in no-place, and the play dares us to think that that is all we ever are. And yet all of these plays ultimately affirm our mutuality – *Tender Napalm* ends by showing us the beginning of the relationship and allows us to piece together the two characters' fantasized hostility as a way of coping with trauma, but it does so without sentimentality, since this affirmation is supported by the sense of togetherness fostered by the performers' skilled co-presence. These plays stage ethical relationships, asking whether we are altruists or egoists, individuals or members of a common ethical community.

Character and personhood

If the ethical nature of these relationships is placed under scrutiny by the two-hander, so too is the nature of the individuals between whom these relationships take place. Tim Crouch's *ENGLAND* is a strange kind of two-hander. In the first half, the two actors, a man and a woman, alternate the lines, jointly playing a single character. It is a rounded, interesting character with humour, personality, a story, but because of the nature of the text and the two performers, we do not know their gender. It is a two-hander for one character. Something similar happens with Fiona Evans's play *Scarborough*. In the first half a schoolboy and his older teacher are in a hotel room in Scarborough. He is underage; the relationship is forbidden and at moments they are plagued by doubts. In the second half, we watch almost exactly the same scene, but this time it is a girl and an older male teacher. Are these the same events happening separately? Or are we watching the same event in two different ways? The latter seems much the more intriguing thought, that the play is asking us to combine the two acts into a single play inflected but not led by gender.

In turn, this recalls David Greig's *Mainstream* (2013), written for Suspect Culture. The story follows a record company employee and a personnel consultant. They conduct a formal interview in a hotel, go for a drink, have sex, and make awkward small talk over breakfast. But these two characters are played by a cast of four, two men and two women. The scenes are splintered, multiplied; we watch events several times with variations, played by different combinations of men and women. The play is intensely fractured yet some general sense of character seems to lift above the particular corporeal enactments we see before us. Nick Payne's *Constellations* asks similar questions, presenting the same characters making different choices in alternative universes.

Another iteration of this device comes in Caryl Churchill's *A Number*, in which a father is confronted by a succession of his cloned sons. It is a play that turns a question of casting into a question of bio-ethics. How many characters does this play have? Two (a father and son)? Or four (a father and his three cloned sons)? This is in turn a question about ethical obligations: how far do we ground our respect for another person in their unique personhood? Are we and is he to care equally for visibly and genetically indistinguishable persons?

All of these plays seem to be asking, what do we need to know about a person to care about them? That this issue is explored in playwriting is unsurprising because the ethical question is also a dramaturgical one. Playwrights typically have to develop, either consciously or unconsciously, a sense of how much they need to individualize a fictional character to allow an audience to engage with them and care about the choices they make, and how far a character needs to be general enough to seem typical or plausible. But there is a yet deeper metaethical question here. What is it about a person than compels our moral regard? For a philosopher like Immanuel Kant it is simply the humanity of the other person, and their rational autonomy, that commands our moral attention. This universalizing principle is rejected by thinkers as diverse and Alain Badiou and Richard Rorty, who claim that we can only ground a sense of obligation to another person in their particularity.[5] Such ideas have been taken up by postmodernist and other thinkers seeking to reconcile ethics with strict anti-universalism.

How plausible is this position? In *Contingency, Irony and Solidarity* (1989), Richard Rorty argues that our selves, our language, our communities and all other components of our identity are contingent, culturally and historically; for that reason, 'human nature' is a metaphysical fiction that may sometimes be useful for political reasons but must not be taken seriously (pp. 192–5). If we do feel obligations to others it will be on the morally local grounds of their similarity to us: being fellow countrymen and women, fans of the same football club, co-religionists, or something similar. He does suggest that there is value in attempting to expand these circles of moral attention: 'This is a process', he says, 'which we should try to keep going' (Rorty, 1989, p. 196). However, he does not explain where the force of the obligation (embodied in the word 'should') comes from. If common humanity is not something we can 'recognize' but only 'create' (p. 169), there seems to be no more value in expanding our moral attention to other people than there is in expanding our moral attention to biscuits or radiators.

One might also object that while similarity might be a ground for paying attention to someone, it seems to deprive that obligation of any specifically ethical character. Suppose, for example, I feel such kinship with other fans of West Ham United Football Club that I start to feel that they deserve special attention. I might frame this in ways that begin to resemble moral judgements: 'thou shalt not kill a West Ham fan' or 'thou shalt not covet a West Ham fan's silverware'. But the very particularity of these judgements seems to deprive them of true moral force; they are not moral principles, just arbitrary rules. As R.M. Hare shows in *The Language of Morals* (1952), properly framed moral judgements cannot contain particulars. This kind of judgement only takes on a fully ethical character if understood to rest on a universalizing syllogism: (a) thou shalt not kill human beings, (b) West Ham fans are human beings, therefore (c) thou shalt not kill a West Ham fan.

Norman Geras has also argued against Rorty's position, noting that it seems hard to understand why an American might be able to identify with all other Americans but not with all other humans: 'it is just not credible that the significant threshold in this matter, where compassion and solicitude will go no further, lies somewhere beyond several hundred million people' (1995, p. 78). He agrees with Rorty that we cannot meaningfully identify ourselves with 'humanity' in the same way that we can with family and close friends but adds that we cannot identify with any very large group in that same way, so Rorty's objection to grounding obligation in common humanity would also seem to rule out grounding it in one's co-religionists, fellow football fans, and so on.

The plays discussed so far in this chapter, through the very structure of theatrical attention that they engender, give us reason to favour the Kantian over the Rortian position. In these plays, what we know about the characters is stripped back almost to nothing and yet we still find ourselves capable of recognizing them as people worthy of our moral attention. All of these multiplied and fractured two-handers – four people playing two, two people playing one or dozens, one person playing *both* one *and* three – are organized and displayed through the iconic image of two people on stage, through which the limits and possibilities of our moral concern are tested.

The differend

In Dennis Kelly's duologue *After the End*, we are in a nuclear fallout shelter. A young man and a young woman are hiding from some devastating event. Initially, she is shocked and grateful but soon becomes suspicious and demands to be let out. The man, seeking, so he says, to protect the woman, forcibly restrains her and eventually assaults her. Two incompatible beliefs about the nature of the world outside the shelter are at work in the play: one, that it has been destroyed in a devastating nuclear event and he is her saviour; the other, that it has not and that he is her abuser. In the final moments, the play is resolved in favour of the latter. But what if the play did not resolve the predicament? What if the play simply brought two quite different incommensurable views of the same event into collision and left them there? There have been a few plays that stage this kind of radical difference and the form in which they characteristically do so is through the two-hander.

Perhaps the starting point for such plays was David Mamet's *Oleanna* (1992), a two-hander set in a university. In the first scene, a student comes to see her lecturer because she is concerned about her marks. In the second scene, we discover that the student has filed a complaint about sexual harassment, based on the events of scene one. By the third scene, the lecturer is about to be sacked and he seeks to explain himself; this becomes a confrontation which leads to the lecturer attacking the student physically and verbally. The play arrived at the Royal Court in 1993 accompanied by a great deal of publicity from its American run (see, for example, Billington 1993), where it was loved and hated as an attack on political correctness in general and feminism in particular. However, in Harold Pinter's careful production, it was, to my mind, neither of those things but instead a complex and finely-balanced play about radical difference and the writer in the theatre.

The key moment in scene one that forms the centrepiece for Carol's complaint against John, her lecturer, is a moment where John, as the script puts it, *'goes over to her and puts his arm around her shoulder'* (Mamet, 1993, p. 36). What is striking about this stage direction is what it *does not* say. It does not say that he 'goes over to her and puts his arm around her shoulder in a purely professional way'. Nor does it say he 'goes over to her and puts his arm around her shoulder in a sexually invasive manner'. Mamet gives us only a sketch of what John has done, not what it means. As a result, the text does not arbitrate between John and Carol, leaving us with two incompatible and unreconciled interpretations of the event. One might think that in production the meaning of John's action might have to be decided one way or the other, but Pinter directed it so that the actor's body blocked the audience's clear view of his arm, so we could not know precisely what had happened either.

Sarah Kane's *Blasted* unfolds entirely in duologue: the characters never meet as three. This allows for one of the central puzzles of the play: how the room remains unchanged throughout but the outside moves from Leeds to somewhere outside Britain altogether. When the Soldier enters, he brings with him an entirely different landscape of the world outside the room and Cate is not there to arbitrate. There is a possibility that much of the second half may be taking place in a dreamscape, perhaps the place that Cate goes to when she has her seizures, yet at no point is there a third character who might decide this for

us. Similarly, Martin Crimp's *The Country* is a three-hander told entirely
through two-handers. We never see all three sides of the tangled emotional triangle at the same time. As a result, we never get agreement on
exactly what the nature of the relationships is in the play, which leaves
us with radically divergent viewpoints and no common understanding.
At the end of each of the play's five scenes, Crimp prints either '(. . .
stone), '(. . . paper)' or '(. . . scissors)' (2000, pp. 15, 26, 41, 57 and 81)
as if, like the child's game, there is only a series of bilateral and circular
battles without end.

These kinds of unresolved and unresolvable differences of understanding, language, and interpretation have affinities with Jean-
François Lyotard's concept of the differend. Lyotard is still perhaps
best known for his *The Postmodern Condition* (originally published in
1979), in which he declared 'war on totality' arguing that the grand
all-embracing narratives of the Enlightenment had given way to the
micronarratives of the present postmodern age. In his next two books,
Just Gaming (originally published in 1979) and *The Differend* (originally
published in 1983), he explores the significance of this condition for
ethical thought. *The Differend* is another attack on totality but this time
in the form of universality in ethics. Lyotard argues that grand talk of
justice is nonsense in an age which has abandoned the grand narrative.
Instead of living in one big narrative we live in separate and incompatible language games. The things we say and do within each language
game cannot be translated from one to another. And, he insists in *Just
Gaming*, 'there is no metalanguage' (Lyotard and Thébaud, 1985, p. 28), no
larger language game in which all other games would fit and through
which they could all be translated. This means that if someone judges
an action in one language game using the criteria from another, they
will inevitably distort and misjudge that action. Thus, ethical judgement can only take place accurately within a language game, and the
idea that there are general principles that guide our action must be
abandoned. The confrontation between two heterogeneous positions
he calls the differend and it is irresolvable. All we can do is 'bear witness
to the differend' (Lyotard, 1988, p. xii).

For Lyotard, this is profoundly different from the philosophical
positions – say, deontology or consequentialism – that have dominated
Western philosophy for the last few hundred years. These previous traditions typically involve various kinds of universal ethical principles.
Their ideas are (supposedly) applicable everywhere. For Lyotard, this
alone is where they fall into error, because there is no all-encompassing
language game in which these ideas could operate. In practical terms,

what this will have meant is the colonial and neocolonial application of Western, patriarchal, bourgeois values onto people with entirely different cultures and values – in Lyotard's terms, onto people in a different language game. Indeed, injustice, for Lyotard, can only mean something within a language game, although there is a yet more profound kind of injustice, which is to allow one language game to impose its rules on another. Perhaps this is what we are seeing in these particularly radical two-handers, like *Blasted*, *Oleanna* or *The Country* – a vision of a new kind of ethics, in which we bear witness to the differend.

To test this idea, I want to consider another two-hander, *Blackbird* by David Harrower, which opened in 2005 at the Edinburgh International Festival, directed by Peter Stein. The situation in *Blackbird* is that a middle-aged man is confronted at his workplace by a woman with whom he had a sexual relationship when she was twelve. The first half of the play concerns their incompatible views of this event, and when Una describes the trial she seems to be describing the imposition of one language game on another:

> I feel like a ghost.
> Everywhere I go.
> I wrote that in my letters too.
> You made me into a ghost.
> People talked about me as if I wasn't there.
> Wouldn't let me speak.
>
> (Harrower, 2005, p. 15)

In Stein's production, as each character gave their lengthy and quite different account of the last night they spent together, the other hid their face, as if acknowledging that both accounts cannot exist simultaneously. It is a shifting and ambiguous text but it is possible to read it as one in which the truth of their relationship is never decided. In *Blackbird*, then, or in any of these sharply contrasted two-handers, do we bear witness to the differend?

I think not. Rather than impassively bearing witness to the differend, my experience of these plays is that we are impelled to judgement by the intense polarities with which they present us. What shocked the first critics of *Blasted* was, if read carefully, not the violence, but the fact that the violence was not editorialized. Kane did not tell us that the violence was wrong; what the critics were not used to and did not see was that the task of judgement had been passed on to the audience.

Indeed, this is where Lyotard's concept of the differend unravels rather seriously. As noted, he believes that all we have are a large number of different language games and that judgements cannot be applied from within one language game to another. He compares the multiplicity of language games to an 'archipelago' rather than a connected mainland (1988, pp. 130–5). But from what position is Lyotard observing this archipelago? Who is looking at all of the language games? If indeed there is 'no common measure' (Lyotard and Thébaud, 1985, p. 50) between language games, how can we be sure they are all language games? Is the discourse of the language game itself just another language game or is it in fact a grand narrative encompassing all micronarratives within it? If it is a grand narrative, then it has contradicted itself and should be discarded. If it is just another language game, then by its own admission it cannot be used to judge anything else and the idea that the differend is a fundamental injustice is invalid. The theatrical duologue has a particular significance here, because, through the intensity of the form, the felt experience of co-presence and mutual alienation, it affirms the desire and possibility of locating a common language (for which the theatre space often stands in) in which our rival ethical demands may be expressed.

The postmodern condition did not take place

Lyotard's curiously anti-ethical ethical theory is part of his diagnosis of the postmodern condition. For Lyotard and others, the Holocaust was the point where modernity's drive towards total control revealed itself: Auschwitz 'is the crime opening postmodernity' (1992, p. 31). As a result there has been a crisis of legitimation for the grand narratives that were supposed to liberate us – enlightenment, progress, revolution, reason, ethics – and instead of grand theory and universals we have micronarratives and particularity. Lyotard urges us to show 'respect for the event' (1992, p. 112) and elsewhere cautions us against 'prejudging the *Is it happening?*' (1988, p. 181; emphasis original).

The politics of postmodernism have been much debated. It seems to me striking to note the homology between this postmodern view and the ideology of neoliberalism. One might look at the way that certain market fundamentalists have suggested that politics or morality cannot restrain the actions of markets; the role of governments, says Kenichi Ohmae, 'has changed from protecting their people to ensuring that their people have the widest range of choice among the best and the cheapest goods and services from around the world' (1990, p. x). For

Norman Barry, capital has no need of ethical regulation because it is 'morally self-sufficient and it develops its own codes of conduct', adding that its conventions 'produce the optimal supply of virtue' (2001, p. 58). In other words, free-market capitalism is very much against universalism in ethics, assuming that local acts of market consumption will reveal their own appropriate local moral virtue. (These are the relativist arguments used to explain why working 14 hours a day in a sweatshop is morally acceptable in China, but not in the US.)

If we can only say 'it is happening', as Lyotard puts it, we are powerless against the actions of the free market, deprived of the ability to think of the world other than it is. This is, of course, a key ideological manoeuvre: think of the Thatcherite slogan 'There Is No Alternative', which aimed to assert the free market as the only viable policy. More recently we have been repeatedly and falsely told that austerity economics is the only way to get out of recession: 'There is No Plan B'. Theodor W. Adorno, a generation earlier, captured the deadliness of this kind of thought: 'that's-how-it-is is the exact means by which the world dispatches each of its victims' (1974, p. 212).

These ethical debates – about the nature of our obligations to one another, the possibility of moral judgement, what makes us worthy of moral regard – are therefore also urgent political questions. Indeed, as I have elsewhere argued, a return to universalism in ethics is a radical position, profoundly resistant to unfettered, aggressive, free-market capitalism (see Rebellato, 2009). Lyotard's vision of a world divided into language games, in which no one can judge anyone else and we are left able only to bear witness to the differend, is one entirely complicit in the destruction of all values but market values. What the plays discussed here do, through the intensity of two people facing each other on a stage, is reveal the precarious but vital need for a common humanity to be expressed and felt.[6]

Notes

1. Simon Stephens, the author of *Wastwater*, also provided the English version of *I am the Wind*.
2. Whether Marxism is a moral theory has been much debated. See Wood, 2004, pp. 127–42 and Cohen, 1983 for opposing views.
3. It is tempting to offer a simple economic explanation for the rise of the duologue: they are cheap. However, through the 1990s and 2000s, British theatre was relatively well-resourced, with National Lottery funding coming in during the 1990s and a significant uplift in the 2000s, especially to the 'regions'. As I and my colleagues showed in *Writ Large*, a report on new

writing commissioned by the Arts Council, new plays were very successful at the box office and played on the very largest stages. If you saw a new play in Britain during 2003–2009, 9 out of 10 times you would have been sitting in a main house, not in a studio theatre (Edgar et al., 2010, pp. 58–9).

4. A similar effect may be seen in Leo Butler's *Faces in the Crowd*, in which a woman comes to visit the husband who abandoned her a decade earlier. The play takes us through the ebb and flow of their recrimination, guilt and residual feeling. It is set in the kitchen/living room, bedroom, and bathroom of the husband's Shoreditch apartment; the couple spend much of the play in separate rooms and this apartness becomes emblematic of the metaphorical distance that has grown between them. In Clare Lizzimore's original production for the Royal Court Theatre Upstairs, the audience were placed above and around the action looking down on the flat. For us, then, the walls and doors were insubstantial barriers, and the coexistence of the two performers in space, having to synchronize their performances with each other, being on stage for one another, provided a corrective opposing force to the characters' isolation.

5. I discuss Alain Badiou's *Ethics: An Essay on the Understanding of Evil* (2001) in the conference paper 'Doing Justice and Injustice' (2006), which can be read at http://www.danrebellato.co.uk/doing-justice-an-injustice.

6. I would like to express my gratitude to Mark Berninger and to Helen Iball at whose invitations I was able to rehearse some of the ideas in this chapter.

Works cited

Adorno, T.W. (1974) *Minima Moralia: Reflections from Damaged Life*, trans. E.F.N. Jephcott (London: Verso).

Barry, N. (2001) 'Ethics, Conventions and Capitalism' in B. Griffiths et al., *Capitalism, Morality and Markets* (London: Institute of Economic Affairs), pp. 57–77.

Billington, M. (1993) 'Man Trouble', *Guardian*, 12 June, pp. 7–9.

Butler, L. (2008) *Faces in the Crowd* (London: Methuen).

Cartwright, J. (1996) *I Licked a Slag's Deodorant* (London: Methuen).

Churchill, C. (2008) *Plays Four (Hotel, This is a Chair, Blue Heart, Far Away, A Number, A Dream Play, Drunk Enough to Say I Love You?)* (London: Nick Hern).

Cohen, G.A. (1983) '*Karl Marx* by Allen W. Wood', *Mind: A Quarterly Review of Philosophy*, 42, pp. 440–5.

Conversi, D. (1996) 'Moral Relativism and Equidistance in British Attitudes to the War in the Former Yugoslavia' in T. Cushman and S. G. Meštrovic (eds) *This Time We Knew: Western Responses to Genocide in Bosnia* (New York: New York University Press), pp. 244–81.

Crimp, M. (2000) *The Country* (London: Faber).

Crouch, T. (2011) *Plays One (My Arm, An Oak Tree, ENGLAND, The Author)* (London: Oberon).

Davis, T.F. and K. Womack (eds) (2001) *Mapping the Ethical Turn: A Reader in Ethics, Culture, and Literary Theory* (Charlottesville and London: University Press of Virginia).

Edgar, D. et al. (2010) *Writ Large: New Writing on the English Stage 2003–2009* (London: Arts Council England).

Evans, F. (2008) *Scarborough* (London: Nick Hern).

Fosse, J. (2011) *I Am the Wind*, trans. S. Stephens (London: Oberon).

Garber, M., B. Hanssen and R.L. Walkowitz (eds) (2000) *The Turn to Ethics* (New York and London: Routledge).

Geras, N. (1995) *Solidarity in the Conversation of Humankind: The Ungroundable Liberalism of Richard Rorty* (London: Verso).

Greig, D. (2013) *Mainstream* in G. Eatough and D. Rebellato (eds) *The Suspect Culture Book* (London: Oberon), pp. 188–246.

Hare, R.M. (1952) *The Language of Morals* (Oxford: Oxford University Press).

Harrower, D. (2005) *Blackbird* (London: Faber).

Holman, R. (2008) *Jonah and Otto* (London: Nick Hern).

Kane, S. (2001) *Complete Plays (Blasted, Phaedra's Love, Cleansed, Crave, 4.48 Psychosis, Skin)* (London: Methuen).

Kelly, D. (2008) *Plays One (Debris, Osama the Hero, After the End, Love and Money)* (London: Oberon).

Kirkwood, L. (2009) *it felt empty when the heart went at first but it is alright now* (London: Nick Hern).

Lavery, B. (2007) *Stockholm* (London: Oberon).

Lyotard, J.-F. (1984) *The Postmodern Condition: A Report on Knowledge* (Manchester: Manchester University Press).

—— (1988) *The Differend: Phrases in Dispute* (Manchester: Manchester University Press).

—— (1992) *The Postmodern Explained for Children: Correspondence 1982–1985* (London: Turnaround).

Lyotard, J.-F. and J.-L. Thébaud (1985) *Just Gaming* (Manchester: Manchester University Press).

Mamet, D. (1993) *Oleanna* (London: Methuen).

Marx, K. and F. Engels (1976) *Collected Works Volume 5, 1845–47* (London: Lawrence & Wishart).

Neilson, A. (1997) *The Censor* (London: Methuen).

—— (2002) *Stitching* (London: Methuen).

Ohmae, K. (1990) *The Borderless World: Power and Strategy in the Interlinked Economy* (London: Collins).

Payne, N. (2012) *Constellations* (London: Faber).

Ravenhill, M. (2001) *Plays One (Shopping and Fucking, Faust is Dead, Handbag, Some Explicit Polaroids)* (London: Methuen).

Rebellato, D. (2006) 'Doing Justice an Injustice', http://www.danrebellato.co.uk/doing-justice-an-injustice (accessed 22 May 2013).

—— (2009) *Theatre & Globalization* (Basingstoke and New York: Palgrave Macmillan).

Ridley, P. (2011) *Tender Napalm* (London: Methuen).

Rorty, R. (1989) *Contingency, Irony and Solidarity* (Cambridge: Cambridge University Press).

Stephens, S. (2011) *Wastwater* (London: Methuen).

Wood, A.W. (2004) *Karl Marx*, 2nd edn (London and New York: Routledge).

6
The Undecidable and the Event: Ethics of Unrest in Martin Crimp's *Attempts on Her Life* and debbie tucker green's *truth and reconciliation*

Martin Middeke

Contemporary ethics no longer follows metaphysical presumptions of origins, priorities, standards, subordination, hierarchies and dualisms. It does not prioritize presence or purity to contingency or complexity (see Derrida, 1998, p. 236 and also 1982, p. 195). We no longer look upon human beings as either congenitally good or bad. However, even though we live in a world of competing, contradictory and often even mutually exclusive opinions, we still have to be capable of judging singular situations, of providing arguments and, ultimately, of making decisions, for better or worse. What effects do such antagonisms have on the judgement of the ethical potential of contemporary drama? In order to find systematic answers to this question it seems worthwhile to recall four pivotal theoretical/philosophical positions on contemporary ethics first: Zygmunt Bauman, Emmanuel Levinas, Jacques Derrida and Alain Badiou. In my discussion of two of the most experimental contemporary British playwrights, Martin Crimp and debbie tucker green, and two of their plays, *Attempts on Her Life* (1997) and *truth and reconciliation* (2011), I then elaborate on three major ethical concepts – Otherness, undecidability, and the Event – and their concomitants which, as is shown, are crucial ethical concerns of these two plays. I conclude on the ethical appeal function emanating from the contents and the structure of both plays.

Theoretical preconsiderations

Bauman has pointed out that human beings are morally ambivalent and that human face-to-face relationships are likewise equivocal.

Moral phenomena, for Bauman, are non-rational, aporetic and non-universalizable, so there are no guarantees of moral behaviour – we have to learn to live with the absence of both a perfect human nature and society (see Bauman, 1993, p. 10). This absence, however, does not lead to moral arbitrariness, but rather makes the ethical horizon discernible: 'Moral responsibility – being *for* the Other before one can be *with* the other – is the first reality of the self, a starting point rather than a product of society' (p. 13; emphasis original). Bauman responds to the ambiguity of human reality by asserting a moral capacity of human beings that he locates in human intuition. Although he otherwise seeks to circumnavigate the assumption of universals, he nevertheless appears to reintroduce such a universal when he concludes that 'if in doubt – consult your conscience' (p. 250). Although in other respects he takes his cue from Levinas, here Bauman seems to overlook the fact that the subject, in Levinas's understanding, has no possibility to opt for a response (to the Other). Responsibility, consequently, is neither something that can be rejected, nor does it indicate an intentional act of a hyposthesized subject, nor can it be reduced to the instance of individual conscience. For Levinas ethics is precisely no catalogue of rules, no maxims to be generalized, no mere theory of reflection of morals and morality (see Luhmann, 1990, p. 20). Ethics results from the encounter with other human beings, which Levinas describes as the moment when through the 'face' of the other a bridge is built to a more general Other. This Other is no simple alter ego of the ego – to be Other it must be allowed to remain Other. Levinas points out that the encounter with the Other not only transcends totality into infinity, it also constitutes the only way in which a Self can fully actualize itself:

> The face is present in its refusal to be contained. In this sense it cannot be comprehended, that is encompassed. [. . .] The Other remains infinitely transcendent, infinitely foreign; his face [. . .] breaks with the world that can be common to us, whose virtualities are inscribed in our *nature* and developed by our existence. (Levinas, 1969, p. 194; emphasis original)

Such Otherness, which does not spring from an intentional attribution of meaning in consciousness and, thus, is prenominal, features a decisive appeal function – the prenominal language of the 'face' of the Other requests us to answer it. This answer both bestows responsibility (that is, *response*-ibility) to our actions (*towards* the Other) and constitutes our subjectivity (in interaction *with* the Other). The Self, then, is *performatively* established in the moment of opening up to the Other. The Other, above all, is singular and unique. Its singularity and uniqueness entail that our responsibility has to be decided upon anew each time we encounter the Other.

Jacques Derrida radicalized this insight by accentuating that our responsibility and all ensuing decisions must pass through an undecidability facilitated by the encounter with the Other. For Derrida there is a tenuousness or precariousness involved in any decision-making. A decision requires a leap of faith that, were it not precarious in itself, would neither be a faith nor a decision at all (see Derrida, 1995, p. 80). To illustrate this, Derrida chooses the 'hyperethical sacrifice' (p. 71) Abraham has to make, the decision of offering his son Isaac on Mount Moriah. Abraham, Derrida argues, is responsible to his son and, thus, fails in his responsibility to 'all the others, to the ethical or political generality' (p. 71):

> What binds me to singularities, to this one or that one, male or female, rather than that one or this one, remains finally unjustifiable (this is Abraham's hyperethical sacrifice), as unjustifiable as the infinite sacrifice I make at each moment. [. . .] And yet we also do our duty by behaving thus. There is no language, no reason, no generality or mediation to justify this ultimate responsibility which leads us to absolute sacrifice; absolute sacrifice that is not the sacrifice of irresponsibility on the altar of responsibility, but the sacrifice of the most imperative duty (that which binds me to the other as a singularity in general) in favour of another absolutely imperative duty binding me to the wholly other. (Derrida, 1995, pp. 71–2)

Just as a successful deconstructive reading is able to suspend an ultimate choice (in interpretation) as it oscillates between openness and logocentric totality (see, for instance, Derrida, 1978, p. 84), ethical responsibility results from enduring the weight of an undecidable decision which would, just like Abraham's impossible choice, necessarily have particular and communal needs cancel each other out. According to Derrida, neither decision can ever be wholly justified. In his seminal *The Ethics of Deconstruction*, Simon Critchley points out that for Derrida the context of a decision cannot be arrayed by a dominant referent. Critchley locates the ethical moment of deconstruction exactly in this absence, but also in its affirmative 'Yes' to the Other, to Otherness and to undecidability (see Critchley, 1999, p. 40). For Critchley, this 'Yes' is the one unconditioned categorical imperative running through the otherwise hypothetical ones which Derrida's concept of *différance* lays bare. *Différance* denotes the unnameable, which must be encountered neither with nostalgia nor with hope: 'The ethical moment that motivates deconstruction is the Yes-saying to the unnameable, a moment of unconditional affirmation that is addressed to an alterity that can neither be excluded from nor included within logocentric conceptuality' (p. 41).

Whereas in Levinas and Bauman the Other functions as the supplement to the Self, and in Derrida writing functions as the supplement of speech, Badiou looks upon the Event as the supplement of being.[1] What these four approaches to ethics undoubtedly have in common is, firstly, that they look upon ethics as a *process in time, an absence*, a procedure of continuing negotiation and oscillation that can never be completed precisely because it remains subjected to temporality, transitoriness and irreversibility. This entails, secondly, that Otherness is given preference to sameness and, thirdly, that being is grounded in the *multiplicity of experience* of a likewise *infinitely multiple number of singularities*. However, whilst ethics in Bauman, Levinas and to a large extent, Derrida, remains a matter of theoretical reflection, Badiou's ethics is much more overtly interested in human practice. He seeks to go beyond an 'ethics of difference' which would, for him, rather predictably aim at deconstructing essentialisms or culminate in 'good old-fashioned "tolerance"' (Badiou, 2001, p. 20). Badiou's ethics centres around three major terms: the Event, truth and Evil. Unlike everyday or even traumatic events, Events are 'irreducible singularities, the "beyond-the-law" of situations' (p. 44). If being equals a multiplicity of a given situation, the Event supplements it, as it on the one hand pertains to a situation and on the other hand remains outside the specific rules of that situation. Thus, an Event denotes something hitherto inexistent, something different from received situations, opinions and knowledge, something 'which compels us to decide a *new* way of being' (p. 41; emphasis original).[2] Events are unpredictable supplements vanishing in time as soon as they appear. Badiou sees Events taking place in the areas of politics, scientific invention, art and love and gives the following examples:

> The French Revolution of 1792, the meeting of Héloïse and Abélard, Galileo's creation of physics, Haydn's invention of the classical musical style. [. . .] But also: the Cultural Revolution in China (1965–67), a personal amorous passion, the creation of Topos theory by the mathematician Grothendieck, the invention of the twelve-tone scale by Schoenberg. [. . .] (2001, p. 41)

The truth process inherent in an Event needs to be authenticated by practice and action. This is where Badiou introduces the term 'fidelity'. In order to be entitled to feature a truth-value, a decision must henceforth be taken to relate to a situation from the perspective of its evental supplement. Fidelity, in other words, implies acting faithfully to an Event; the truth of the Event, therefore, implies practical acknowledgement and verification. Faith in a political Event, for instance, implies the practice of politics in the spirit of that Event; Faith in an artistic Event (such as the Theatre of the Absurd) implies that you cannot go back to nineteenth-century realism as if nothing had happened; faith in a scientific Event (for example, Einsteins's Theory of Relativity) implies that you cannot *naively* practise physics in a traditional Newtonian fashion any longer, even though pragmatic everyday needs might force you to do so. Fidelity to an Event, thus, entails faithfulness to its novelty, 'a real break (both thought and practised) in the specific order within which the event took place (be it political, loving, artistic or scientific [. . .])' (Badiou, 2001, p. 42). As such, truth (as fidelity to an Event) moves forward in time and 'proceeds *in* the situation'; the break established by the Event is an *'immanent break'* (p. 42; emphasis original) that discards hitherto prevailing language and knowledge. Subjectivity emerges in the process of subjects exposing themselves to such a 'post-evental fidelity' (p. 46). In other words, not only have we got to *persevere* in what is and what we know already, but also in what follows for us from the encounter with the Event and, hence, in what we do not know. We have got to submit our perseverance 'of what is known to a duration [*durée*] peculiar to the not-known' (p. 47). More precisely, fidelity to the truth in an Event equals consistently juxtaposing the known with the unknown: 'It is now an easy matter to spell out the ethic of a truth: "Do all that you can to persevere in that which exceeds your perseverance. Persevere in the interruption. Seize in your being that which has seized and broken you"' (p. 47).

Badiou's ethics is *optimistically* grounded in the positive evaluation of the human capacity for Good, that is, the ability to be faithful to the rupture procured by the Event. Human beings, for Badiou, are capable of breaking boundaries, of imaginatively transgressing conservatism and of identifying Evil. Good is not defined through Evil; on the contrary, Evil 'arises as the (*possible*) *effect of the Good itself*' (p. 61; emphasis original). Evil, for Badiou, has three names: terror, betrayal and disaster. Terror is a fidelity to a simulacrum of an Event. Badiou gives the example of the German Nazi regime, which called its 1933 takeover a 'revolution', but conceived it as characterized by a plenitude and absoluteness based on blood, soil and race, thus perverting the idea of the Event albeit offering a structural resemblance to it. Betrayal, for Badiou, is the failure to live up to the fidelity to an Event, 'the temptation to *betray* a truth' (p. 79; emphasis original), be it under pressure, for convenience, out of cowardice, or simply because common, everyday interests collide with the disinterestedness involved in being true to the Event and the process of truth it instigates. Thirdly, Badiou speaks of disaster when truth is identified with total power. Truth-processes generated by Events can never be anything but multiple; they must always pass through the language of a singular situation and can, hence, never be total, completed, objective, rigid or dogmatic because they are liable to temporality and, thus, to change in the world (pp. 82–3). In Badiou's terms, the subject (who is capable of persevering to the fidelity to the Event) is always in a fight with the human animal (who is not) – the mortal besieges the immortal; ordinary interests beset the 'disinterested-interest' (p. 78) involved in holding on to the truth-process. Gibson describes the ethics arising from these collisions as 'a condition of furious restlessness' (1999, p. 149).

On the basis of this diagnosis of an 'ethics of unrest', I can now cogently formulate the openness of the ethical horizon at work in contemporary literature and, in particular, in contemporary drama. The ethical in literature can be approached by analysing the equivocal conditions of 'in-between-ness'. Taking its cue from Bauman, Levinas and Derrida as well as Badiou, an ethical perspective does not aim at fixating texts on the axis of a clear-cut moral message or aesthetic strategy, but rather investigates those restless gaps, blanks, hinges or breaks that remain ambiguous, multiple and undecided both with regard to their aesthetic structures and with regard to their reception and the interpretation of their semantic potential. Hence, contemporary literature in general and contemporary drama in particular become ethically liminal spaces of unrest as they entangle (implicit) authors, texts, and (implicit) readers/spectators in a complex, non-harmonizable, ultimately inconclusive network of dialogue and communication. This literary ethics of unrest, then, involves aesthetic demands, but also satisfies mimetic claims of fiction to the lifeworld, that is, the world that we experience together.

Martin Crimp's *Attempts on Her Life* and the triumph of undecidability

Martin Crimp is one of the most versatile, creative, aesthetically prolific and challenging playwrights of our time. Aleks Sierz called *Attempts on*

Her Life 'the best play of the decade' (2006, p. 49), and Mary Luckhurst argues that the play is 'the most radically interrogative work in western mainstream theatre since Beckett' (2003, p. 49). Shaun Usher finds that Crimp 'goes even farther [than Luigi Pirandello], doing away with character as such, not to mention a recognisable plot' (1997, pp. 312–13). Crimp describes the structure of the play as 'Seventeen Scenarios for the Theatre', which underlines its radical departure from traditional formats, including its redefinition of traditional concepts of subject, author, gender and ethics. These scenarios, in which we encounter messages, elliptic sentences, advertising copy and patter, stage directions, non-sequential, hermetic and also highly poetic clusters of words and collage-like snapshot images, present seventeen opposing or unrelated outlines for the life of someone called Anne (or Anya, Annie, Anny and Annushka), with the ever-absent 'protagonist' adopting such diverse roles as those of a film heroine, a civil war victim, a megastar, an international terrorist, an artist, a survivalist, a porn star, or even a car or a victim of aliens. Such apparent arbitrariness notwithstanding, each scenario presents us with incoherent, albeit thoroughly recognizable images of everyday life, reminiscent of the ready-mades of Conceptual or Minimal Art (see Escoda Agustí, 2007, p. 149, and Middeke, 2011b).

Already the first scenario, ambiguously named 'ALL MESSAGES DELETED', is crucial because of its likewise equivocal ontological status. We encounter eleven messages on Anne's answering machine, which provide contradictory information from which we can barely infer a context. As if Crimp wanted to increase the incoherence of these messages and the opaqueness of the scenario, he notes that in performance the first scenario may be cut (see Crimp, 2005, p. 202). If this is done, any possible origin or causal connection between the fragmented messages and the following scenarios is completely annihilated. Much in this vein, the title of the first scenario, if read literally, denotes an absence already, a void; if read allegorically, it is a pun, a proleptic marker reflecting on the absence of all clear-cut messages in the play.

Throughout the play, notions of sameness are deflected into Otherness, as countless instances of *repetition* – the most important rhetorical trope in the play – make clear. In scenario 9, the obsessive repetition of the phrase 'Is this the same [little] Anne' (Crimp, 2005, pp. 241, 242, 244) implies a change in the life of (an) Anne, who apparently has turned terrorist and thereby proceeds 'with all the terrible detachment of an artist' (p. 242). This again echoes scenario 11, in which a conceptual piece of artwork is discussed and considered 'pornographic' (p. 255). The pornography motif is taken up in scenarios 5, 14 and 16. In scenario 3, we witness a treatment of a film (or a documentary?) and shocking imaginary out-lines of sickening atrocities in a country apparently torn by civil war, in the midst of which there is a woman named Anya, who curses the oppressors who have killed her family. The exact wording is repeated in scenario 12, where a woman, whose hair is smeared with blood, is held up by soldiers on her way to the airport out of a bombed city and aggressively asked to reveal her identity. She answers that she is taking her daughter Anne/Annushka to the airport; the girl is apparently in two bags on the back seat of her red Cadillac. The motif of the car is repeated in scenario 6, where 'MUM AND DAD' recall their daughter Annie's wish 'to act like a machine, [. . .] pretending to be a television / or a car' (p. 230) and, most prominently, in scenario 7, which is a mul-tilingual, sugar-coated advertisement for a car, 'THE NEW ANNY', with obviously racist undertones as it has no space for 'gypsies, Arabs, Turks, Kurds, Blacks' (p. 237).

Such an interpretative effort to identify instances of repetition and interrelations between scenarios in the play could go on seamlessly – these few examples sufficiently highlight Crimp's aesthetic strategy. Reminiscent of Julian Barnes's extraordinary *A History of the World in 10 ½ Chapters* (1989), Crimp devises a dense network of leitmotifs and cross-references, but he isolates every repetition from its context. Each scenario delineates a new context, whose inner coherence as well as its coherence with the other scenarios in which particular signifiers resur-face with variations are no longer commanded by a dominant referent. Each rudimentary context that is given can, thus, no longer mediate between a word, a signifier and a concept, let alone a transcendental signified. Keeping in mind that Barnes called his novel '*A*' (rather than '*The*') *History of the World in 10 ½ Chapters*, it seems more than notewor-thy that in *Attempts on Her Life* the alleged protagonist's name is Anne, a homophone of the indefinite article 'an', or Annie, which forms a pho-netic minimal pair with 'any'. Indeed, the detected absence of context may conjure up any presence or any context – Annie can be *any* Annie or even *any*one; Anne is just *an* Anne, an isolated singularity among other singularities of nameless speakers. Each repetition is a repetition *with a difference* – a medium of undecidability.

In this regard, Gilles Deleuze has argued that repetition strives for consensus but, at the same time, makes the notions of similarity and identity appear as derivational and conceivable only on the foundation of an all-encompassing difference (see Deleuze, 1994). As a leitmotif, the signifier 'attempts' hints at such an interlacing of identity and dif-ference in repetition. 'Anne/Anya/Annie/Anny/Annushka' constitute empty, floating signifiers that stress what Derrida called the 'iterability of the signifier', emphasizing that even in everyday speech performative speech acts are the rule rather than the exception and that signifiers, thus, lack ultimate authority (see Derrida, 1995, p. 9). For Derrida, and for Crimp, the iterability of a signifier implies that each sign could be isolated from the sequence or chain of written speech in which it appears and be 'grafted' onto other sequences, other chains (see Derrida, 1995, p. 9). No context surrounding a sign can ever captivate it completely and, hence, representation, meaning and (complete) understanding are displaced. Taking up signifiers from one context of speech and grafting them onto other contexts is exactly what happens in *Attempts on Her Life* and the chain of its scenarios. In this interplay, even the symbolic qualities of metaphorical reference become deflected into the realm of the allegorical. In allegory, following Walter Benjamin, '[a]ny person, any object, any relationship can mean absolutely anything else' (1998, p. 175) – Crimp's Annie can indeed mean 'absolutely anything else', since in this allegorical ghost-like rendering of what formerly used to be called a dramatic 'character', Crimp makes 'materiality, signifier, and signified diverge' (Fischer-Lichte, 2008, p. 145).

Such undecidability undoubtedly presents abundant material inviting interpretation. Crimp coaxes the reader/spectator to try an 'attempt' on Anne/Annie/Anny/Anya/Annushka's life, that is to say, to try to find some hidden explanation, some detail that would illuminate an explanatory source of all the different repetitions. One could stress the countless metadramatic references and from there highlight the self-reflexive and autopoietic force of the play (see Middeke, 2011b). With equal ease, however, one could, in a neo-Marxist, Baudrillardean or Jamesonian fashion, emphasize the elements of social satire that focus on a debunking of a postmodernist, late capitalist world of simulation or consumerism, or emphasize issues such as gender (that is, the male gaze), hyperreality, the 'culture of contentment' or the 'society of spectacle' (see, for instance, Sierz, 2006; Escoda Agustí, 2007 and 2013). Vicky Angelaki (2007, 2008, 2012) has done important research on techniques of defamiliarization in Crimp with a view to redefining the nature of the political in his work as well as in contemporary drama in general. Heiner Zimmermann (2002) and Eckart Voigts-Virchow (2010) have pointed to the metabiographical as well as postdramatic features of the play. All of these readings are important contributions to the understanding of the play.

My point here is that the best readings of the enigmatic '*Mene, Mene, Tekel, Upharsin*' that the play confronts us with are those which account best for the undecidability of the text, for its ineluctable heterogeneity, its oscillation between different possible readings which might or might not be interconnected but are in any case logically incompatible so that in whatever way one might set out to illuminate the obscurity of the play, 'the darkest place is always under the lamp' (Crimp, 2005, p. 251). A vital example of such undecidability is the passage in 'PORNÓ' (scenario 16) when, in a moment of transitory confusion, the female speaker stops performing what she is apparently being prompted to say. This seems to be emblematic, but emblematic of what? Is this woman having a breakdown? Is she a victim of the porno industry, of late capitalism, of (self-)alienation, of heteronomy? Or should we not put some faith in the play-acting and in the view that pornography may be really building for some women 'the kind of security and independence many women would envy' (p. 271) – a stance, by the way, brought forward by no less than Angela Carter in her polemical preface to *The Sadeian Woman* (2006, pp. 3–37)? Characteristically, Crimp leaves the question why the girl stops speaking entirely unanswered, and the stage directions emphasize that '*it should not be clear whether she's suffering stage fright or true distress*' (p. 273).

The same ambiguity holds true for the aesthetics of ready-mades which Clara Escoda Agustí (2007) diagnoses, because much in Marcel Duchamp (and in Crimp's play) could of course be read as a revolt against capitalism and mass production, but this alone would underrate the sheer playfulness that underlies Duchamp's *Fountain*, for instance, or schools like Surrealism, Dadaism and Minimal Art, whose stylistic features of collage and mosaic-like fragmentation function as intermedial sources for Crimp's work. The play itself addresses the issue of conflicting interpretations, most notably in 'UNTITLED' (scenario 11), which centres on a woman artist whose work is made up of suicide notes, polaroids of objects with which she has attempted to kill herself and video recordings of the actual attempts on her life. Various singular, nameless speakers deliver their judgements, which range from pornographic self-fashioning and 'pure narcissism' to the acknowledgement of 'cryptic' yet 'moving', 'distressing', even 'funny' and 'entertaining' aspects which render the piece a 'landmark work' (Crimp, 2005, pp. 249 and 250). The debate ends in a *cul-de-sac* of the undecidable: echoing 'PORNÓ', the speakers leave it open whether the woman is a victim or is just play-acting, and any judgement of her art based on a moral evaluation of this victim/play-acting dichotomy becomes a matter of an unruly normativity. Crimp's play – ethically – frustrates such normative moral stances just in the same way as it ironically encounters all the references to the downfall of the genre of classical tragedy (see, for instance, Crimp, 2005, pp. 212, 214, 218, 223, 224) from a disinterested, metadramatic distance. Any attempt at pigeon-holing Anne's life – *any*one's life – would come close to murdering it; likewise, any interpretation that would assume that there is a single, unified, logically coherent meaning to be found in the play turns out to be built on sand.

Evidently, the ethics of unrest which *Attempts on Her Life* confronts us with results in a metahermeneutic projection of undecidability onto the reader/spectator – an avenue, as it were, for the possibility of pos-sibilities. Readers and spectators are invited to attempt to read structure and meaning into the polyphony of impressions, voices, opinions and judgements across a radically polymorphous stream of scenarios. In Derrida's sense, *Attempts on Her Life* produces responsibility in the reader/spectator through the acts of deferral of meaning they have to go through. Responsibility in *Attempts* most of all calls for an affirma-tive openness to Otherness and undecidability, and it is derived from enduring competing interpretations without making attempts at taking refuge in logocentric dichotomies. By accentuating the undecidability of the choice between social satire and self-reflexive play/minimalist experiment, for instance, Crimp makes an ethical statement insofar as he summons readers and audiences alike to reflect on whether or not that 'composition of the world beyond the theatre' is adequate or whether 'the world we're living in' (Crimp, 2005, p. 254) as it is repre-sented in the play is liberating or fatal. Crimp's fidelity to his own aes-thetics is corroborated by the fact that there is not a single instance in the play in which both author and text give up their detached, entirely disinterested stance in favour of a clear-cut (moral) decision. None of the incidents we encounter in the play qualifies as an Event in Badiou's sense. On the contrary, from a Jamesonian perspective one could argue, accentuating Crimp's critique of contemporary consumerism, that some scenarios rather describe simulacra of Events. Those scenarios, one might also argue, which resemble treatments of film scripts go some way towards writing Events in that they at least mention human resilience and resistance. Each of these events, however, falls short of becoming an Event as they lack the consequence of action – truth, which, as fidelity to the Event, is not a path that manifests itself in the irruption of an event alone; rather, truth for Badiou is that post-Evental consequence which all of the speakers/singularities in *Attempts on Her Life* are profusely lacking.

debbie tucker green's *truth and reconciliation* and the fidelity to the event

The ethics of debbie tucker green's 2011 *truth and reconciliation* take a different route from *Attempts on Her Life*, although aesthetically both have many things in common. In *truth and reconciliation* there is hardly a plotline to speak of; the different scenes show different, also nameless speakers who are not presented as psychologically coherent dramatic 'characters', but appear as singularities in their respective cultural, communal, national, as well as historical and political backgrounds and predicaments. Forward slashes indicate overlapping dialogue, while silence becomes an integral part of the dramaturgy of the play as words printed in brackets refer to intentions only and are not to be spoken, so that they become eloquent silent testimonies of shame, guilt and bewilderment. Similar to Crimp, tucker green's style is sparse, stylized, and its minimalist, condensed simplicity and accumulation is thoroughly poetical. Whereas in Crimp's play, however, history and contemporary historical incidents form but an occasional condition rather than a causal framework or point of reference, the starting point of *truth and reconciliation* is historically verifiable catastrophe. The play consists of five strands of action which take the reader/spectator to post-Apartheid South Africa in 1998, Rwanda in 2005, Bosnia in 1996, Zimbabwe in 2007, and Northern Ireland in 1999 – to the aftermath, as it were, of conflict, to places 'where truth and reconciliation are longed for but desperately hard to come by' (Mountford, 2011, p. 935). The five strands are crosscut into 19 episodes, which produces an interwoven succession of scenes and places which breaks up the linearity and chronology of the play's development. In this, the play succeeds in generating the impression of simultaneity and even universality beyond cultural, national or political boundaries. All episodes remain open and inconclusive.

Each strand of action deals with gross human rights violations in the past; each centres on a moment of confrontation when a victim is meant to meet face-to-face with the perpetrators of violence. The historical details are not given, but are deducible from historical knowledge. A South African mother and her family appear at a hearing that is obviously initiated by the Truth and Reconciliation Commission (TRC) in order to give a statement about their experience and gain information about what happened to their young daughter, who was killed in 1976 – what is meant is quite distinctly the Soweto Uprising by high-school students on 16 June against Apartheid, in which an estimated number of up to 700 children found their deaths. A Bosnian woman encounters two Serbian ex-soldiers, one of whom made her pregnant when both raped her in the last year of the Bosnian War. A Zimbabwean wife faces terrible consequences for speaking up against political persecution during the Mugabe regime. A Tutsi Rwandan Widow, ten years after the Rwandan Genocide, faces the Hutu Man who killed her husband. Finally, two Northern Irish women and men – Catholic and Protestant – blame each other for the deaths of their children in the Irish Troubles. Each episode focuses on the *temporal difference* between the present and a moment in the past that changed the life of these singularities. tucker green is not interested in historical analysis, but rather in the emotional impact of the incident of personal loss in the past in terms of the acknowledgement of truth and an eventual ethical opportunity for responsibility, reconciliation and forgiveness in the present.

On the whole, all five stories cast a devastatingly pessimist glance at the chance of such reconciliation. The play unapologetically makes it clear that moral/ethical experience actually has a content in reality, visible, for example, in the indignation and outrage with which we react to injuries and witness these injuries turn into resentment if no apology is made for them. 'In general', P.F. Strawson argued in a famous essay on 'Freedom and Resentment', 'within varying limits, we demand of others for others, as well as of ourselves for others, something of the regard which we demand of others for ourselves' (1974, pp. 15–16; see also Habermas, 1983 and Middeke, 2011a, p. v). In all five stories, the violations of human rights not only flout Strawson's ethical imperative, they also disregard that 'for-the Other' or 'with-the Other' which Bauman and Levinas consider the prenominal conditions of being.

The five strands of action all have the same setting, '*[t]hree wooden chairs face one solitary wooden chair*' (tucker green, 2011, p. 4), which manifests the gap of resentment, hate and fear between a clearly demarcated 'us' (the victims) and 'them' (the perpetrators). For the most part, the time of waiting for the face-to-face encounter between victim and perpetrator is filled with talk about indifferent topics, but even simple matters such as a decision whether and where to sit down are political statements as they are charged with hierarchies and attempts to preserve one's dignity: '[s]he needs to sit down by me', the South African grandmother tells her daughter, 'standing will stand for nothing' (p. 5). When the Bosnian woman sees her rapists in front of her, she indignantly asks, 'Are they waiting for me to speak first?', and insists that 'it's for them to speak. [. . .] for them to say something to / me' (pp. 18 and 19). In the Northern Ireland episode there is so much resentment between the opposite parties, which ironically have suffered the same fate, that any communication seems impossible, as the overlapping dialogue makes clear (see, for example, tucker green, 2011, p. 64).

Only one of the five stories qualifies as an Event in Badiou's sense: the Soweto Uprising in 1976. The Bosnian War, the Irish Troubles, Zimbabwean totalitarianism and the Rwandan Genocide are perversions of Events, examples of Evil in the sense of terror and disaster, because they involve either absoluteness on the basis of ethnicity and religion or claims to total political power. Truth, however, becomes visible in the unconditional fidelity by which the South African mother has been persevering for more than twenty years to be told about the fate of her child and the circumstances of her death: 'I want to hear from him' (tucker green, 2011, p. 26). In a slight variation on Badiou's theory, truth appears also in what I would call 'fidelity to the rebellion against a simulacrum or perversion of an Event' – in other words, in the perseverance to resist injustice, totalitarianism and any other form of oppression that would set out to quiet such resistance. There is the example of the brave Zimbabwean wife, who has publicly spoken what '"needed" to be said' because 'somebody had to speak' (p. 15). The decision that she is making is actually as impossible as Abraham's on Mount Moriah because her perseverance in what is true and ethical estranges her from her responsibility to her husband, whose life is as threatened as hers. Not only has she got to rebel against political totalitarianism, she also has to revolt against being engrossed by hierarchical gender constructions and family structures – a leitmotif which resurfaces in the Rwandan, South African and Bosnian episodes, in which *female* perseverance in the fidelity to rebellion is persistently rejected, scrutinized, interrogated, or at least, doubted by men with remarks such as 'I wouldn't let you', 'let your unsure mind – tell your unsure mouth to surely be quiet', '[t]here are people who say things better than you', 'this isn't helping the dead', '[t]here are things that I would lose what we had for' or '[t]his isn't helping me' (pp. 8, 15, 16, 27, 35, 38). The examples of the South African mother, the Zimbabwean wife and the Rwandan widow are all epitomes of Events in Badiou's understanding and, hence, signs of ethical hope because these women do what many others shirk (see also Bauman, 1993, p. 84).

tucker green, however, is as adamant in her analysis of why reconciliation or even forgiveness are respectively hard to accomplish and impossible. As the examples of the Bosnian rapists or the Zimbabwean husband forcefully explain, the truth produced by the fidelity to an event can simply be betrayed by denying or suppressing it. Furthermore, responsibility, which is generated in the space of human face-to-face encounters, is nullified by simply shunning the face-to-face situation. The South African mother never meets the person responsible for her daughter's death because he never comes, which she laments in a long monologue which is certainly one of the most sublime, moving, poetic moments in the play (see tucker green, 2011, pp. 41–4). What is more, the Zimbabwean woman, whom the husband asks for information after his wife has been taken away, presents herself as just a representative of an abstract, distant, faceless bureaucracy which never has to face the effects of its decisions. In this context, Bauman speaks of 'adiaphoriz-ing' (2008, p. 107) strategies which seek to suspend responsibility.[3] Marginalizing or segregating individuals or groups from the quantity of 'faces' which ask for our responsibility is another adiaphorizing strategy, one that constitutes a leitmotif in every episode of *truth and reconciliation*.

As far as forgiveness is concerned, tucker green is realistic about the aporia inherent in the internal logic of the idea of 'forgiveness'. As there is an unbridgeable gap of temporal difference between an act itself and the act of its forgiveness, there cannot be atonement in the sense of at-*one*-ment. Further, 'genuine forgiveness must engage two singularities: the guilty and the victim. As soon as a third party intervenes, once can again speak of amnesty, reconciliation, repara-tion, etc., but certainly not of forgiveness in the strict sense' (Derrida, 2001, p. 42), or as one of the Northern Irish women in the play puts it, 'what he did was unforgivable and you're unforgivable for not saying something sooner that could have stopped / it' (tucker green, 2011, p. 67). In *truth and reconciliation* the radically singular confron-tation between victim and perpetrator is realized only in the Bosnian episode. All other episodes involve the deaths of the victims, which precludes a literal confrontation between victims and perpetrators. The absence of such a confrontation is bridged by mediating parties such as the families or representatives of bureaucracy like the Zimbabwean woman. Consequently, tucker green deflects the impossibility of for-giveness into the (utopian) realm of the imaginary as she resolves her play by two equally shocking and touching episodes which go back in time and in which the living perpetrators meet with their victims, the dead husband in Rwanda and the dead child in South Africa (see tucker green, 2011, pp. 70–4 and pp. 75–80). In the stunning, unforgettable final tableau, the dead child wrenches a promise from her murderer that he will go and tell her mother what has happened (p. 80). Sadly, as we know by now, he never did.

Conclusion

Both *Attempts on Her Life* and *truth and reconciliation* emphasize that ethics involves facing up to undecidables while making decisions and admitting to the difficulties and aporias involved in our responsibility for the Other. Both plays centre on moral ambivalences, equivocal face-to-face encounters, the non-universalizability of moral problems, and the multiplicity of experience of an infinitely multiple number of singularities of which the examples given in the plays are but synecdoches. By devising open, innovative aesthetic structures both plays in fact become such an Other acknowledging the impact of contingency and paradox on their ethical predications. Their ethics, however, does not exhaust itself in the intrafictional relationships and interactions they devise. Both plays are characterized by a decisive appeal structure, which projects the notion of undecidability onto the reader/spectator, setting in motion a complex, inconclusive, and, thus, restless transformation process in the reception of the plays. Not only does this transformation process confront us – as readers and spectators – with intrafictional gaps which we have to fill or with Events or their simulacra, it also turns the plays themselves into Events asking for our own post-Evental consequence and perseverance.

Both plays, as literary/theatrical Events, constitute liminal spaces of negotiability between the fictive and the imaginary by alienating us from received modes of perception and knowledge in order to create new ones that may change the way we experience the world. In the London production of *truth and reconciliation* at the Royal Court Theatre Upstairs, directed by tucker green herself, audience members sat on the same hard wooden chairs as the cast did. Outside the auditorium the walls bore the names of victims that had died in conflicts including Rwanda and Northern Ireland, forcing the audience members to bear witness. For readers and spectators of art/literature/theatre, this could be the ethical chance to become the 'some-one' Badiou speaks of, who is capable of truth, capable of fulfilling an immanent break, '*this* spectator whose thinking has been set in motion, who has been seized and bewildered by a burst of theatrical fire, and who thus enters into the complex configuration of a moment of art' (Badiou, 2001, p. 45).

Notes

1. I capitalize 'Event' to indicate Badiou's understanding of the term. 'Good' and 'Evil', to which I turn subsequently, are capitalized by Badiou himself.
2. For further commentary see also Gibson, 1999, pp. 146–58.

3. This is 'a term borrowed from the language of the medieval Christian Church, [which] originally meant a belief that was "neutral" or "indifferent" in the matters of religious doctrine. Here, in our metaphorical use, "adiaphoric" means amoral: subject to no moral judgment, having no moral significance' (Bauman, 2008, p. 138).

Works cited

Angelaki, V. (2007) 'Performing Phenomenology: The Theatre of Martin Crimp' in D. Watt and D. Meyer-Dinkgräfe (eds) *Theatres of Thought: Theatre, Performance and Philosophy* (Newcastle: Cambridge Scholars Publishing), pp. 6–12.

—— (2008) 'Subtractive Forms and Composite Contents: Martin Crimp's *Fewer Emergencies*' in E. Redling and P.P. Schnierer (eds) *Non-Standard Forms of Contemporary Drama and Theatre* (Trier: Wissenschaftlicher Verlag Trier), pp. 31–46.

—— (2012) *The Plays of Martin Crimp: Making Theatre Strange* (Basingstoke and New York: Palgrave Macmillan).

Badiou, A. (2001) *Ethics: An Essay on the Understanding of Evil* (London and New York: Verso).

Barnes, J. (1989) *A History of the World in 10 ½ Chapters* (London: Jonathan Cape).

Bauman, Z. (1993) *Postmodern Ethics* (Oxford: Blackwell).

—— (2008) *The Art of Life* (Cambridge: Polity Press).

Benjamin, W. (1998) *The Origin of German Tragic Drama*, trans. J. Osborne (London: Verso).

Carter, A. (2006) *The Sadeian Woman: An Exercise in Cultural History* (London: Virago).

Crimp, M. (2005) *Plays Two (No One Sees the Video, The Misanthrope, Attempts on Her Life, The Country)* (London: Faber).

Critchley, S. (1999) *The Ethics of Deconstruction: Derrida and Levinas* (Edinburgh: Edinburgh University Press).

Deleuze, G. (1994) *Difference and Repetition*, trans. P. Patton (New York: Columbia University Press).

Derrida, J. (1978) *Writing and Difference*, trans. A. Bass (Chicago: Chicago University Press).

—— (1982) *Margins of Philosophy*, trans. A. Bass (Chicago: Chicago University Press).

—— (1995) *The Gift of Death*, trans. D. Wills (Chicago and London: Chicago University Press).

—— (1998) *Limited Inc.*, ed. G. Graff, trans. S. Weber (Evanston, IL: Northwestern University Press).

—— (2001) *On Cosmopolitanism and Forgiveness* (New York and London: Routledge).

Escoda Agustí, C. (2007) '"head green water to sing": Minimalism and Indeterminacy in Martin Crimp's *Attempts on Her Life*' in C. Henke and M. Middeke (eds) *Drama and/after Postmodernism* (Trier: Wissenschaftlicher Verlag Trier), pp. 149–63.

—— (2013) *Martin Crimp's Theatre: Collapse as Resistance to Late Capitalist Society* (Berlin and Boston: De Gruyter).

Fischer-Lichte, E. (2008) *The Transformative Power of Performance: A New Aesthetics*, trans. S.I. Jain (New York and London: Routledge).

Gibson, A. (1999) *Postmodernity, Ethics and the Novel: From Leavis to Levinas* (London and New York: Routledge).

Habermas, J. (1983) *Moralbewußtsein und kommunikatives Handeln* (Frankfurt am Main: Suhrkamp).

Levinas, E. (1969) *Totality and Infinity: An Essay on Exteriority* (Pittsburgh, PA: Duquesne University Press).

Luckhurst, M. (2003) 'Political Point-Scoring: Martin Crimp's *Attempts on Her Life*', *Contemporary Theatre Review*, 13 (1), pp. 47–60.

Luhmann, N. (1990) *Paradigm Lost: Über die ethische Reflexion der Moral* (Frankfurt am Main: Suhrkamp).

Middeke, M. (2011a) 'Introduction', *Anglia*, 129 (1–2), pp. v–x.

—— (2011b) 'Martin Crimp' in M. Middeke, P.P. Schnierer and A. Sierz (eds) *The Methuen Drama Guide to Contemporary British Playwrights* (London: Methuen), pp. 82–102.

Mountford, F. (2011) 'Review of *truth and reconciliation*', *Theatre Record*, 31 (34), p. 935.

Sierz, A. (2006) *The Theatre of Martin Crimp* (London: Methuen).

Strawson, P.F. (1974) *Freedom and Resentment and Other Essays* (London: Methuen).

tucker green, d. (2011) *truth and reconciliation* (London: Nick Hern).

Usher, S. (1997) 'Review of *Attempts on Her Life*', *Theatre Record*, 17 (6), pp. 312–13.

Voigts-Virchow, E. (2010) 'Postdramatisches Theater: Martin Crimp' in M. Tönnies (ed.) *Das englische Drama der Gegenwart: Kategorien – Entwicklungen Modellinterpretationen* (Trier: Wissenschaftlicher Verlag Trier), pp. 158–71.

Zimmermann, H. (2002) 'Martin Crimp, *Attempts on Her Life*: Postdramatic, Postmodern, Satiric?' in M. Rubik and E. Mettinger-Schartmann (eds) *Discontinuities: Trends and Traditions in Contemporary Theatre and Drama in English* (Trier: Wissenschaftlicher Verlag Trier), pp. 105–24.

Part III
Spectatorial Ethics

7
Playing with Proximity: Precarious Ethics on Stage in the New Millennium

Clare Wallace

An intensified consciousness of ethical dilemmas and political failures has indelibly stamped the inaugural years of the twenty-first century. While philosophy and critical theory has been gripped by an ethical turn for some time, digesting the implications of postmodern relativism and Francis Fukuyama's bold assertion in 1992 that the end of history (or more accurately, ideology) had been reached, such developments may seem far removed from mundane experience. Indeed, this is exacerbated by the multiple valencies attributed to the term 'ethics', which seems to lend itself to promiscuous couplings with almost any noun: is ethics the natural inheritor of moral philosophy and criticism, should one regard such a turn as a welcome rerouting of relativism towards judgement and value, or does the current validation of ethics displace or, worse still, neutralize the political as theorists like Jacques Rancière (2006) or Chantal Mouffe contend (2000)? In the twenty-first century so far, those apparently abstract concerns have been met with a deluge of concrete ones. Fed by the terrorist attacks of September 2001, the War on Terror, Guantánamo, the ever more blatant inequalities of neoliberal globalization and corporate capitalism, a chain of financial crises and the apparent implosion of moral principles in the popular media, the stream of ethics-based debate has unquestionably overflowed the banks of academic or philosophical discourse. This chapter investigates how that intensified consciousness is inscribed in work by a cluster of theatre makers since 2006. That work demonstrates a pronounced, but heterogeneous, preoccupation with the slippery surfaces of ethics, and suggests that existing debates around ethics and aesthetics are far from concluded. As a prelude to the analysis of specific pieces, I want to trace some of the debates that underpin the present discussion of such ethical speculations.

Alan Read opens his book *Theatre and Everyday Life: An Ethics of Performance* with an arresting question, one that goes to the heart of the matter of theatre and ethics: 'Is the theatre good?' (1993, p. 1). Obviously not necessarily, obviously not universally – so how and when is theatre 'good'? Where, in other words, does its ethics lie? Amidst the burgeoning proliferation of transient images and experiences offered by postmodernity, theatre can only, according to Read, 'distinguish' itself by 'an ethical stance' (p. 6). For Read that stance is manifest when theatre 'enables us to know the everyday in order to better live everyday life' (p. 2); it does this by 'offer[ing] alternative realities and insights to the everyday' (p. 7). At the conclusion of *Postdramatic Theatre*, Hans-Thies Lehmann also reflects upon theatre's current social function, arguing that its ethical promise resides in challenging the logic of spectacle, '[t]he basic structure of perception mediated by media [in which] there is no experience of a connection between the receiving and sending of signs; there is no experience of a relation between address and answer' (2006, p. 185). Although their destinations are undoubtedly different, what is salient to both these critical interventions is the primacy of relationality to their analyses of theatre's role, and the fundamental significance of responsibility at work here. For Read:

> Good theatre stands face to face with its audience. [. . .] An ethical theatre cannot be produced in the purpose-built design of another time. It can only be built as a response, and with a responsibility, to its traditions with constant attention to a vocabulary drawn from the frontier disciplines that press upon its borders, new ways of describing the problematics of place, aesthetic value and audience that are central to its continued existence. (1993, pp. 6–7)

Lehmann's conclusions closely echo this – theatre's potential (and indeed future) resides in 'an *aesthetic of responsibility (or response-ability)*' that can 'move the *mutual implication of actors and spectators in the theatrical production of images* into the centre and thus make visible the broken thread between personal experience and perception' (2006, pp. 185–6; emphasis original). In other words, theatre's ethical promise lies in illuminating and enacting forms of relationality and connection. While relational ethics underscore relationships of interdependence, intersubjectivity and responsibility, this plaiting of theatre, ethics and relationality also recalls the work of Nicolas Bourriaud. His analysis of 1990s art in terms of 'relational aesthetics' foregrounds 'a set of artistic practices which take as their theoretical and practical point of departure the whole of human relations and their social context, rather than an independent and private space' (2002, p. 113). Relationality in this instance might be seen as implicitly resistant to the alienating effects of commodified representation, yet the extent of the efficacy of aesthetic relationality remains a point of contestation. Notably, Bourriaud's assertions have drawn criticism for their alleged disinterest in the nature of the relations produced (see, for example, Bishop, 2004, p. 65), highlighting a continuing dissonance surrounding the role of relationality, and its politics, in contemporary creative practice.

What interests me is the simultaneous vitality and fragility of connection, or drawing together, that forms the basis for discussions of ethics in theatre, and the ways certain British playwrights and performers in the new millennium have attempted to create such moments of precarious connection. The exploration of such moments is elaborated here via four examples: Mark Ravenhill's *pool (no water)* (2006), Caryl Churchill's *Seven Jewish Children* (2009), Tim Crouch's *The Author* (2009) and David Greig's *Fragile* (2011). Though widely divergent, each play crucially engages with what Lehmann terms 'the politics of perception' (2006, p. 185) within zones of ethical ambivalence. My argument is that in all a triangular configuration can be identified, the points of which are representation, proximity and violence, and at the centre of which an ethics of responsibility/'response-ability' is unsteadily balanced.

Proximity and face-to-face relations

Proximity is, of course, a key node in many conceptions of ethics, not least the one embedded in Read's assertion of the value of the face-to-face encounter. The philosophy of Emmanuel Levinas supplants the tradition of conceiving ethics as self-realization or being with an alternate obligation. For Levinas, the foundation of ethics lies in the open-ended relation to what he describes as the face of the Other: 'The approach to the face is the most basic mode of responsibility' (Levinas and Kearney, 1986, p. 23). This face is neither a specific one, nor is it confined to the human; it is, as Richard Kearney states, 'undecidable' but nevertheless presents an inexorable ethical demand, a responsibility. As Kearney goes on to explain, '[a]n other in need makes the ethical demand upon me – "where are you?" – before I ask of the other the epistemological question – "who are you?"' (1998, p. 362).

That relationship of co-presence, responsibility and 'response-ability' can be seen to underwrite many of the claims made for theatre's ethical possibilities. Read observes that a 'conception of ethics as centred in the "face-to-face" relation is particularly appropriate to theatre' (1993, p. 91). Nicholas Ridout similarly comments on how 'what looks like a "face-to-face encounter" has encouraged a consideration of the relationship between spectator and actor, audience and performance' (2009, p. 54), and several recent publications like Helena Grehan's *Performance, Ethics and Spectatorship in a Global Age* (2009) and Katharina Pewny's *Das Drama des Prekären* (2011) continue, to varying degrees, in this vein.

That said, as each of these scholars is careful to note, in spite of conceptual rewards, a Levinasian model of ethical relation cannot be transposed wholesale to theatre. Even without rehearsing the further complications that derive from this complex philosophical domain, the matter of the validity of the theatre situation of encounter as an ethical one presents itself. It is hard to ignore the import of Levinas's 1948 essay, 'Reality and its Shadow,' in which he criticizes art in general as the substitution of images for reality; 'art', which he sees as 'essentially disengaged, constitutes, in a world of initiative and responsibility, a dimension of evasion' (Levinas, 1989, p. 141). To be fair, 'Reality and its Shadow' is a minor part of Levinas's oeuvre. It undoubtedly speaks to its time, originating in a desire to challenge 'the contemporary dogma of knowledge through art' and to raise the problems of 'committed' art or literature immediately after the Second World War (p. 131). The erosion of such 'dogmas' in the era of the postmodern, however, precipitates an impulse to reevaluate what 'committed' art might be for both artists and critics. I concur with Read, Ridout and Grehan's work in marking this scepticism about the aesthetic while contesting that it need not stand unchallenged. Moreover, as Ravenhill, Churchill, Crouch and Greig show, in practice aesthetics and ethics, ethics and politics, politics and aesthetics are not necessarily or simply aligned in mutually exclusive configurations.[1]

Vulnerabilities and violence

Less easy, perhaps, to reconcile with the theatre situation is the injunction that accompanies the face-to-face relation with the Other, the injunction against violence. Levinas suggests that 'the face of the other in its precariousness and defenceless, is for me at once the temptation to kill and the call to peace' (1996, p. 167). The centrality of vulnerability here is fruitfully explored by Judith Butler in her essay 'Precarious Life', where she states, '[t]o respond to the face, to understand its meaning, means to be awake to what is precarious in another life, or, rather, the precariousness of life itself' (2004, p. 137). With the War on Terror in mind, Butler considers how Levinas may offer ways 'of thinking about the relationship between representation and humanization', and by extension, dehumanization and the uses of the face to these ends (pp. 140–1). Looking at how representation can dehumanize she reflects on how the media, through personification, projection, essentializing and invitations to dis/identification, can generate 'images that seem to suspend the precariousness of life' (p. 143). Such representation elides reality and forecloses a sense of proximity, creating instead irreality and distance: 'The derealization of loss – the insensitivity to human suffering and death – becomes the mechanism through which dehumanization is accomplished. This derealization takes place neither inside nor outside the image, but through the very framing by which the image is contained' (p. 148). That process, defined by the logic of spectacle flagged at the beginning of this chapter, constantly shadows attempts to engage ethics in both theatre making and theatre criticism.

Given prevalent experiences of vulnerability in politics and economics, it is small wonder that the term precarity is gaining some critical momentum. Current work on performance and ethics invests its energies in unravelling, rerouting and extending understandings of the modalities of precarity suggested by Levinas and latterly by Butler. Pewny (2011) contends that the ethical in contemporary theatre appears not only in terms of content but in forms that make the precarious palpable and perceptible. Still more recently, the winter 2012 issue of *TDR* spotlights the term. The issue's editors, Nicholas Ridout and Rebecca Schneider, aver:

> Precarity has become a byword for life in late and later capitalism – or, some argue, life in capitalism *as usual*. [. . .] At the same time, 'creative capital' invests a kind of promise in precarity with words like 'innovation,' 'failure,' 'experiment,' and 'arts.' The links here between creativity and terror, art and structures of risk and insecurity, point also to connections with performance and the embodied balancing act of the live performer. (2012, pp. 5–6; emphasis original)

Such an appraisal of the precarious fruitfully extends its use as a relational condition belonging to the philosophy of ethics. Consciousness of precarity as a socioeconomic and political phenomenon that bears upon all spheres comprehends a deep ambivalence about the dependencies and insecurities it implies, as well as a recognition of interdependence and the non-totalizing impulse of provisionality. It is this complex of reflections on proximity and precarity that provides the lens through which the ensuing analyses of theatre works are projected. Diverse as they are, these plays each exhibit a desire to reflect upon, reveal and generate senses of precarity through their excavations of the relationships between representation, violence and vulnerability.

Beyond empathy? The art of suffering

Mark Ravenhill, who was positioned by Aleks Sierz at the epicentre of 1990s 'in-yer-face' theatre (2001), has rarely shied away from dissecting the pathologies of postmodernity – its relentless logic of consumption, its disorientating disjunctions between self and place, its rudderless relativity and obsessive superficialities. First performed in 2006, *pool (no water)* continues to explore many of these targets by mapping them in a pseudo-confessional play about art, friendship and aesthetic opportunism. At the same time, because *pool (no water)* was generated in collaboration with the physical theatre company Frantic Assembly, it is also a departure for Ravenhill, one he describes candidly in an article in the *Guardian* at the time of the play's first production (Ravenhill, 2006). In that article Ravenhill charts the uneven initial phases of his co-operation with the company and how his ideas for the project fell into place, not after a week of studio work, but rather in response to a book of photographs by American artist Nan Goldin. The playwright neatly sums up the result: 'A group of friends, who have become very close at art college, feel huge jealousy as one of them becomes a massively successful artist. They go to stay with her and when she is badly injured in an accident, realise they can use her as material for their next work of art' (2006). This deceptively simple synopsis masks the complexities of the piece's engagement with proximity, representation and violence, which overflow the bad case of *schadenfreude* blighting its trendy art opportunists.

At an obvious level, *pool (no water)* is a play about making art, the relation of art to life and the ethics of that relation. The unnamed artist at the hub of the narrative has made a career of absence – 'It's that quality in her work that sells. [. . .] Absent. And yet somehow – recognised by the world' (Ravenhill, 2008, p. 295). That commercial success, catalysed by her artistic use of her friend's 'blood and bandages and catheter and condoms' (ibid.) after he dies of AIDS, suggests an ambivalent aestheticization of pain, suffering and vulnerability, even before the gruesome incident at the pool. Notions of absence are intricately networked through the play. The storytellers remain nameless, their successful friend is never accorded a speaking part in the unfolding of the story, and permeating the fabric of the piece is a keen sense of ethical vacuity. Following the violent accident in the pool, physical proximity is juxtaposed with emotional distance. They reflect on how

> we wanted to feel what she was feeling – she is one of us, we are artists – no, we're people – we wanted to feel what she was feeling – share the pain.
> But it didn't happen.
> We stood. We stood and we watched the jerking and we heard the screams. And we stood and we watched. All of us.
> We couldn't do anything. Couldn't touch her. But we could have felt something. A life without empathy is [. . .]
>
> (Ravenhill, 2008, p. 302)

Ravenhill allows the ellipsis to carry his satirical point home in lieu of an object. What is a life without empathy? From this point, the artist herself, already ventriloquized by the performers, becomes not only an Other to whom they feel compelled to respond, but also an object. Notably, their first response to her vulnerability is a violent verbal outburst – a nasty admission of exhilaration in the presence of another's suffering. While this gives way temporarily to the performance of care, the seduction of aestheticization invades the intensive care ward: 'The purple of the bruise [. . .] It appeals. It tempts. There is beauty here' (p. 306).

Arguably, in both the marketable work of the absent artist and in the group's creative recording of her suffering and convalescence, the precariousness of life becomes a product, and dehumanization and desensitization take its place. As the artist regains agency, she exerts her ownership of the images her friends have produced of her broken body, yet this does not mark a shift away from dehumanization or desensitization. Rather it is a reorientation more akin to a turn from a pseudo-Nan Goldin aesthetic to a pseudo-Cindy Sherman mode of performance photography. The shift is from voyeurism to self-objectification, but both share an ego-driven opportunism. Strikingly, the artist becomes present for her companions only after they destroy the art work in a fit of drug-addled jealousy. Yet even at this juncture, when allegedly '[s]he is totally [. . .] there', there is no direct speech; instead, they are caught in her gaze and judged: 'her eyes take us in. And it's as if we can hear her say – her mouth is closed, but still I, we, I, heard' (p. 322).

The nuances of speaking and listening in this final moment of epiphany where the artists hear the judgement of the other *through closed lips* point to the instability of the play's situation of responsibility and 'response-ability'. Ravenhill produces an open, narrative text in which character is displaced by voices and possible choral effects that flow together to tell a story. Commenting on the Frantic Assembly production, Allison Vale remarks on how 'the actors complete each other's sentences and thoughts without ever sacrificing their own distinct identities' (2006). Those apparently distinct identities, however, are deliberately blurred by Ravenhill and this, I would contend, dovetails with the erosion of individuality that the spectacle of suffering implies and its consequent ethical disjunctions. Simultaneously, the confessional flavour to the narrative disallows a complete evasion of individual responsibility even when the convention of dramatic character (signalling distinct identity) is sidestepped. The reliance on 'we', so prominent throughout the play, is definitively ruptured in the moment of being 'taken in' as the oscillation between subject positions – 'I, we, I' – indicates. The subsequent dominance of first person in the final sections of the play may be seen as a tentative acceptance of responsibility.

Frantic Assembly brought to the debut of *pool (no water)* an intensely visually dynamic and physically energetic interpretation that used music, dance and light effects. As Michal Lachman observes, the production foregrounded a 'robust physicality' which featured performers in constant motion: 'The spectacle soars from extremely natural gestures and realistic, mundane delivery of lines to the heights of prolonged sequences of intensified, unbearable emotions. The text of the play is spoken with artificially prolonged vowels and shouted words' (2013, p. 158). While *pool (no water)* has been performed since in various styles by other companies and groups of performers, the resonances of Frantic Assembly's performance style warrant attention because they were so intrinsic to the gestation of the work. Unquestionably the design and choreography of that interpretation are impressive, creating a rich texture of visual and aural stimuli. Philip Fisher concludes his praise of the show's high production values with the remark that 'it is primarily a Frantic Assembly work with music and dance adding immensely to a simple story' (2006). And yet there is a dissonant tension, a potential remainder which places a strain on the play's aesthetic of risk and 'response-ability'. The communication of ethical ambivalence towards the aestheticization of pain and, to paraphrase Butler, the dehumanizing and derealizing capability of spectacle through sheer kinetic energy presents a potential paradox. The 'dialogue going on in the writing' that Ravenhill describes as happening 'with an audience' (2006) rather than between characters is questionably displaced by the visually compelling 'balletic physicality'

(Vale, 2006) of Frantic Assembly's performance. Arguably, like the characters in the play, the audience is drawn into an ethically undecidable appreciation of the body as object.

Rogue speech acts and anti-Semitism

Caryl Churchill's *Seven Jewish Children*, first performed at the Royal Court in February 2009, cast itself openly as a response to the Palestinian-Israeli conflict in Gaza in January of that year. It is a piece that stirred fiercely divergent reactions and has been criticized as an incendiary act of anti-Semitism – a charge Churchill has strongly rejected (2009b). The play is divided into seven scenes, each of which refers to a different historical moment, and each of which involves a different set of speakers and a different, absent, child addressee. Beginning with the Second World War, the Holocaust and its aftermath, the scenes indirectly allude to the settlement of Palestine and subsequent crisis points in Israeli history up to the current invasion of Gaza. With no fixed cast of characters, no action and no dialogue, the play is motored by a litany of competing views of what should or should not be told to the child at each of these seven moments in order to convey the truth of the situation. The rhythmic refrain 'Tell her'/'Don't tell her'/'Don't frighten her' across the scenes (Churchill, 2009) unmasks each cluster of speakers 'grappling', as Antony Lerman puts it, 'with questions of right and wrong' in the midst of brutality (2009). With its confluent political, ethical and aesthetic aspects, *Seven Jewish Children* is undeniably a deeply ambivalent and polemical gesture that continues to generate extremely polarized responses and raises multiple questions about responsibility. The extent and ferocity of the reaction to this ten-minute work (which Churchill made available for free and as a result was widely disseminated) confirms, if nothing else, the acute sensitivity of the territory with which the play precariously engages.

That territory is perceptively surveyed in Butler's essay 'The Charge of Anti-Semitism: Jews, Israel, and the Risks of Public Critique' in *Precarious Life*, which uncannily preempts the debates surrounding the ethics of *Seven Jewish Children*. Butler attempts to unravel the politics of perception and reception of particular speech acts at the centre of which lies the force of the charge of anti-Semitism and how it can be used to 'quell public criticism' (2004, p. 104). She goes on to consider the paradoxical 'distinction between intentional and effective anti-Semitism' and contends that 'it would seem that effective anti-Semitism can be understood only by conjuring a seamless world of listeners and readers who take certain statements of Israel to be tacitly or overtly *intended* as anti-Semitic expression' (p. 105; emphasis original). Consequently, the meaning of anti-Semitism 'as a crucial and effective instrument' to contest prejudice is distorted and diminished (p. 110). Associated with the charge of anti-Semitism is the problematic conflation of all 'Jewish people with the state of Israel' (p. 111) or with its current policies – 'It is important to remember', Butler cautions, 'that the identification of Jewishness with Israel, implied by the formulation that maintains that to criticize Israel is effectively to engage in anti-Semitism, elides the reality of a small but dynamic peace movement in Israel itself' (p. 115), as well as those outside the state who may support its transformation.

Many of the criticisms and defences made during the initial stormy reception of *Seven Jewish Children* tread remarkably similar paths to those traced by Butler. Howard Jacobson damningly reviewed the play as an 'audacious [. . .] encapsulation of Israel's moral collapse – the audacity residing in its ignorance or its dishonesty', and as 'Jew-hating pure and simple' (2009). Dave Rich and Mark Gardner criticize the 'dishonesty and amorality of the adult voices' in the play and see it as a renovating of 'blood libel' (2009). Conspicuously, they argue that although Churchill 'almost certainly does not intend it' the play has 'anti-Semitic resonances' (2009). Both criticisms recall the paradoxical distinction between intentional and effective anti-Semitism debated by Butler, and its attendant problems. Churchill's response to Jacobson refutes his assertion that criticism of Israel is default anti-Semitism, and argues that the views held by the speakers are heterogeneous and not simply to be accepted as representative (2009b). Yet *Seven Jewish Children* deliberately touches a nerve. Even in their impassioned defence of the play, Tony Kushner and Alisa Solomon are forced to admit that 'there are passages, particularly in an ugly monologue near the play's conclusion, that are terribly painful to experience, especially for Jews' (2009).

Seven Jewish Children clearly creates a zone of discomfort heightened by the condensation of its form and focus. That form and focus have been dismissed as 'psychobabble' that glibly maps the transformation of trauma and victimhood into a Zionist defensiveness and aggression (Jacobson, 2009). But the play's aesthetic challenge may also work, as Enric Monforte observes, to 'underline the ethical' (2012, p. 101). Although still hotly disputed, its poetic form serves to keep ethical dilemmas in play and open, in a manner that may awaken a sense of precarious life precisely through its confrontational mode. This is substantiated by the fact that the instructions about how to tell the story and what should be represented as the truth of each historical moment are consistently divergent and incongruent, as is vividly highlighted in section two of the play:

> Tell her there are still people who hate Jews.
> Tell her there are people who love Jews.
> Don't tell her to think Jews or not Jews.

> (2009a, p. 3)

The rhetorical manoeuvre of oscillation between diametrically opposed proposals, as well as the fact that as proposals they are future orientated and therefore not closed or final, refuses to homogenize, resolve or stabilize attitudes to Jews.

The final and seventh section of *Seven Jewish Children*, which treats the conflict in Gaza, is the one most frequently cited as evidence of Churchill's malicious message and intent. The scene builds to a tense crescendo where finally a single speaker is afforded a monologue in which a hatred of those seen to threaten his/her world is vented. There is no way to deny the vengeful tone of this outburst, yet immediately following are statements that are easy to overlook but are vital in their refusal of this provocative bid for violence and their reiteration of love:

> Don't tell her that.
> Tell her we love her.
> Don't frighten her.

> (Churchill, 2009a, p. 7)

(Not) offending the audience

'The idea was to have the spectators [. . .] thrown back upon themselves. What mattered to me was making them feel like going to the theatre more, making them see all plays more consciously and with a different consciousness. My theatrical plan is to have the audience always look upon my play as a means of testing other plays', states the playwright (Joseph, Handke and Ashton, 1970, p. 58). The provocative play he refers to involves a minimum of four speakers and undertakes an active deconstruction of our expectations in the theatre. The audience is told:

> You will hear what you usually see.
> You will hear what you usually don't see.

> You will see no spectacle.
> Your curiosity will not be satisfied.
> You will see no play.
>
> (Handke, 2003, p. 7)

The play is not Tim Crouch's *The Author*, but Peter Handke's *Offending the Audience* (1966); I cite it because the parallels and contrasts between them are so salient. Both are experimental metatheatrical works that tackle spectatorial complicity and both attempt to dismantle dramatic illusion with a view to an ethical reorientation of perception and response akin to what was outlined at the beginning of this chapter. Where Handke and Crouch differ is in the treatment of the audience and in the working through of response and responsibility. Handke commits openly to his stated task of offending or more accurately insulting the audience, rising to a fantastically excessive barrage of taunts and name-calling, whereas Crouch distils a disconcerting encounter by crafting an empathetic space of communication and shared responsibility. Ironically Crouch's play is deeply disturbing at a level Handke's never achieves.

While *Seven Jewish Children* obviously polarized audiences along ethico-political lines, later in 2009 and also at the Royal Court opened *The Author*, a play that inaugurated widespread and ongoing debate about ethics, the role of the playwright and spectatorship and which has attracted considerable critical commentary since, including a special issue of *Contemporary Theatre Review* in 2011. A prime quality of the piece is the ambiguous effect of its ludic attitude to truth/illusion and the complications of the games it initiates. In the play, Crouch performs himself, while three other roles – two actors, one audience member – are delivered by performers using their own names. There is no stage, just a bank of seats where actors and audience sit together.

Two metaphors suggest themselves as ways to approach what takes place in *The Author* – the play as a set of Russian dolls, where each figure contains another, and the play as a telescope expanding to enable the distant to be perceived as proximate. The first enables an appraisal of the storytelling and performance situation, the second an apprehension of its effects. The outermost layer of the performance situation is the audience themselves. This is where the 'play' actually begins, with Adrian, a loyal and enthusiastic patron of the Royal Court, encouraging other spectators to communicate, to share their experiences of theatre-going, their expectations of the work they are about to see and their feelings about actors as they wait for the performance. In contrast to *Offending the Audience, The Author* discreetly opens spaces for audience response even before they may believe the play to have begun and continues to do so throughout the narrative performance. This is emphasized visually when the lights come up for the show proper and the audience find themselves 'beautifully lit' (Crouch, 2009, p. 21) as Crouch launches into his first monologue.

Crouch's story about a visit to a flotation tank segues to the next level, unfolding a collage narration of the development, performance and consequences of an earlier play by Crouch for the Royal Court. This play centres on a graphically abusive relationship between father and daughter. Via that story, processes of brutalization, led and fostered by the playwright, become visible. While Crouch defends the play as a 'poem' and a 'personal lament' (p. 30), it becomes clear that his methods of research and obsession with representing 'what was happening in the real world' (p. 32) in order to make an extreme theatrical statement has detrimental effects on the actors and the audience and, ultimately, culminate in the author's decision to commit suicide in the flotation tank he describes at the outset.

Already in the embedded structure of the narratives presented, *The Author* promotes self-consciousness about being a member of an audience. This was accentuated by the performers' disarming sensitivity to spectators, inviting ease and empathy, politely pausing at moments that might cause embarrassment or asking permission to continue, thus opening a space within the performance to unpredictability and precarity. It is also ameliorated, at times quite amusingly, with various references and in-jokes about British theatre culture and specifically Royal Court traditions of provocative new writing. Progressively though *The Author* builds a discomfiting sense of complicity by linking the conventions of British theatrical provocation with voyeuristic consumption of dehumanizing images and then with the revelation of the playwright's weakness for internet child pornography. The juxtaposition of these two provocations (one 'acceptable', one despicable) and the implication of their connectedness create an electrifying sense of proximity. The result is a type of ethical short circuit in the comfortably generated communication space the performance has so subtly engineered.

What makes *The Author* both ambivalent and resonant, therefore, is the way it confrontationally tackles the ethics of performance and spectatorship not through direct attack, but by actively soliciting audience participation in a self-conscious theatre game. Through the narration of the creation of the play-within-the-play, the limits of that participation are tested; as descriptions of atrocities and their incorporation into the play-within-the-play accumulate, so too does an uneasiness with collusion in such a game. Paradoxically, the play-within-the-play attains this ambivalent proximity precisely because it is not performed. Its images are reconnected with ethical outcomes. As Crouch himself has stated, '*The Author* is a play about responsibility, how active we are as spectators and how responsible we are for what we choose to look at' (2010). Patently it touched a nerve in many audience members as regards their own convictions – be they concerned with what a play ought to deliver, with being deceived or seduced by a performance, or with the considerable force of violence and abuse recounted during the performance. Being personally implicated in, as Crouch puts it, 'the culpability of the eye' (qtd. in Kinskey, 2011) here challenges not the saturation of spectacle in the abstract, but as I have suggested elsewhere, in the specific and hallowed minority community of the theatre (Wallace, 2012, p. 63).

Enlisted spectators

David Greig's *Fragile* was written for Theatre Uncut, 'a politically motivated collective' (Price, 2011, p. 7) that in March 2011 organized a nationwide creative initiative to protest radical cuts in public spending in Britain. Like *Seven Jewish Children*, then, its initial impetus was seeded in a moment of political crisis, to which it sought to provide an aesthetic response. A cluster of eight short plays were performed at the Southwark Playhouse from 16 to 19 March, and around Britain and elsewhere on 19 March. Primary among Theatre Uncut's aims was to open debate about important contemporary political issues, to create a space for new work on political themes to be shared, and to instigate action (see www.theatreuncut.com). Although hardly controversial or provocative as the plays already discussed, if, as Butler asserts, '[p]recarity exposes our sociality, the fragile and necessary dimensions of our interdependency' (Puar, 2012, p. 170), then *Fragile* is a piece of theatre that works significantly to make the precarious palpable.

Greig's play presents a tense exchange between Jack, a young man reliant upon mental healthcare services, and Caroline, a therapist at the community support centre which has just lost its funding. Upset by the news, Jack has broken into Caroline's home at night. After some discussion Jack proposes a protest that would make the plight of vulnerable citizens like himself unignorable for the government. He has come prepared with a flask of diesel – ironically stowed in a recyclable 'supermarket "bag for life"' (Greig, 2011, p. 53) – and plans to immolate himself just like Mohamed Bouazizi (whose suicide catalysed the Tunisian Revolution in 2010). Caroline, faced with this unstable man soaked in diesel, tries to persuade him to give her the cigarette lighter, arguing that other forms of action would be more feasible.

The scenario gathers force because Greig assigns the role of Caroline to the audience. In an 'Audience Briefing' it is explained that 'in the spirit of the big society' the playwright would like the audience to participate (p. 51). By means of a PowerPoint presentation, the audience are asked to rehearse some lines and non-verbal character directions before the play gets underway. Immediately this process realigns relationships in the theatre space, casting the audience as a community but also more obliquely as agents. The lines spoken by the character Caroline under these circumstances take on new significances. Presumably those attending Theatre Uncut's event are also those who do not agree with government austerity policies that in fact disenfranchise the vulnerable while leaving wealthy elites and institutions unscathed. If they participate as planned, the audience are obliged to explain the very situation they themselves are protesting by their presence at the Theatre Uncut performances. They become implicated in Caroline's apologetic explanations of the rationale behind the cuts, her resigned and defeatist attitude to a lost 'dream of Britain' (Greig, 2011, p. 61). They must also face Jack's frustrated responses. Still more compelling is the dramatic turn in this conversation when the audience as Caroline find themselves desperately trying to convince Jack that less radical forms of protest than public suicide can truly be effective. Following her admission of an overwhelming sense of pessimism and powerlessness, her promise that '*We'll use the internet/We'll start a campaign.* [. . .] *We'll protest*' (p. 63; emphasis original) is not particularly convincing.

In contrast to the plays considered above, *Fragile* enlists spectators as a community of participants, bringing them face to face with and making them responsible for the inexorable ethical demand of the Other noted by Kearney by reference to Levinas at the beginning of this chapter. Via Jack, precarious life is foregrounded. Indeed, at the play's conclusion his fate still hangs in the balance as he has not relinquished the lighter. Through their choral and collective engagement in the performance, audience members may come to countenance the necessity to respond to the vulnerable other, and to take responsibility for their political actions and compromises as a step towards envisioning social change.

Proximity – too close for comfort?

There is, inevitably, no single formula to encapsulate attitudes to ethics in contemporary British theatre. Nevertheless each of the four plays examined here are points on an expanding map of that context. They testify to their playwrights' conscious exploration of the ethical resonances of performance and their engagement in a diverse politics of perception. Each is attuned to the risks that journey involves, confronting the ambivalence of looking, listening and speaking *as* action. Repeatedly the mechanisms used to create such a confrontation derive from the rendering of states of proximity and precarity that are both intrinsically and radically uncomfortable. Ultimately that process, contested and incomplete as it may be, asserts the essential quality of relationality and is grounded in the imperative to respond.[2]

Notes

1. See Jacques Rancière's opposition of ethics to politics in his 'The Ethical Turn of Aesthetics and Politics' (2006).
2. The publication of this chapter was supported by the 'Programme for the Development of Research Areas at Charles University, P09, Literature and Art in Intercultural Relations,' sub-programme 'Transformations of the Cultural History of the Anglophone Countries: Identities, Periods, Canons' (Tato kapitola bylo vydáno v rámci Programu rozvoje vědních oblastí na Univerzitě Karlově č. P09, Literatura a umění v mezikulturních souvislostech, podprogram Proměny kulturních dějin anglofonních zemí identity, periody, kánony).

Works cited

Bishop, C. (2004) 'Antagonism and Relational Aesthetics', *October*, 110, pp. 51–79.

Bourriaud, N. (2002) *Relational Aesthetics*, trans. S. Pleasance and F. Woods (Paris: Les Presses du Réel).

Butler, J. (2004) *Precarious Life: The Powers of Mourning and Violence* (London and New York: Verso).

Churchill, C. (2009a) *Seven Jewish Children* (London: Nick Hern).

—— (2009b) 'My Play is Not Anti-Semitic' in 'Letters: Jacobson on Gaza', *Independent*, 21 February, http://www.independent.co.uk/voices/letters/letters-jacobson-on-gaza-1628191.html (accessed 11 January 2013).

Crouch, T. (2009) *The Author* (London: Oberon).

—— (2010) 'Interview: Tim Crouch', by S. Mansfield, *Scotsman*, 21 July, http://www.scotsman.com/news/interview-tim-crouch-theatre-director-1-820005 (accessed 3 January 2013).

Fisher, P. (2006) 'Review of *pool (no water)*', *British Theatre Guide*, http://www.britishtheatreguide.info/reviews/poolnowaterLH-rev (accessed 18 January 2013).

Grehan, H. (2009) *Performance, Ethics and Spectatorship in a Global Age* (Basingstoke and New York: Palgrave Macmillan).

Greig, D. (2011) *Fragile* in *Theatre Uncut* (London: Oberon), pp. 48–64.

Handke, P. (2003) *Plays One (Offending the Audience, Self Accusation, Kaspar, My Foot My Tutor, The Ride across Lake Constance, They Are Dying Out)* (London: Methuen).

Jacobson, H. (2009) 'Let's see the "Criticism" of Israel for what it really is', *Independent*, 18 February, http://www.independent.co.uk/voices/commentators/howard-jacobson-letsquos-see-the-criticism-of-israel-for-what-it-really-is-1624827.html (accessed 11 January 2013).

Joseph, A., P. Handke and E.B. Ashton (1970) 'Nauseated by Language: From an Interview with Peter Handke', *TDR*, 15 (1), pp. 57–61.

Kearney, R. (1998) *The Wake of the Imagination* (London: Routledge).

Kinskey, R. (2011) 'Tim Crouch is "The Author" and the actor at Kirk Douglas', *LA Stage Times*, 16 February, http://www.lastagetimes.com/2011/02/tim-crouch-is-"the-author"-and-the-actor-at-kirk-douglas (accessed, 17 January 2013).

Kushner, T. and A. Solomon (2009) 'Tell Her the Truth', *The Nation*, 13 April, http://www.thenation.com/article/tell-her-the-truth (accessed 11 January 2013).

Lachman, M. (2013) 'Absent Body: Ravenhill's Phenomenology of Carnality', *Journal of Contemporary Drama in English*, 1 (1), pp. 149–60.

Lehmann, H. (2006) *Postdramatic Theatre*, trans. K. Jürs-Munby (London and New York: Routledge).

Lerman, A. (2009) 'Antisemitic Alarm Bells', *Guardian*, 4 May, http://www.guardian.co.uk/commentisfree/2009/may/04/caryl-churchill-antisemitism-play (accessed 11 January 2013).

Levinas, E. (1989) 'Reality and its Shadow' in S. Hand (ed.) *The Levinas Reader* (Oxford: Blackwell), pp. 129–43.

—— (1996) 'Peace and Proximity' in A.T. Peperzak, S. Critchley and R. Bernasconi (eds) *Emmanuel Levinas: Basic Philosophical Writings* (Bloomington: Indiana University Press), pp. 161–70.

Levinas, E. and R. Kearney (1986) 'Dialogue with Emmanuel Levinas' in R.A. Cohen (ed.) *Face to Face with Levinas* (Albany: State University of New York), pp. 13–34.

Monforte, E. (2012) 'Ethics, Witnessing, and Spectatorship in David Hare's *Via Dolorosa* (1998), Robin Soans's *The Arab-Israeli Cookbook* (2004), and Caryl Churchill's *Seven Jewish Children* (2009)' in M. Berninger and B. Reitz (eds) *Ethical Debates in Contemporary Theatre and Drama* (Trier: Wissenschaftlicher Verlag Trier), pp. 91–104.

Mouffe, C. (2000) 'Which Ethics for Democracy?' in M. Garber, B. Hanssen and R. Walkowitz (eds) *The Turn to Ethics* (New York: Routledge), pp. 85–94.

Pewny, K. (2011) *Das Drama des Prekären: Über die Wiederkehr der Ethik in Theater und Performance* (Bielfeld: Transcript Verlag).

—— (2012) 'The Ethics of Encounter in Contemporary Theater Performances', *Journal of Literary Theory*, 6 (1), http://www.jltonline.de/index.php/article/view/483/1219 (accessed 12 January 2013).

Price, H. (2011) 'Introduction' in *Theatre Uncut* (London: Oberon), pp. 7–8.

Puar, J. (ed.) (2012) 'Precarity Talk: A Virtual Roundtable with Lauren Berlant, Judith Butler, Bojana Cvejic, Isabell Lorey, Jasbir Puar, and Ana Vujanovic', *TDR*, 56 (4), pp. 163–77.

Rancière, J. (2006) 'The Ethical Turn of Aesthetics and Politics', *Critical Horizons*, 7, pp. 1–20.

Ravenhill, M. (2006) 'In at the Deep End', *Guardian*, 20 September, http://www.guardian.co.uk/stage/2006/sep/20/theatre1 (accessed 18 January 2013).

—— (2008) *Plays Two (Mother Clap's Molly House, Product, The Cut, Citizenship, pool (no water))* (London: Methuen).

Read, A. (1993) *Theatre and Everyday Life: An Ethics of Performance* (Basingstoke and New York: Palgrave Macmillan).

—— (2009) *Theatre, Intimacy and Engagement: The Last Human Venue* (Basingstoke and New York: Palgrave Macmillan).

Rich, D. and M. Gardner (2009) 'Blood Libel Brought up to Date', *Guardian*, 1 May, http://www.guardian.co.uk/commentisfree/2009/may/01/carylchurchill-theatre (accessed 11 January 2013).

Ridout, N. (2009) *Theatre & Ethics* (Basingstoke and New York: Palgrave Macmillan).

Ridout, N. and R. Schneider (2012) 'Precarity and Performance: An Introduction', *TDR*, 56 (4), pp. 5–9.

Sierz, A. (2001) *In-Yer-Face Theatre: British Drama Today* (London: Faber).

Theatre Uncut (2012) http://www.theatreuncut.com (access date 26 April 2013).

Vale, A. (2006) 'Review of *pool (no water)*', *British Theatre Guide*, http://www.britishtheatreguide.info/reviews/poolnowater-rev (accessed 18 January 2013).

Wallace, C. (2012) 'Uncertain Convictions and the Politics of Perception' in M. Berninger and B. Reitz (eds) *Ethical Debates in Contemporary Theatre and Drama* (Trier: Wissenschaftlicher Verlag Trier), pp. 55–64.

8
Witness or Accomplice? Unsafe Spectatorship in the Work of Anthony Neilson and Simon Stephens

Vicky Angelaki

Anthony Neilson and re-locating the audience

In the summer of 2008, the Royal Court Theatre staged the type of eerie play that seems predestined to incite high emotions. Billed as '[n]ot recommended for anyone under the age of 16' (Royal Court Theatre, 2008), Anthony Neilson's *Relocated* only took 90 minutes to affect London theatre critics in different ways, in one notable case leading them to the point of exasperation.[1] In his review Michael Billington described the play as 'repellent', adding that in his opinion this was inextricably linked to the 'hideously inappropriate' disconnection between form and subject matter (2008). From Billington's viewpoint, Neilson's choice of using a 'Gothic thriller format' as the representational vehicle for violence against children was sensationalistic and beyond justification. Even in the context of Billington's emphasis on detail and explication (emerging consistently if we examine his reviews of certain contemporary plays that follow a dramatically unconventional path), the question of 'to what end we were being scared other than to give us a morbidly indecent thrill and to tickle our jaded theatrical appetites' still rings relevant. Can it be that the feeling embossed in the play's form and content is that of a desperate desire to convince us to care – a controversial attempt to entice an audience exposed to multiple options, spectacles and interpretations by combining a subject that is guaranteed to stir emotions with a dramatic method that was certain to escalate them? The question of whether as audiences we have become all too complacent is fascinating. Beyond our potential complacency as citizens, as spectators of our everyday lives that it points towards, the question also asks whether we have embraced a misconstrued hedonism in our relationship to art and our viewing habits. The issue emerging from Billington's critique is that if the play has a validity of argument in the notion that when it comes to incidents of child abuse 'society resorts to facile condemnation without examining the causes' (2008), it is irrevocably compromised by a representational method which encourages that very same viewing attitude amongst spectators.

Billington concludes that the play left him equally 'shaken and spiritually diminished' (2008). The already sensitive subject matter was made more precarious still through the play's topical affinities as well as retrospective resonance in a combination that caused it to become overwhelmingly potent.[2] In her account of the performance, written not as review but invitation to dialogue on the *Guardian Theatre Blog*, Lyn Gardner wonders whether it is her personal sensibilities that lead her to take issue with *Relocated* (2008). She emphasizes a well-known fact about Neilson's work process, namely that he allows the text to be re-morphed throughout rehearsals. As other critics note, *Relocated* came to be formulated by the company 'through research and workshopping' over the period of one month (Fricker, 2008). Neilson's is not only a method of ensuring performability or fostering a sense of collective responsibility for the creative team. It is also dramatic leeway for making insertions to the piece until much later in the process than is considered standard, a point particularly relevant to *Relocated* and its context.[3] Gardner questions the extent to which the play's nonexistent temporal distance from actual events is the issue; she suggests, rather, that it is a somewhat vapid sense of contemporaneity, injected in the play so as to add to its cool appeal – in both senses of the word – that is unpalatable. Between this note and Karen Fricker's observation that *Relocated* gave the impression of being prematurely completed, the emerging question is whether there is such a notion as 'too of the moment' in contemporary theatre (Fricker, 2008). Can performance be timely in a way that, beyond being resonant, risks not hubris, but superficiality disguised as social comment? We need to consider to what extent this may alienate the audience (not in the Brechtian sense), or how contemporaneity may act as oppression for them and whether, beyond impression-making, theatre such as *Relocated* possesses the raw materials that may resonate more deeply, attacking conventional ways of seeing.

It is not my intention to treat the plays in this chapter as isolated case studies through which to account for how spectatorial behaviours and responses are conditioned, but rather, to probe the changing field of text-based theatre on the basis of the interrelationship it establishes with the audience. It is on this ground that much of contemporary

resonant performance interrogates our ethics and modes of engagement and response. We should recognize that audiences are more alert
because of recent radical developments in dramatic representation, but
also more demanding by means of these; to an extent, I would contend,
they have become more empowered, seeing beyond the outwardly
experimental (text-based or not) and making active, informed choices
on where to invest their time.

The device of using the time leading up to performance in ways that
serve to envelop the audience in the experience is far from unique to
Relocated. In the contemporary period we have seen recurring trans-
gressions against neutral time and space, communicating to spectators
that the theatre is not safe and aiming for complete immersion. As a
technique for audience engagement, it can work well, especially in cases
where a theatre space is already familiar, associated in our mind to a
number of productions we have seen, and therefore is almost homely,
or harmless. Regarding the question of how the theatre can surprise and
keep us at the edge of our seats, this production's answer was to appeal
to primal instincts. The choice to stage *Relocated* in a venue – the Royal
Court Theatre Upstairs – whose flexibility is an open challenge to any
designer when it comes to upsetting audience expectations by offering
up something they had not witnessed before was crucial, as it added to
the discomfort. Different critics offer varying views for how this was
achieved; in itself, this is an allusion to how the play clashed with individual sensibilities. For Andrew Haydon, an unnaturally low, artificial
ceiling created a claustrophobic effect, which, as Natasha Tripney adds,
was made all the more intense for the 'black-walled, featureless room'
framing the spectators' path on their way to their seats (Haydon, 2008;
Tripney, 2008). What achieved the most impact, however, was the way
the production conceptualized and established its obscurity from the
start – visually, metaphorically, critically, practically. Critics unfailingly
mention the use of gauze, a semi-translucent, manipulable material,
which, in this production, caused the stage action to unexpectedly shift
from visible to invisible. It was a crafty find for the manifestation of what
is right in front of us, easily discernible if we pay close enough attention,
but just as easily missed and contained within, away from prying eyes.[4]

The gauze functioned to disorientate the spectator through an artificial as much as imperceptible sense of distance, augmented or reduced
at moments completely outside of our control. In an immersive performance setting such as this one, we were enticed to conceptualize
ourselves as much as part of the action as extrinsic to it – from insiders
to outsiders and witnesses to eavesdroppers. By deftly accentuating the

act of seeing, at times facilitated while at others impeded, the gauze emphasized a key theme in the play: voyeurism. It was a subtle shift, like the one caused by the change of lighting on the tissue of the gauze, between titillation and a genuine act of criticism of this very attitude – the problem in the play on which a number of critics concurred. It is as difficult to say where Neilson positioned himself in this, if anywhere at all, as it is to establish whether this was a conscious effort to pose a question, or whether the play fell victim to its own boldness and devices. Then again, in the context of this piece the gauze was in fact a very raw and sincere material, manifesting the issue at the heart of the play from the start: the open wounds from hideous crimes, inwardly directed atrocities that our societies are reeling from. Through Miriam Buether's set, the play seemed to pose the question of how much gauze it takes to cover up the collective wounds brought on by such violently transgressive acts. It asked for how long such an act can remain concealed and what is the shared responsibility in an attentive society to discover it. Ultimately, the play focused on where the imperceptible divide lies between failing to notice and becoming effectively guilty of complacent not-seeing. Through different staging methods, *Relocated* did not negotiate the issue but rather forced it on the spectators, testing, through sensory means, the point at which pleading ignorance by claiming not to see or hear becomes invalid. Through the form and content of the play the issue was conceptualized at the very level of theatrical spectatorship, and here we may begin to detect an analogy. Perhaps *Relocated* was something more than whispers in the dark, or sensationalist cat and mouse games. Severe simulated unease was an extreme device deployed in the play, but it was also a way of probing our spectatorial responsibilities envisaged in direct parallel to our societal duties. The sensory precariousness that the play cultivated in its spectators, however intense, still paled in comparison to the larger issue it served to foreground: the contingency between watching and witnessing, between failing to see and becoming complicit.

There is nothing in Neilson's oeuvre that conveys a need to be universally liked; in fact, the kind of provocation he delivered with *Relocated* is not unusual, though its format certainly proved to be. Still, there *is* a sense of an ongoing imperative emerging, more to do with the playwright's responsibility to earn and retain the spectators' attention. Neilson writes, for example, that '[b]oring the audience is the one true sin in theatre' (2007). While this may sound like a mission statement, one not unlikely to be followed by an expression of dedication to the immersion or involvement that performance can induce, Neilson is reliably controversial. He openly questions the notion that the theatre ought to have what he perceives as an oppressively instructive character that causes it to be seen as civic duty rather than entertainment. 'It is not that a play cannot be quasi-educational, or even overtly political', he observes, 'just that debate should organically arise out of narrative. But this reductive notion persists and has infected playwriting root and branch' (2007). Neilson is not particularly forgiving of what he terms 'debate-led theatre', emphasizing that though the playwright's role is deeply social, it does not entail sermonizing (2007). He is not particularly forgiving either of what in his text is treated as an academic tendency for over-explanation, but he does insist on the playwright's 'responsibility' to 'stimulate [. . .], refresh [and] engage' (2007). Neilson also stresses that an elemental feature in the constitution of a play should be 'accessibility'. The debate between high-, middle- and low-brow art is revisited and what emerges strongly from Neilson's words is that the only commitment a playwright ought to feel is to the paying audience. Spectators are the ones who matter and, therefore, their needs ought to be prioritized. Such a stance, despite the fact that the statement I am referring to was published in 2007, predating *Relocated* and not written in defence of that play specifically, has continued to define Neilson's theatre. It also sets up the scene for the relentless revisiting of what makes sense in theatrical representation today; of the means towards the overarching end of, firstly, attracting a broad spectatorship and, secondly, not disappointing them by staging a piece so trite that they may feel their time has been wasted. In Neilson's playwriting universe, method meets function and they are both geared towards ensuring that a spectator will return to the theatre – that one 'flat' show will not forever dissuade them from performance.

It is intriguing to place this within the context of what some reviewers criticized as deployment of horror film tactics, a populist medium by any standards, within *Relocated*. In the context of an increasingly politicized understanding of theatrical representation, Neilson's description of himself and his playwright peers as 'entertainers' (2007) sounds brazen, even controversial. In the context of *Relocated*, the form through which the story was told invited the audience in and pulled them close so that they might partake in the plot perceptually – a term that within a phenomenological context, most notably, implies both intellectual and physical response. Neilson prioritizes the *story*: the one that demands to be told and that the playwright feels compelled to share with the spectators. In an article published the same year as Neilson's statement (therefore also predating *Relocated*) Brian Logan provides an insightful description of Neilson as a playwright with 'twin obsessions', whose work 'express[es] psychological [indeed psychopathic, on occasion] states on stage and us[es] the techniques of vaudeville to do so' (2007). The description rings true if we home in on *Relocated* through this lens, always in the broader framework of how, through his work, Neilson proposes to reconcile the incentives behind a playwright's creative process with the kind of theatre that contemporary audiences will find inviting and worth their time. The impetus is inscribed on the fibre of Neilson's writing process: '[m]y stuff is designed to be done in the heat of the moment, with a certain passion. It's drive-yourself-to-the-point-of-breakdown theatre writing', he says (qtd. in Logan, 2007). Such a description provides some context for the tribulations Neilson submits his audience to in *Relocated*: since this is the process that the playwright endures, it seems only fitting that the spectator experience an equally intense rollercoaster in the course of watching a play. It is unconventional and open to criticism as a method, but at the same time unequivocally honest in how it carries out the attempt to attack the safe divide between stage and audience, fostering the sensation that we all form part of a unified experience, from inception to execution and reception. Therefore, the thrills should be the same for all involved, with no one party benefiting from a more privileged perspective. If Neilson and the creative team have but a vague understanding of what the play will become when going into the process, it is only fair that the same be true of the spectators. The 'precarious [creative] process, with no guarantees' (Logan, 2007) is the one enduring narrative in the work of a playwright who deplores being dubbed as didactic. Its affect is written into what becomes a script and does not fade when the piece comes into contact with its recipients, *by* and *for* whom it is re-instigated.

The unmitigated shock tactics that form the basis of a piece like *Relocated* may to an extent be a dramatic ploy for keeping spectators on the edge of their seats, but a false sense of real complicity is better than a false sense of safety or distance from the real problem. Such a technique falls neatly within the narrative of what Neilson discusses as the theatre's task to rise above the analytical dissection of the everyday more suited to other outlets of debate, like the media, and instead strive for the stimulation of 'liveness' (Neilson, 2007). Though it would be tempting to dismiss Neilson as merely creating a framework within which to conveniently situate his own work, it seems far more purposeful to consider the value of the dramatic language he is proposing. A play arising from the prerequisites he cites in his 2007 statement will be an experiment that fails or succeeds. Perhaps immaterial to this, and supremely more important, are the motive and effort themselves. In theatre inextricably bound to its moment in time, like Neilson's, certain subjects will strike us as more taboo than others – leading to a play like *Relocated* being predominantly seen as tasteless. Pierre Bourdieu's consideration of types of performance and audiences is particularly resonant when he contrasts boulevard performance to 'experimental theatre, which attracts a young, "intellectual" audience to relatively inexpensive shows that flout ethical and aesthetic conventions' (1986, p. 234). It is fascinating that both *Relocated* and the play which I discuss in the next section, Simon Stephens's *Three Kingdoms* (2012), did not only clash with an audience they would have been anticipated to clash with (a spectator more used to the boulevard play), but also unsettled the expectations of what would have been their more natural spectator base. This was arguably because the flouting of conventions, both ethical and aesthetic, occurred on an altogether new ground, which even the more receptive spectators would have had no prior indication of, or exposure to.

In the theatre of resonance and collectivity, the play becomes the vehicle for the question: beyond watching, what is it that may compel us into action? What indeed, if not to feel that we are turned into parts of the story in ways that are not making us feel entirely comfortable, as they evoke a sense of near complicity through our convention-enforced silence? The follow-up to this kind of self-interrogation is another question – the consideration of how, in situations of genuine anguish, abuse and subjugation, we can help break the cycle of silence by taking a more active involvement in our roles as citizens. This is a state engendered through the kind of active spectatorship that Neilson's work encourages. It would be naïve to assume that because a playwright denounces the sociopolitical comment as the intended crux of the play, the play itself does not operate broadly on that level.

An attitude that Neilson's 2007 statement openly attacks relates to the assumption that a text operating within a less tightly controlled formal framework, the type of play that we might categorize as abstract/experimental, possesses a certain artistic superiority over a text following the classic format of a middle, beginning and end. As Neilson argues, the traditional type of play carries the potential of appealing to more spectators because it can be readily understood. The lack of formal fluctuation should not automatically deduct from the artistic value of the piece – if the audience has rapport with the play, this is all that matters. Nor should it be an imperative, Neilson continues, that a playwright artificially impose an open structure on the play in an attempt to heighten its assumed artistic merit. Though his own plays have more often fallen within what, however loosely defined, can be deemed unconventional, the observation is interesting as it applies to the work of some of Neilson's peers, who have developed new avenues between the conventional and the subversive, where the latter relies more on content than form. In such plays, the audience is drawn in and despite first impressions the issues informing the plays run deep, potently generating disquietude. At the same time, such plays prove popular – there is an audience for them that is far from reducible to the type of spectator that is only an occasional visitor of the theatre. In plays like these, the issues may be carefully hidden, not given away by an adventurous format, but a series of quiet explosions take place nonetheless – for an audience to feel complicit, they need not have necessarily been through the experience of a piece like *Relocated*. Seemingly simpler pieces can achieve an equal level of discomfort.

Simon Stephens and the discomfort of seeing

The work of Simon Stephens is indicative of this representational trend. Ranging from the decidedly unconventional to the almost social-realist, Stephens's plays inhabit a territory where the co-existence of seemingly irreconcilable forms of theatre appears manageable. Trish Reid makes the observation, in relation to Neilson's work, that there is a certain 'commitment to exploring the materiality of the live event' (2008, p. 489). This astute comment is equally relevant to the work of Stephens. Particularly in plays like *Three Kingdoms* (2012), which features intensely visceral stage moments, the implications of such a 'commitment' to the raw 'materiality' of performance are strongly resonant. In this play, there is a sense of dangerous exposure shared amongst the characters and gradually instigated within the spectators. By the standards of contemporary text-based theatre especially, where the duration of most plays rarely exceeds two hours, this is a long piece in the course of which the lead characters (police officers on a quest to solve the murder of a prostitute) experience an extraordinary trajectory of transformation. By the end of performance the notions of perpetrator, persecutor and vigilante have become irretrievably blurred. For the spectators the play is a sensory journey conceptualized as a nightmare – and by the end of performance not much is resolved. The expressionistic eruption is not only unpredictable on the basis of the realist opening interrogation scene, but it also radically undermines any dramatic authority that the scene may at first be felt to possess. Returning to Reid's proposition, through the unpredictable ways it unfolds *Three Kingdoms* emits the impression that anything and everything could happen on stage, or indeed to those audience members sitting at an unsafe distance from it, as objects and substances begin to interfere, making the stage-scape into a much more fluid territory than it appeared at the beginning.

The original production, directed by Sebastian Nübling, encouraged a feeling of constant contingency. There are different ways in which *Three Kingdoms* makes us feel complicit. Beyond its unrestrained textual boldness, these also depend on the unapologetic *tour de force* of the staging. Perhaps under a different director – a premise itself difficult to imagine as Nübling and Stephens have developed a distinctive form of collaboration with shared impact on the final product – the play might become somewhat tamer. As seen in its original context, though, it was a ferocious show whose direct experience almost made us feel increasingly depraved, in a way. In *Theatre Audiences*, Susan Bennett discusses how conditioning factors, both cultural and spectator-specific, determine our attitude towards a given performance. However, this is far from the only context for our interaction with the show and any impression we form. As Bennett argues, 'the direct experience of [a] production feeds back to revise a spectator's expectations, to establish or challenge conventions, and, occasionally, to reform the boundaries of culture' (1997, p. 207), an observation that resonates in the context of a play like *Three Kingdoms*: it is a piece from which it is difficult to imagine a turning-back point, the kind of work that has the power to cause a shift of our ethics, aesthetics and sensibilities. It should be said that in her influential book, Bennett mainly discusses types of performance that are different to the kind of theatre discussed in this chapter, or to contemporary text-driven theatre more broadly. In an indicative statement that merits the lengthy quotation, she notes:

> The playwright invariably shapes a text and the director [. . .] a production to provoke particular expectations and responses within an audience. The interactive nature of theatre is particularly evident from the rewriting a playwright often [. . .] chooses (or is called) to do while a play is in rehearsal and from the cuts or changes a director makes after previews, try-outs, or, indeed, during a run. Clearly, then, the audience affects not only the performance but the dramatic text too. Here, however, it is intended to concentrate on the audience's relationship with performance (or, at least, text-in-performance) rather than with specific dramatic texts. Much contemporary theatre occurs without a text available for academic study and deliberately so. In the explosion of new venues, companies, and performance methods,

there is a non-traditional theatre which has recreated a flexible actor–audience relationship and a participatory spectator/actor. The practices of these theatres are as valid as those of any mainstream operation in designating theatrical art. (1997, pp. 18–19)

The position merits discussion in various respects in the context of the current chapter, which focuses on playwright-driven theatre within the field of audience engagement. Firstly, Bennett's suggestion that our impression of a play is conditioned by playwright and director, in different yet equally powerful ways, is entirely accurate. Indeed, it relates to the point I make above about Stephens and Nübling's collaboration, one that relies heavily on an 'improvisational' model of work that the director contributes (Stephens qtd. in Curtis, 2012). However, and once more taking that collaboration as vehicle, there is more to say. It is becoming increasingly common for playwrights to develop collaborative webs, whether reliant on an author/director partnership, as in the case of Stephens and Nübling, or on an author/company model, as in the case of Neilson. Both are indicative rather than exhaustive examples of such working methods. One could argue, therefore, that the result emerges instinctively and is not readily divisible into 'playwright', 'director' or 'company' categories. While it has been both important and necessary to challenge the hegemony of the text, it is equally crucial to allow the space for the understanding of how dialectical, emerging forms of text-based theatre have redefined the field, not least in terms of the ways a spectator is invited to engage with them. In that respect, the playwright-authored piece that relies on the 'conventional' production schema of an author/director/standard venue collaboration carries the potential of being far from predictable.

The question of how a play in this (however broad) category can render us, beyond spectators, witnesses and, even beyond that, accomplices is difficult to answer, but at least part of the method relates to how the production team works to render us its co-conspirators. We have a sense of vested interest in whether the play succeeds or fails and a responsibility for either outcome; at no point in performance are we reassured that a conventional conclusion is guaranteed. '[A]s a writer, [. . .] I try to make stories by trying to make sense of the things I am afraid of', Stephens reveals, tellingly (qtd. in Curtis, 2012). As in Neilson's case, this requires a similar investment on the part of the audience. Facilitating the belief within spectators that they are in a *position* of authority due to their privileged *position* in the theatre auditorium is but the flipside of surrendering them to a *position* of critical passivity while watching a performance. Such states of watching are to the same degree perceptually barren and counter-productive when it comes to fleshing out the collectivity of the theatre experience. The playwright, like the spectator, is also a citizen. S/he may provide the forum or vehicle, but the 'things [. . . to be] afraid of' do not differ between the two sides. Therefore, any assumption of a divide between stage and audience is inherently problematic. What such performance provides is the unsafe but necessary ground for the shared exploration of persistent but neglected fears.

A play like *Three Kingdoms* offers no reassurance as it submerges us in its nightmarish journey towards an indeterminate ending. The major issues – sexual exploitation, violence against women, the fragility of the individual in an increasingly globalized world – have not been resolved in our societies. The play is honest in its resistance to providing an arbitrary answer for the purposes of traditional dramatic resolution. And so, it ends with a non-ending, essentially bleeding into our experience as spectators – it has conceived us as its witnesses, but also as a form of jury for the crimes it depicts and/or alludes to. *Three Kingdoms* hints at our complicity-by-silence, an acceptance-by-default of the crimes haunting modern-day developed societies. Though far from Brechtian, through its open form and neo-expressionistic representational methods it reinforces the public nature of the forum that theatre is. As Stephens suggests, we inhabit an era defined by different artistic expressions of the crime or detective narrative – a diverse field to which *Three Kingdoms*, too, may also be seen to belong. He notes, 'I wonder if we are operating in a culture with a sense that something awful has been done, and we want to find out who did it' (qtd. in Curtis, 2012). As *Three Kingdoms* shows, uncovering the perpetrator is a more complex process than we might expect it to be; in our time, as the limits of representation are fading, so is the facile attribution of guilt under the old familiar binary that readily establishes an 'us' and 'them'. Stephens's theatre is far from easily classified under types of playwriting.

Neilson's notion of the writer's imperative to take an intuitive approach to the narrative and assign to it the structure that seems natural, not looking to impress or appear unconventional, provides a context for this style: inaction, the plays suggest, is a conscious decision with very tangible repercussions. The plays, therefore, may not deliver an outright moral, but they do pose an unwavering ethical dilemma. The plot in texts like Stephens's *Motortown* (2006), *Punk Rock* (2009) or *Morning* (2012), in contrast with a lot of Neilson's work, develops mostly linearly. These are plays whose thematically wide appeal is reinforced by relatively accessible form. However, the seeming simplicity far from renders them tedious especially because the issues explored, such as a young soldier's violent return from war (*Motortown*), violence against peers in a broader school context (*Morning, Punk Rock*), or gratuitous urban violence (all of the above), specifically relate to young lives. Consequently, the plays have a stronger chance of appealing to a younger audience. Beyond a playwright's given imperative, it is important to acknowledge the educational capability of such work. Returning to Bennett's discussion of the factors shaping the development of a dramatic text, it seems appropriate to argue that these are more variegated than might initially appear. Other than the changes a play withstands in rehearsals, there is an important element relating to the preparation of the piece and the creative decisions at play in the early stages. These should not be necessarily seen as extrinsic to the audience, made *in spite of* it, but, rather, taken *for* and *with* it in mind. Rather than a process of guiding taste, we may understand this as the manifestation of the interdependence between text and production, playwright and audience.

Returning to Neilson's observation, referred to at the beginning of this chapter, the audience's invested time should be honoured. This, however, is not to take the form of placation but, rather, adventure and exposure. As Stephens argues, there is something to be said about the theatremaker's task 'to unsettle and undermine' (2012d). Certainly the plays discussed as indications of this approach in this chapter work to this affect. It is important to speak of an *affect* rather than *effect*, because the former is more representative of the transformative process we have the prospect of undergoing as audiences.[5] The affect accounts for an experience that is fully corporeal and intellectual, engaging us on different levels at the same time. Stephens underlines the importance of a bold theatre that ventures into such perceptual territories with the spectator. Speaking about his collaboration with Nübling specifically, he emphasizes the 'visceral and individual, authored and alive' approach, which 'brings a muscle of theatricality' to the staged piece that emerges from it (2012d). This is not theatre for the faint at heart, surely, but at the same time it makes no apologies. The moment *Three Kingdoms* makes contact with the spectator it sets off explosions on all fronts: firstly through language, then through the body, all through by testing our critical ability. All this until, at the end of performance, it leaves us with the impression that what we have formed part of as spectators may be far from cohesive but is fully coherent nonetheless – albeit in a highly unconventional way.

Three Kingdoms divided the critics, leading Gardner to sum up its reception as 'split between newspaper critics who – you guessed it – are resistant to the work, and online writers who embrace it fervently' (2012). Bourdieu explores the relationship of reader to critic, probing its symbiotic contingency – for a given publication, critics know whom they are addressing in terms of tastes and expectations. There is a process of mutual identification in which the critic recognizes their readership, while the reader recognizes the voice that legitimizes their set of beliefs (Bourdieu, 1986, pp. 235, 240). If we consider Bourdieu's observation in relation to (especially middle-class) audiences and tastes, standard press critics such as those that Gardner refers to respond predictably. It is tempting to consider *Three Kingdoms* – raw, trendy and as Gardner rightly observes, 'that rare beast, a piece of work that could only be made now' (2012) – as more taste-adjacent to those writers who are themselves outside mainstream publishing. They operate on a different set of expectations and targets and are inclined, perhaps, to respond more warmly to the experimental. At the same time newspaper critics, (arguably) older, less spontaneous and/or impressionable, more tied to deadlines and with an established language of responding to new productions, are also more reserved towards the radical – perhaps because experience moderates enthusiasm. Beyond such classifications, however, the issue seems to be better tackled if we accept that *Three Kingdoms* was destined to be controversial from the point of inception. It was the kind of work that would not even play to the tastes of the audience most likely to respond to it: educated, young or middle-aged, middle-class spectators.

By definition, an internationally conceived, collaborative, festival-supported piece like *Three Kingdoms* is geared towards the experimental and aggressive for good reason. After all, it is about to establish multiple points of contact with international audiences, who will vary greatly in their cultural sensibilities – not to mention individual predispositions.[6] With reference to Bennett's observation, discussed earlier, that in cases where the act of reforming the boundaries of culture 'takes place at the interface of different cultures, the potential to reform those boundaries is heightened, although it may well be that the rendition of a cultural Other might serve just as well to reinforce the spectators' own cultural definitions' (1997, p. 207), I would argue that *Three Kingdoms* took its mission seriously. Its creators refused to produce a feat that would be familiar to any one culture (whether theirs, or the audience's), though many of its spectators might respond, in different ways, to its strangeness. The international scope of the production rendered the understanding of a cultural 'I' and 'Other' not simply difficult to assert but essentially obsolete. Bennett makes a fair point when she notes that, unfailingly, 'the experience of intercultural performance emphasizes those cultural assumptions which underpin any production or reception process' (1997, p. 207). In the case of *Three Kingdoms*, though, these were attacked from within. The play took on cultural stereotypes as much as it worked to disprove, through its unpredictable development, that any assumptions we might make on our cultural superiority can withstand the pressure brought on by a relentless chase of exposition. As audiences, we begin our course conceptualizing ourselves as detectives, with the remit of piecing the puzzle together in this whodunit that seems to spin out of control. By the finale we worry whether we can survive unscathed the crimes committed everyday in the name of aspirational mobility and erasing boundaries. The very nature of the piece is a celebration of diversity, inclusiveness and sharing of geographical and cultural spaces, not shying away from the darker side of this: the cost at which the process has taken place and the individuals mercilessly victimized. As emerges from the ethics and aesthetics of the production, a degree of complicity is involved in embracing the positive aspects of internationalization and turning a blind eye to the brutal truths that hide beneath. The assault that *Three Kingdoms* launched on taste functioned to foster novel ways of staging, but also of seeing – it encouraged a radical shift in our perspectives and a reenvisioning of our collective and individual identities in the context of a globalized society, astutely mirrored in the cultural mosaic that formed the play and production themselves.

Conclusion

Bennett makes the point that, in the context of her study, the analysis of 'many theatrical forms [. . .] indicate[s] the strength and diversity of non-traditional theatres'. She adds, '[w]ithin mainstream theatre, the minimalist experiments of writers such as Beckett and Cage have been accepted and conventionalized. Some oppositional practice has been recuperated and defused' (1997, p. 207). Even in the case of Brecht, she notes, the canon has prevailed, which we might assume means that the risk and impact of the work has been moderated. As for those operating in the Brechtian tradition, Bennett quotes Alan Sinfield, who describes their spectators as divided 'between [their] wish for a radical posture and [their] actual privileged position' (p. 207). The statement hits a nerve, but at the same time it does not indicate that the entire process of active questioning in the theatre is futile, or that audiences who occupy a somehow 'privileged' perspective could not be continuously challenged in new ways.

These should not be seen as precluding the dramatic even though there is immense value in the performance-focused theatrical practices that Bennett devotes the bulk of her analysis to. Certainly, conventions need to be defied for theatrical representation to move forward. However, with the emergence of new dramatic forms such as those discussed here, the proposition that '[n]ow so much non-traditional theatre restores the [spectator's] participative energies [and s/he] has become the subject of the drama' invites attention (p. 209). I doubt that it is purposeful to argue whether an immersive, 'non-traditional' piece such as *Roadkill*, for example, is more affective than *Three Kingdoms* in its suitably aggressive, visceral criticism of sexual slavery.[7] Both are stingingly powerful, albeit through different methods. With reference to Bennett's suggestion that 'recent developments [in performance and its study] have [. . .] marked an encouraging emancipation from previous devotion to the dramatic text' (p. 211), it is worth underlining that within the textual, or dramatic, there are various degrees of nuance, too, and these deserve understanding and recognition. 'Those practices which share little with traditional theatre and which cannot be absorbed into institutional playing spaces have, for a long time, been ignored', notes Bennett (p. 208). Certainly this is accurate, especially considering when *Theatre Audiences* was first published. However, the field has moved quickly. The multiplicity characterizing contemporary theatrical representation has reinforced the importance of critical frameworks that do not treat one type of theatre as intrinsically superior or inferior to another.

My aim in this chapter has been to address how, in the contemporary period, the individual spectator and/or collective audience have benefited from this diversity, even if, in the process, they may feel less detached or safe than they may have previously felt. As for the type of 'institutional playing spaces' that Bennett refers to, many of these have expanded their scope to a noticeable degree to include the type of play that has re-invigorated the form – plays like Neilson's *Relocated*, Stephens's *Three Kingdoms*, Tim Crouch's *The Author* (2009), debbie tucker green's *truth and reconciliation* (2011), Lucy Kirkwood and Ed Hime's *Small Hours* (2011), or any of the further examples readily available.[8] They have achieved this by interrogating 'traditional' viewing relationships encouraged by the authored text and invading the mainstream – if we accept that such a thing exists. What such plays have in common is that they have brought the performance uncomfortably close to the spectator, and vice versa. They have instigated a thought and sensory process which compels us to ask whether and when we should intervene in what we are witnessing, and what the direct implications of tacit acceptance are for ourselves. As Katie Mitchell, who directed *Small Hours*, suggests, in the intimate performance experience there is a 'mild sensation of imprisonment' (2011), a physical and spatial manifestation of our liability as audience, and this can happen even in the 'traditional' theatre venue, under the right circumstances. 'Traditional' is becoming increasingly difficult to define, but on the basis of how audiences have been challenged by playwrights in the recent period, it is fair to argue that the 'non-traditional' can be equally taken to mean both non-textual and new, radical, text-driven forms of theatre. What we are looking at is far more dangerous than we might suspect.

Notes

1. *Relocated* ran at the Royal Court Theatre Upstairs from 6 June to 5 July 2008. The play has not been published.
2. Critics reviewing the play unfailingly mention documented cases of violence against children in the UK and Europe as points of allusion throughout the piece.
3. Gardner (2008) makes this point particularly strongly in relation to the sensitive subject matter that *Relocated* negotiates.
4. As Tripney (2008) notes, for example, 'precise shifts in the lighting cause [the gauze] to shift from transparent to opaque, concealing scene changes'.
5. Stephens (2012c) speaks of the transformative process that performance has the power to generate.
6. The internationalist aspect of the play and production is emphasized by Stephens (2012d).
7. *Roadkill* is a performance piece first staged at the Traverse, Edinburgh, in 2010, conceived and directed by Cora Bissett. It boldly and viscerally delves into issues of sexual exploitation and abuse, taking spectators on a physical and conceptual journey whose objective is to capture the horror of the experience.
8. *Small Hours*, arguably the lesser known of the three plays, takes place in a young woman's living room, realistically recreated for the spectators in a highly intimate space within the theatre. For a more detailed discussion of this play, see Mireia Aragay's introduction to this volume (Chapter 1).

Works cited

Bennett, S. (1997) *Theatre Audiences: A Theory of Production and Reception*, 2nd edn (Abingdon: Routledge).
Billington, M. (2008) 'Review of *Relocated*', *Guardian*, 18 June, http://www.guardian.co.uk/stage/2008/jun/18/theatre.reviews (accessed 22 January 2013).
Bourdieu, P. (1986) *Distinction: A Social Critique of the Judgement of Taste*, trans. R. Nice (Abingdon: Routledge).
Crouch, T. (2009) *The Author* (London: Oberon).

Curtis, N. (2012) 'Simon Stephens Talks on His New Play *Three Kingdoms*', *Evening Standard*, 3 May, http://www.standard.co.uk/goingout/theatre/interview-simon-stephens-talks-on-his-new-play-three-kingdoms-7707198.html (accessed 12 February 2013).

Fricker, K. (2008) 'Review of *Relocated*', http://www.variety.com (accessed 22 January 2013).

Gardner, L. (2008) 'When Should a Playwright's Compassion Step in?', *Guardian Theatre Blog*, 25 June, http://www.guardian.co.uk/stage/theatreblog/2008/jun/25/relocated (accessed 22 January 2013).

—— (2012) '*Three Kingdoms*: The Shape of British Theatre to Come?', *Guardian Theatre Blog*, 16 May, http://www.guardian.co.uk/stage/theatreblog/2012/may/16/three-kingdoms-shape-british-theatre-or-flop (accessed 28 February 2013).

Haydon, A. (2008) 'Review of *Relocated*, *Postcards from the Gods*, 24 June, http://postcardsgods.blogspot.co.uk (accessed 22 January 2013).

Logan, B. (2007) 'The Outside Man', *New Statesman*, 6 December, http://www.newstatesman.com/arts-and-culture/2007/12/british-theatre-neilson (accessed 12 February 2013).

Mitchell, K. (2011) 'Welcome to My Front Room: Why I Love Directing in Small Spaces', *Guardian Theatre Blog*, 19 January, http://www.guardian.co.uk/stage/theatreblog/2011/jan/19/directing-small-spaces-katie-mitchell (accessed 4 March 2013).

Neilson, A. (2007) 'Don't Be So Boring', *Guardian*, 21 March, http://www.guardian.co.uk/theguardian/2007/mar/21/features11.g2 (accessed 12 February 2013).

Reid, T. (2008) '"Deformities of the Frame": The Theatre of Anthony Neilson', *Contemporary Theatre Review*, 17 (4), pp. 487–98.

Royal Court Theatre (2008) http://www.royalcourttheatre.com/whats-on/relocated (accessed 21 January 2013).

Stephens, S. (2006) *Motortown* (London: Methuen).

—— (2009) *Punk Rock* (London: Methuen).

—— (2012a) *Morning* (London: Methuen).

—— (2012b) *Three Kingdoms* (London: Methuen).

—— (2012c) 'theartsdesk Q&A: Playwright Simon Stephens', interview by J. Rees, *Artsdesk.com*, 29 July, http://www.theartsdesk.com/theatre/theartsdesk-qa-playwright-simon-stephens (accessed 28 February 2013).

—— (2012d) 'Deutsch Courage: Why German Theatre Dares – and Wins', *Guardian Theatre Blog*, 9 May, http://www.guardian.co.uk/stage/theatreblog/2012/may/09/german-theatre-dares-three-kingdoms (accessed 28 February 2013).

Tripney, N. (2008) 'Review of *Relocated*', *MusicOMH*, 1 June, http://www.musicomh.com/extra/theatre/relocated-royal-court-london (accessed 22 January 2013).

tucker green, d. (2011) *truth and reconciliation* (London: Nick Hern).

9
Witnessing, Sexualized Spectatorship and the (De)construction of Queer Identities in *Mother Clap's Molly House*, *The Pride* and *Cock*

Enric Monforte

(De)constructing sexual identities

In the last decade, a number of plays have opened on British stages that scrutinize the complicated fashioning of gay/lesbian/queer identities. Often labelled as 'queer' and seen as a result of a 'post-AIDS conscious-ness' (Roberts, 2000, p. 178) which inherited the legacy of the gay thea-tre produced in the post-Stonewall period, these texts have digested and transformed such an inheritance, adapting to their times and critically responding to them.[1] In this way, they can be said to bear witness to the complex, painful (de)construction of the homosexual subject. This chapter focuses on the way in which Mark Ravenhill's *Mother Clap's Molly House* (2001), Alexi Kaye Campbell's *The Pride* (2008) and Mike Bartlett's *Cock* (2009) pose relevant, thought-provoking, even diverging questions about queer identities both in present-day Western societies and in those belonging to times past. In doing so, special emphasis is placed on the plays' immediate socio-cultural contexts, on the role of witnessing and on the ethics of spectatorship.

Michel Foucault and Jeffrey Weeks have studied the construction of sexuality at different levels (medical, legal, social, cultural, historical, among others). As is well known, in his seminal *The History of Sexuality*, Foucault refers to sexuality as an 'historical construct' (1990, p. 105), places its creation as an 'apparatus' (p. 106) in the eighteenth century and describes how the homosexual became a 'species' (p. 43) and a 'category' (p. 101) in the late nineteenth and early twentieth centuries, when psychological, psychiatric, medical, legal and literary discourses began to be applied to homosexuality. That was therefore the moment

when 'a recognizably "modern" male homosexual identity was beginning to emerge' (Weeks, 1989, p. 115), the specific juncture when the
homosexual became 'a new subject of social observation and specula-
tion', even though it also 'opened up the possibility of new modes of
self-articulation' (p. 102). In any case, we are significantly talking of
'human subjects, subjected' (p. 7).

The vital importance of the social regulation of sex deserves particular attention. Weeks mentions how the individual is 'a product of
social forces, an "ensemble of social relations"' (p. 3), and hence how
central the 'socio-cultural' contexts are to sexuality. As a consequence,
he argues that '[t]he social not only defines, but actually in part constructs [sexual unorthodoxy]' (p. 97). Attention should thus be paid to
the effects of social categorization, to 'the social reactions to the sexed
individuals that emerge in any particular form of society, and the ways
in which these shape individual meanings' (p. 97). Therefore, when
approaching homosexuality, 'what matters is not the inherent nature
of the act but the social construction of meanings around that activity,
and the individual response to that' (p. 117).

Witnessing and sexualized spectatorship

Besides tracing the effects of the construction of sexuality and the
social regulation of sex, this chapter argues that the plays under discussion also share the fact that, through setting up processes of bearing
witness and, to varying degrees, experimental modes of representation,
they turn spectators into 'fully lucid, unaffected witness[es]' (Felman
and Laub, 1992, p. 81) who become potentially aware of the diverse
discourses inf(l)ecting the construction of queer identities since the
early eighteenth century, with a particular emphasis on contemporary
times.

In *Testimony: Crises of Witnessing in Literature, Psychoanalysis, and
History*, Dori Laub divides the act of bearing witness to the traumatic
historical event of the Nazi Holocaust into three levels. The third one,
'the level of being a witness to the process of witnessing', defined as 'one
in which the process of witnessing is itself being witnessed' (pp. 75–6),
lends itself well to the theatrical situation. In this light, the spectator,
through watching and listening, has the potential to embody the 'total
presence of an *other*' (pp. 70–1; emphasis original) and become a witness
to the events represented on stage. As such, s/he may become 'a party to
the creation of knowledge *de novo*. [. . . T]he blank screen on which the
event comes to be inscribed for the first time' (p. 57; emphasis original).

Bearing this in mind, the plays analysed are significant in as much as they situate spectators – both men and women, both gay and straight – as double witnesses, that is, witnesses to that which they are watching and listening to and, inevitably, to their own process of witnessing (p. 58). Thus, the plays have the potential to interpellate spectators by nudging them into sexualizing – and perhaps, inevitably, queering – their spectatorial positions, prompting them to ask themselves questions about their own sexual identities as well as to interrogate established assumptions of sexual and gender identity over time.[2] This may lead to acts of resubjectivization on the part of spectators as a result of their witnessing the particular representations offered by the plays in question, acts that ultimately would afford them the possibility of creating 'new forms of gendered or sexual citizenship' (Warner, 2002, p. 57). In the case of straight spectators, this would involve engaging in an imaginary encounter with the 'face' (Levinas, 1989, pp. 75–87) or even recognizing Otherness in themselves, thus becoming aware of their own potential for '*response-ability*' (Lehmann, 2006, p. 185; emphasis original). The outcome would be to involve all spectators, irrespective of their sexualities, in a process of active rethinking of dominant discourses on sexuality, eventually leading to their own empowerment.

From this perspective, the theatre is seen as a place characterized by the '*mutual implication of actors and spectators in the theatrical production of images*' (Lehmann, 2006, p. 186; emphasis original), 'a community site' made up of capable individuals (Rancière, 2009, pp. 16–17) endowed with a definite ethical potential. Thus, according to Jacques Rancière, 'The spectator also acts, [. . .] She observes, selects, compares, interprets. [. . .] She participates in the performance by refashioning it in her own way – [. . .] They are thus both distant spectators and active interpreters of the spectacle offered to them' (p. 13). In other words, to argue that *Mother Clap's Molly House*, *The Pride* and *Cock* may prompt acts of sexualized resubjectivization on the part of spectators amounts to taking for granted their intrinsically active position as both individuals participant in the action and 'agents of a collective practice' (p. 8), an agency that entails ethico-political emancipation.

Mother Clap's Molly House and the queer (de)construction of identity

The publication of *Anti-Gay* (1996) constituted a shock in the Anglo-American gay world of the time. Edited by Mark Simpson, the book, a collection of essays written by a mixture of British, American and

Canadian journalists, photographers, film directors and critics, writers and activists, all of them 'disgruntled non-heterosexuals' (Simpson, 1996, p. xix), aimed a sharp critique at the gay community of the time, the constant demand for positive images of gay people, the utter commodification and standardization of gay identities – '[n]owadays, gay is *goods*' (p. xiv) – and the replication of Western, late capitalist heterosexual institutions, while calling for 'a new dialectic, a new conversation with the world' (p. xix). Contributors to *Anti-Gay* share profound misgivings about the state of contemporary gay communities and gay culture for being a 'political-, media-, business-constructed monolith' (Manning, 1996, p. 115) which interpellates the gay community '[t]hrough its political and financial imperatives' (p. 108). In addition, they demand the replacement of 'separate, mutually exclusive, rival orientations and identities' (Tatchell, 1996, p. 44) by 'a more all-inclusive, polymorphous and fluid sexuality' (p. 36), all this leading to the claim, possibly underpinned by Judith Butler's (1990) and Eve Sedgwick's (1990) deconstruction of binary thought in relation to sexuality, that '[t]he ultimate queer emancipation is the abolition of homosexuality and the eradication of the homosexual' (Tatchell, 1996, p. 35). *Anti-Gay* needs to be placed in the context of a broader (post-)queer theoretical debate regarding the way in which gay and lesbian existence has evolved into assimilation, empowerment and inevitable instrumentalization by mainstream, neoliberal capitalist culture since the life-changing events of Stonewall, with critical voices putting forward instead an 'anti-assimilationist thesis' on the basis of the necessity of imagining 'a queer ethos at odds with heteronormativity' (Walsh, 2012, p. 92; see also Warner, 2000 and Edelman, 2004).

Mark Ravenhill's *Mother Clap's Molly House* (2001) may be approached as a text that responds to the various dissenting attitudes voiced in *Anti-Gay* and in the (post-)queer movement generally, and puts forward a queer deconstruction of a commodified, bourgeois gay identity that replicates the schema of heteronormative, homophobic, patriarchal society. Ravenhill returns to some of his favourite topics: the contrast between queerness and the gay bourgeoisie, the issue of parenting (Rebellato, 2001, p. xiii) and the creation of alternative families. As in *Handbag* (1998), the play presents audiences with an intertextual game, the action taking place on two different temporal planes, early eighteenth-century London at the time of Restoration city comedy – according to Peter Tatchell, '[the] embracing of a gay identity had its beginnings in eighteenth-century European cities' (1996, p. 37) – and the beginning of the twenty-first century, thus encompassing 'a continuum of gay history'

(Saunders, 2012, p. 180). An 'iconically gay' (Ravenhill, 2007, p. 101) play, *Mother Clap's Molly House* carries out a queer imaginative exploration of Britain's gay subculture by investigating the thriving world of 'molly houses', establishments where homosexual men got together, wore female attire, socialized and had sexual intercourse with each other (see, for example, Bray, 1995, pp. 81–114; Norton, 2006, pp. 86–112, 144–69 and *passim*; Trumbach, 2007, pp. 78–94), and by establishing comparisons with the present-day gay world, represented by a sex party that takes place in the household of an affluent gay couple. As in *Handbag*, the play interrogates the reproduction of bourgeois, heteronormative structures by sexual minorities, suggesting that a search for alternative formations needs to be carried out. From another perspective, as 'a fantasia on historical themes which [. . .] asks fresh questions about sexuality and the market place' (Ravenhill, 2008, p. x), the play analyses that specific proto-capitalist moment and the turning of bodies into commodities as precisely reflected in the 'emerging power of the mercantile bourgeois class in the later post-Republic period' (Billingham, 2007, p. 142), as well as in its depiction of the millennial *angst* and moral vacuum.

The 'bawdy rapturously Hogarthian' (Svich, 2011, p. 411) part of the play devoted to the eighteenth century shows how a recently widowed Mrs Tull, as a consequence of the downturn in business in the tally shop where she rents dresses to prostitutes, and of her late husband's squandering of their money on whores, drink and gambling, ends up by opening up a molly house and changing her identity into that of Mother Clap. The success of the establishment in the London of the time, *'a city of business and enterprise'* (Ravenhill, 2001, p. 5) where, according to God, 'profit reigns supreme' (p. 56), allows her, at the end of the play, to leave London for the countryside, where she plans to create an alternative type of family. We also witness Mrs Tull's gradual abandonment of a sexist, homophobic position represented by a submissive attitude towards her husband, an adherence to traditional gender division strictures and a hostility towards Princess Seraphina, *'a large man in a dress'* (p. 7) who comes to the tally shop looking for work and whom she mistakenly considers to be a 'sodomite' (p. 9), when in fact William – his real name – is heterosexual and uses drag to give himself 'a character' (p. 23).

The eighteenth-century section is also interesting in that it introduces the notion of 'pretend' family – a copy of 'the "real" heterosexual original' (Rayner, n.p.) – represented by the characters of Kedger and Philips, working men who come to the molly house to socialize, and their 'son' Orme, who give spectators glimpses of gay life in the

London of the time. This family unit contains specific allotted roles for each member, with Kedger being Father and Philips fulfilling the role of Mother. Graham Saunders has questioned the subversive potential of such 'pretend' families, since they 'never seriously challenge the innate legitimacy of the traditional family' (2012, p. 184). In fact, the play itself articulates such a critique through having Martin and Orme, the two apprentices, perform a mock wedding ceremony in the molly house which ends up with Martin in drag as Susan Guzzle giving birth to their own child, a *'wooden doll'* that *'is pulled out from Martin's skirts'* (Ravenhill, 2001, p. 76).

In the contemporary part of the play, which takes the form of 'a [bitter] bourgeois comedy', Ravenhill wanted to find out 'where you would end up if you followed through the process that starts in the molly house in the eighteenth century' (2007, p. 100). Spectators bear witness to the preparations and development of a sex party in Josh and Will's stylish 'loft apartment' (Ravenhill, 2001, p. 57). The couple's open relationship is shown to be declining and mostly devoid of sex, with Will, who longs for 'a form of relationality modelled on a heteronormative template' (Walsh, 2012, p. 92), looking for a commitment that Josh refuses to give. Thus Will feels compelled to carry on with the sex parties, depending on a non-stop drug supply to help him cope with the situation – 'Got to be something, make this bearable' (Ravenhill, 2001, p. 102). The couple works as a mirror image of that composed by Martin and Orme in the eighteenth-century section, with Martin willing to create a more committed relationship and Orme refusing to do so, eventually staying in London and carrying on with the hedonistic lifestyle of the molly house.

Through Tom, a contemporary character recently come out in the gay clubbing and drug scene, the play also articulates a lambasting critique of the bourgeois gay community, aimed this time not at the queer replication of heteronormative structures, but instead questioning the challenging potential of random, noncommittal relationships. Thus, when a drugged Tom is forced to perform oral sex on Will, he reacts:

I was really looking forward to this evening. This is all I ever wanted. All them years stuck at home listening to me dad: Fucking poofs this, fucking queers that. And I thought: You're history, you. Cos I'm a poof, but I in't telling you. Oh no. One day I'm just gonna up and go. Stick a note on the fridge. 'Fuck the family'. Little husband with his little wife and their little kids. That's history. And I'm the future. This is the future. People doing what they want to do. People being who they want to be. So why [. . .]? Why do you have to make it wrong? (Ravenhill, 2001, pp. 85–6)

Once he recovers from his crisis, however, he decides to plunge again into the world of sex and drugs offered by the club scene, a kind of '[g]lobal Disco Family' (Ravenhill, 2001, p. 101). Tom's words are reminiscent of those uttered by Orme, which close the play, '[o]h yes. Dance. Dance. Dance. And on for ever more' (p. 110). The ending of the contemporary part of the play is utterly bleak, with 'damned and doomed' gay characters (Ravenhill, 2007, p. 101) only valuing a self-ishly hedonistic lifestyle based on 'absolute sexual liberty but no sense of pleasure or of relationships whatsoever' (p. 99). The ending of the play, merging the two worlds by making the molly house become '*a rave club*' (Ravenhill, 2001, p. 110), underlines the striking similarities they share – both are moral vacuums pervaded by lack of commitment and the urge for instant satisfaction of desire, all this in a capital-ist framework (early and late, respectively) in which bodies become commodities.

The deconstruction of gender and sexual identities can clearly be seen in the final section, when some of the eighteenth-century characters decide to escape the advent of early capitalist regulations and live differ-ent, less constricted existences by leaving London behind and moving to the countryside. Thus, Mrs Tull, passing on her business to Amelia, will work in the fields, while her lover Princess Seraphina/William will take charge of the domestic sphere. They will be accompanied by those that do not fit in – Martin, the young apprentice, who will take on the role of the couple's son, and Amy, a former prostitute dressed as a man, who will undertake the function of protecting them from outside perils. As Mrs Tull puts it, '[s]o now we can move on. Away from this world. And on to the new. Whatever we are' (Ravenhill, 2001, p. 105). As Ravenhill summarizes, '[t]hose characters who are polymorphous are the ones who are prepared to go and have a pastoral existence at the end' (2007, p. 100). The deconstruction of sexual and gender identity is perhaps best signalled by Mrs Tull/Mother Clap's shedding of her former identities at the end of the play. When they are ready to leave, she realizes that she does not have an identity any longer – 'who am I?' (Ravenhill, 2001, p. 105) – since none of the previous ones can actually account for the complexities of her new self. She will therefore have to come up with a new name. It is this notion of the fluidity or intrinsic instability of sexual and gender identity that Mrs Tull suggests when kissing William – the out-of-drag Princess Seraphina – and endowing him with a different identity each time they embrace – 'Man. Woman. Hermaphrodite. [. . .] Want all of 'em. All of you' (p. 99).

The ending of the play brings up once again the theme of parenting and the creation of families, the latter understood as 'structures that need reinventing' in a queer context (Saunders, 2012, p. 184). The family unit created by the group of dissident survivors is, as has been seen, a non-canonical one, that perhaps being the key to survival. Francesca Rayner discusses how such '[q]ueer resignifications of the family' are inevitably 'overtly parodic and deconstructionist' (n.p.). She shows how Judith Butler's study of Jennie Livingston's documentary *Paris is Burning* (1991) about drag subculture in New York City exemplifies the notion of 'the parodic inhabiting of conformity' while warning nevertheless about the risk of it leading to a 'relapse into injury' (Butler qtd. in Rayner, n.p.; Butler, 1993, pp. 122–3). Nevertheless, according to Butler, 'the resignification of the family [. . .] is not a vain or useless imitation, but the social and discursive building of community, a community that binds, cares, and teaches, that shelters and enables' (1993, p. 137). This dovetails with Ravenhill's social vision (Rebellato, 2001, p. x), his view of human bonds not driven by economic exchange as small spaces of subversion and sites of resistance, and his emphasis on our responsibility as members of a society, '[b]eing a social being, being part of a society, is the only truly adult form of existence' (Ravenhill, 2007, p. 93).

In any case, it is through Ravenhill's detached 'moral' view (Billingham, 2007, p. 135; Rebellato, 2001, p. x; Sierz, 2001, p. 144; Svich, 2003, p. 92; Svich, 2011, p. 419), one that rather than comment, merely shows through the interstices left by his harsh critique, that a space emerges for spectators to define their own ethico-political position. By rejecting capitalist structures, by showing the constraining effects of established definitions of sexual and gender identity and by emphasizing instead playful, less hierarchical, more elusive queer identifications, *Mother Clap's Molly House* manages to elude modern categorizations.

The Pride: bearing witness, escaping regulation

Alexi Kaye Campbell's *The Pride* (2008) offers an insight into the pernicious effects of the social regulation of sex and, in doing so, poses relevant questions about the survival of gay/queer identities through historical hardship. At the same time, the play openly questions some aspects of contemporary queer existence. With the play alternating between two different temporal axes, the London of 1958 and 2008, the audience witnesses stories of the plight, survival, and subsequent commodification of gay identities in contemporary Britain. In the 1950s section, Sylvia introduces her husband Philip to her colleague Oliver, towards whom she is developing a profound attachment. As a consequence of the effect the encounter has on them, the two men become involved, but after a short span of time Philip finds himself unable to resist the pressures of society, finally rejecting Oliver and looking for help in the medical services. Sylvia finds out about the affair and decides to leave Philip. In the part of the play devoted to the 2000s, we find the alter egos of the three characters fifty years later. This time, Oliver and Philip are in a relationship, with Sylvia being Oliver's close friend. Oliver is addicted to sex, which eventually makes Philip decide to end the relationship. The play closes with the reconciliation of Philip and Oliver, with Sylvia beginning a relationship with a man and with the three characters together at the London gay pride celebration.

Both temporal moments in the play illustrate very well the regulatory regimes described by Foucault in *The History of Sexuality* and show how the conjunction of the medical/clinical and legal discourses on homosexuality, together with the social regulation of sex, became mechanisms of control that have survived into the present. Thus, the section devoted to the 1950s focuses on the effects of the setting up of the Wolfenden Committee for the regulation of sexuality (1957) and reflects the moral panic – the 'official concern and public anxiety' (Weeks, 1989, p. 240) – felt at the time, as the reference to Sylvia's former colleague Richard Coveley's trial for '[g]ross indecency' (Campbell, 2008, p. 55) and subsequent suicide exemplify. Oliver, on the other hand, fights the definition of sexual deviancy that is imposed on him, claiming instead a feeling of 'pride for the person I was' (p. 79). When he talks to a reluctant Philip about his sexual tendencies, he recounts a visit to a place frequented by homosexuals, where he felt like '[a] witness' (p. 78):

> And I thought that some of those men, [. . .] hovering, waiting in that dim flickering light, some of those men would also choose this, [. . .] but [. . .] because they have been told that this is who they are, that they are these men who stand waiting [. . .] to touch another man's skin, that they've believed that's *all* they are, but that what they want, [. . .] is [. . .] an intimacy with someone they can hold onto for a while, that what they want more than anything is to be able to *see* them, to look at them, to look into their eyes and to *know* them. And be known. (Campbell, 2008, p. 79; emphasis original)

Unable to bear the burden of the categorizations imposed on him, Philip decides to visit a doctor, an example of the deep social impact of the medicalization of homosexuality, which 'encouraged would-be cures, from hypnotism through to chemical experimentation and in the 1960s to aversion therapy' (Weeks, 1989, p. 105) and as a consequence of which homosexuals were seen as 'perverts' and defined as sick or mentally ill. Predictably, the doctor labels Philip's homosexuality a *'perversion'* (Campbell, 2008, p. 115; emphasis original) yet is unable to answer Philip's question about 'the other things. The other feelings. [. . . T]he ones that aren't *exclusively* sexual' (p. 116; emphasis original). The treatment consists in Philip being injected apomorphine while looking at homosexual pornography and at a photograph of Oliver. This is the last the audience sees of the Philip of the 1950s, a frightened character who becomes a blank and disappears under the imposed identity he is given by the legal, medical and social discourses at work at the time.

In contrast to the bleakness of the 1950s, in the 2000s the atmosphere has become freer, with the issue of gay pride becoming central. From this perspective, the play focuses on the deconstruction of the socially-, medically- and legally-received gay/queer identity and its subsequent reconstruction. On the one hand, there is a strong critique of the superficiality, lack of commitment and sheer hedonism that seem to be inherent to sections of contemporary bourgeois gay/queer life, a mistaken reaction against the regulation of sexuality. The more combative, intellectually-challenging activist literature produced by the gay community in the 1970s has given way to glossy magazines dealing with topics such as fashion, money – a hint at the 'pink pound' – or physical care that epitomize the late capitalist consumerist atmosphere of the new millennium. Paradoxically, the outcome of the struggle for gay rights has produced a hedonistic subculture not preoccupied in the least with transforming oppressed identities and effecting more profound changes in society. To this is added another shortcoming, namely a common lack of ideological positioning, reflected in Oliver's sexual encounter with a man dressed in a Nazi uniform, or in his lack of remorse for staging sexual fantasies with members of the BNP. As Sylvia eloquently advises him, '[y]ou have to stop sucking the dick of your oppressor' (Campbell, 2008, p. 108).

The Pride, therefore, states that the superficiality and lack of commitment that define a section of contemporary gay life are proofs of '[a]nti-respect' (p. 107), the unwelcome result of the regulation of homosexuality, which has prompted gay people to adopt models of behaviour that are in fact imposed on them. As Oliver puts it:

There's an expected behaviour. People telling you who you are. And you believe them. And then, of course, you become that very person.

> The one they want you to be. [. . .] And the thing is because I needed this person in some way, I keep needing their affirmation. So I try looking for them. [. . .] In all the wrong places. In the parks, and the loos and the saunas. On the internet. (Campbell, 2008, pp. 71, 107–8)

In this way, the play seems controversially to imply that sexual promiscuity is actually related to the perception of homosexuality as a taboo. The fact that the only female character in the play, Sylvia, expands on and elaborates this view underlines the connection between the gender and sexual oppression she and Oliver experience as a woman and a homosexual respectively:

> They reduce you, Oliver, to this person who is shallow. Someone who is defined by his body, by what he does with his body and by his taste in things. [. . .] And I'm thinking of what it was that first made people question things, to push the boundaries, I mean, to stand up for themselves and to really fight and that what they were fighting for can't have been the right to fuck in parks and wear designer clothes . . . [. . .] After all, the only reason you were in parks to begin with was because you couldn't be at home. You were kicked out, as it were. In exile. (Campbell, 2008, pp. 120–1)

The final setting of the play, the London Pride celebration, becomes deeply significant as a platform for the vindication of rights still not acquired, the honouring of past gay figures and the experimentation of new forms of relationality. The 1950s Sylvia closes the play as a sign of hope in times to come, highlighting the connection between the suffering taking place in both temporal planes, whilst pointing at a more congenial future.

Thus, *The Pride* is concerned with the isolation and loneliness of individuals on the margins – women and gays in this case – and poses questions on gender and sexuality that are still relevant to contemporary audiences, seeking to make them aware of the workings of discourses on sexuality and of the effects of the social regulation of sex, potentially enabling them to escape external categorization and achieve some form of agency. Perhaps ideologically closer to a gay identity politics based on binary thought than to a queer emphasis on fluidity and lack of an overt sexual definition, the play takes a political stance on the necessity to protect our tentative, fragile identities in contemporary late capitalist societies by showing the existence of a few precarious queer lives, this way giving contemporary audiences the tools to begin to mend their own damaged subjectivities.

Cock and the que(e)rying of homonormativity

Mike Bartlett's *Cock* (2009) shows the dilemma of John, a man in a long-term gay relationship with M, who, out of the blue, feels profoundly attracted to W, a woman. The play pushes on the (de)construction of queer sexual and gender identities to a satirical querying of homonormativity. Bartlett establishes that spectators are to be 'raked down towards the actors' (2009, p. 4), which places them in a witnessing position in relation to the production of meaning. At the same time, the blurring of strict definitions of identity is reflected in the absence of mimesis and analogy, as reinforced by the playwright's indication that '[t]here is no scenery, no props, no furniture and no mime' (p. 4). Divided into three parts, with the first two subdivided into six shorter sections with a mixed chronology of events, the play presents John – the only character with a full name, thus imbued with an apparently full identity but paradoxically devoid of any kind of agency – in his exchanges with M in Part One and W in Part Two. The other character in the play, F, M's father, appears in Part Three – a dinner party at John and M's in the course of which John is supposed to state his preferences – and tries to convince John to stop seeing W and thus preserve the homonormative family unit he has created with M.

John shifts between rejecting oppressive definitions – 'No I don't think I'm, no I know I'm not. I'm not straight [. . .] I suppose I like both' (Bartlett, 2009, pp. 21–2) – and asserting a fixed sexual identity for himself – by saying 'I'm gay' (p. 44) when trying to leave W. At the same time, the difficulty he experiences choosing between M and W – who seem themselves to be quite confident about their own sexual preferences – may stand as a sign for a queer conception of identity. In Part Three, when W urges him to be himself, he replies, 'But I have absolutely no idea who that is, everyone else seems to have a personality a character but I've never, I've never – ' (p. 63).

At the beginning of the play, John is variously described by M as being 'all gestures and waving' (p. 6), as being like 'fudge' (p. 24), 'a sprawl', '[a] mob' (p. 26), '[w]et' (p. 30); the very John also describes himself as 'a mess' or 'liquid' (p. 10) if he were hit by a car. On her part, W elaborates, '[s]ome people might think you were scrawny but I think you're like a picture drawn with a pencil. I like it. You haven't been coloured in, you're all / Wire' (p. 35). John's fluidity can be read from a queer perspective as being concerned with 'multiple, shifting, and gloriously polymorphous bodies, pleasures, and resistances', the outcome of which will be a focus on 'mutability, instability, and polyvalence'

(Savran, 2002, pp. 153–4). On her part, Sedgwick relates queer to 'the open mesh of possibilities, gaps, overlaps, dissonances and resonances, lapses and excesses of meaning when the constituent elements of any-one's gender, of anyone's sexuality aren't made (or *can't* be made) to signify monolithically' (1993, p. 8; emphasis original). Indeed, *Cock* establishes how John refuses to endow his sexuality with a monolithical meaning whatsoever. He finds himself attracted equally by M and W, and the play also makes clear that his is not a case of bisexuality, since W is the only woman he has ever felt attracted towards. At the same time, the implications lying behind John's dilemma are also spelt out:

> John   I mean if you really think about it tonight could change eve-rything. I turn one way I have children and a normal family
> M   Normal.
> John   I turn the other way and I'll always be wondering if I made the right decision. Our whole lives turn on tonight.
>
> (Bartlett, 2009, p. 69)

The dinner party in Part Three is significant as it signals the way to proceed in the future. F, the old heterosexual patriarch, comes to the aid of M, the younger homosexual one, more affluent and older than John. W, on the other hand, shows agency when she decides where to sit at the table. F urges John to choose a definition of identity – 'I think you need to work out what you are. Fast' (Bartlett, 2009, p. 74). As F puts it – and, interestingly, his son M agrees with him – 'some things are *fundamental* some things are genetic. Baldness, or height, or sexuality. It's built in. You don't choose. [. . .] It's how you're born' (pp. 77–8; emphasis original), to which John replies 'maybe it's not a switch, one way or the other, maybe it's more like a stew, complicated things bub-bling up – ' (p. 78), thus voicing the notion of 'a spectrum of sexuality' or 'a continuum' (Thatchell, 1996, p. 40) intrinsic to a queer position. It is towards the end of the play when John articulates what can be read as a queer questioning of 1970s-style gay liberation:

> When I was at uni and I finally decided I'd do it and *come out*, all these people hugged me and were *proud* of me and said how brave I was and suddenly people were touching me and I was wearing different clothes and I was part of a *scene*, even walking differently I think and everyone said the real me was emerging, that I'd been repressed, and so I thought I must've done the right thing then, but it didn't feel like that to me. I had to make more of an effort than before, and yes

I fancied men, a lot a lot but I never got why that changed anything other than who I wanted to fuck. What did it matter? Gay straight, words from the sixties made by our parents, sound so *old*, only invented to get rights, and we've got rights now so [. . .] They're horrible horrible words what they do how they stop you [. . .] and I can see now I can see that it's about *who the person is.* Not man or woman but *What they're like. What they do.* Why didn't anyone say? I thought I thought your generation was all for that. Peace. Love. So why are you telling me that *what* I sleep with is more important that *who* I sleep with? [. . .] Why are you telling me I have to know what I am? (Bartlett, 2009, pp. 87–8; emphasis original)

Leaving aside the debatable argument that gay rights are on a par with those granted to heterosexuals, the play controversially lambasts identity politics and the achievements of gay and lesbian groups since the 1970s, by pointing forward at the same time at other possible avenues.

However, in the end John is unable to find the necessary strength to give up his comfortable life and start a new one with W. Both the challenges related to this new, uncertain existence and the normative discourses on (homo)sexuality prove too difficult to be overcome, so he finally clings to M and remains in their suffocating, unequal relationship in their cosy, bourgeois abode, thus finally embracing a strict definition of identity. As he says, '[t]his isn't what I want. / I just. / I think this is easier' (Bartlett, 2009, p. 94). At the same time, John and W's rosy dream of a nuclear family reunion at Christmas is eventually accepted by M, who had previously refused to make plans for the future – 'If you want children we can have children and Christmas and whatever all of that, we can have that ourselves, you know we can do anything you want we can' (p. 96). In any case, and apart from the sombre elements that close the play and do away with the humour that had pervaded it until then, in its open questioning of strict definitions of sexual identity and of binary categories *Cock* opens up a breathing space for dissidence – interestingly this time focused on a heterosexual relation – and hints at possible ways for spectators to flee oppressive discourses and regulatory regimes.

Interpellating queer existence, producing sexualized spectators

Through witnessing the exploration of the interstitial spaces between the construction, reconstruction and deconstruction of the queer subject carried out in *Mother Clap's Molly House*, *The Pride* and *Cock*, spectators are placed in a position where they may potentially become intensely aware of their own sexualities – sexualized spectators who may ultimately enact a process of resubjectivization. Although quite sombre in its exposition of the standardization and commodification of gay identities and of the dubious effects of the translation of heteronormative schemes into queerness, Ravenhill's *Mother Clap's Molly House* paradoxically offers some hope in its partly-utopian ending. Concerned with the theme of parenting, the creation of families and the broader state of society, the play problematizes a stable and monolithic gay identity – yet another result of the social regulation of sex – proposing instead a definition of sexuality as multiple, mutant and unstable. Campbell's *The Pride* sheds light on the effects the construction of sexuality and the subsequent social regulation of sex have had on queer individuals from different periods. Finally, Bartlett's *Cock*, in its querying of homonormativity, offers a more humorous, always queer view of the constraints and contradictions lying behind fixed, comfortable definitions of identity. The three plays, to varying degrees, leave leeway for spectators to (re)create their own experiences in the processes of watching, listening and witnessing. In so doing, they create a dissident space where spectators – both gay and straight – can hopefully negotiate their own sexual identities and, defying dominant discourses and regulations, create new, more heterogeneous, ultimately less constraining ones.[3]

Notes

1. For a detailed discussion on the issue of gay/lesbian/queer theatrical practices see, among others, Case, 1996, Clum, 2000, Collis, 1993, Deeney, 2006, de Jongh, 1992, Dolan, 1993, Freeman, 1997, Monforte, 2007, Savran, 2002 and Sinfield, 1999, as well as my interviews with Neil Bartlett, Nicholas de Jongh, Mark Ravenhill and Alan Sinfield in Aragay et al., 2007.
2. I am adapting Jenny Spencer's formulation (2012), following Jacques Rancière, of the notion of the 'racialized spectator'. Spencer discusses the way in which Adrienne Kennedy's plays make spectators distinctly aware of their own racial identities. My thanks to Mireia Aragay for bringing Spencer's article to my attention.
3. Early drafts of this chapter were read at 'Research Day Spring 2007: Theatre & Politics' (Royal Holloway College, University of London, March 2007) and at the conference 'Fractured Narratives: Pinter, Postmodernism and the Postcolonial World' (Goldsmiths College, University of London, November 2009). I am grateful to Chris Megson for mentioning the possible synergies between Ravenhill's plays and Simpson's *Anti-Gay*, to Francesca Rayner for allowing me to quote from her unpublished manuscript, and to Cristina Delgado for supplying texts out of my reach. My thanks to Clara Escoda and

Pilar Zozaya for reading drafts of the chapter and providing me with valuable insights. Research towards this chapter was financed by the Spanish Ministry of Science and Innovation through the project 'The representation of politics and the politics of representation in post-1990 British drama and theatre' (FFI2009-07598).

Works cited

Aragay, M. et al. (eds) (2007) *British Theatre of the 1990s: Interviews with Directors, Playwrights, Critics and Academics* (Basingstoke and New York: Palgrave Macmillan).

Bartlett, M. (2009) *Cock* (London: Methuen).

Billingham, P. (2007) *At the Sharp End: Uncovering the Work of Five Contemporary Dramatists* (London: Methuen).

Bray, A. (1995) *Homosexuality in Renaissance England*, 2nd edn (New York: Columbia University Press).

Butler, J. (1990) *Gender Trouble: Feminism and the Subversion of Identity* (New York and London: Routledge).

—— (1993) *Bodies that Matter: On the Discursive Limits of 'Sex'* (London and New York: Routledge).

Campbell, A.K. (2008) *The Pride* (London: Nick Hern).

Case, S-E. (ed.) (1996) *Split Britches: Lesbian Practice/Feminist Performance* (London and New York: Routledge).

Clum, J.M. (2000) *Still Acting Gay: Male Homosexuality in Modern Drama* (New York: St. Martin's Griffin).

Collis, R. (1993) 'Sister George is Dead: The Making of Modern Lesbian Theatre' in T.R. Griffiths and M. Llewellyn-Jones (eds) *British and Irish Women Dramatists since 1958: A Critical Handbook* (Buckingham: Open University Press), pp. 78–83.

Deeney, J. (2006) 'Lesbian and Gay Theatre: All Queer on the West End Front' in M. Luckhurst (ed.) *A Companion to Modern British and Irish Drama: 1880–2005* (Oxford: Blackwell), pp. 398–408.

de Jongh, N. (1992) *Not in Front of the Audience: Homosexuality on Stage* (London and New York: Routledge).

Dolan, J. (1993) *Presence and Desire: Essays on Gender, Sexuality, Performance* (Ann Arbor: University of Michigan Press).

Edelman, L. (2004) *No Future: Queer Theory and the Death Drive* (Durham, NC: Duke University Press).

Felman, S. and D. Laub (1992) *Testimony: Crises of Witnessing in Literature, Pscyhoanalysis, and History* (New York and London: Routledge).

Foucault, M. (1990) *The History of Sexuality – Vol. I: An Introduction*, trans. R. Hurley (New York: Vintage Books).

Freeman, S. (1997) *Putting Your Daughters on the Stage: Lesbian Theatre from the 1970s to the 1990s* (London: Cassell).

Lehmann, H.-T. (2006) *Postdramatic Theatre* (London and New York: Routledge).

Levinas, E. (1989) 'Ethics as First Philosophy' in S. Hand (ed.) *The Levinas Reader* (Oxford: Blackwell), pp. 75–87.

Manning, T. (1996) 'Gay Culture: Who Needs It?' in M. Simpson (ed.) *Anti-Gay* (London and New York: Freedom Editions), pp. 98–117.

Monforte, E. (2007) 'English Gay/Queer Theatre in the 1990s: Kevin Elyot's *My Night with Reg* and Mark Ravenhill's *Shopping and Fucking*', *Revista Canaria de Estudios Ingleses*, 54, 195–206.

Norton, R. (2006) *Mother Clap's Molly House: The Gay Subculture in England 1700–1830*, 2nd edn (Stroud: The Chalford Press).

Patterson, C. (1997) 'The Rage of Caliban: Eighteenth-Century Molly Houses and the Twentieth-Century Search for Sexual Identity' in T. di Piero and P. Gill (eds) *Illicit Sex: Identity Politics in Early Modern Culture* (Athens and London: University of Georgia Press), pp. 256–69.

Rancière, J. (2009) *The Emancipated Spectator*, trans. G. Elliott (London and New York: Verso).

Ravenhill, M. (2001) *Mother Clap's Molly House* (London: Methuen).

—— (2007) 'Mark Ravenhill', interview by E. Monforte in M. Aragay et al. (eds) *British Theatre of the 1990s: Interviews with Directors, Playwrights, Critics and Academics* (Basingstoke and New York: Palgrave Macmillan), pp. 91–104.

—— (2008) 'Introduction' in *Plays Two (Mother Clap's Molly House, Product, The Cut, Citizenship, pool (no water))* (London: Methuen), pp. ix–xii.

Rayner, F. (n.d.) '"If nature don't provide 'em, we must do what we can": Playing at Family in Mark Ravenhill's *Handbag* and *Mother Clap's Molly House*' (unpublished).

Rebellato, D. (2001) 'Introduction' in M. Ravenhill, *Plays One (Shopping and Fucking, Faust is Dead, Handbag, Some Explicit Polaroids)* (London: Methuen), pp. ix–xx.

Roberts, B. (2000) 'Whatever Happened to Gay Theatre?', *New Theatre Quarterly*, 16 (2), pp. 175–85.

Saunders, G. (2012) 'Mark Ravenhill' in A. Sierz, *Modern British Playwriting: The 1990s* (London: Methuen), pp. 163–88.

Savran, D. (2002) 'Queer Theater and the Disarticulation of Identity' in A. Solomon and F. Minwalla (eds) *The Queerest Art: Essays on Lesbian and Gay Theater* (New York and London: New York University Press), pp. 152–67.

Sedgwick, E.K. (1990) *Epistemology of the Closet* (Berkeley and Los Angeles: University of California Press).

—— (1993) *Tendencies* (Durham, NC: Duke University Press).

Sierz, A. (2001) *In-Yer-Face Theatre: British Drama Today* (London: Faber).

Simpson, M. (1996) 'Preface' in M. Simpson (ed.) *Anti-Gay* (London and New York: Freedom Editions), pp. xi–xix.

Sinfield, A. (1999) *Out on Stage: Lesbian and Gay Theatre in the Twentieth Century* (New Haven, CT and London: Yale University Press).

Spencer, J. (2012) 'Emancipated Spectatorship in Adrienne Kennedy's Plays', *Modern Drama*, 55 (1), pp. 19–39.

Svich, C. (2003) 'Commerce and Morality in the Theatre of Mark Ravenhill', *Contemporary Theatre Review*, 13 (1), pp. 81–95.

—— (2011) 'Mark Ravenhill' in M. Middeke, P.P. Schnierer and A. Sierz (eds) *The Methuen Drama Guide to Contemporary British Playwrights* (London: Methuen), pp. 403–24.

Tatchell, P. (1996) 'It's Just a Phase: Why Homosexuality Is Doomed' in M. Simpson (ed.) *Anti-Gay* (London and New York: Freedom Editions), pp. 35–54.

Trumbach, R. (2007) 'Modern Sodomy: The Origins of Homosexuality, 1700–1800' in M. Cook et al. (eds) *A Gay History of Britain: Love and Sex between Men since the Middle Ages* (Oxford and Westport: Greenwood World Publishing), pp. 77–105.

Walsh, F. (2012) 'Queer Publics, Public Queers', *Performing Ethos*, 2 (2), pp. 91–4.

Warner, M. (2000) *The Trouble with Normal: Sex, Politics, and the Ethics of Queer Life* (Cambridge, MA: Harvard University Press).

—— (2002) *Publics and Counterpublics* (New York: Zone).

Weeks, J. (1989) *Sex, Politics and Society: The Regulation of Sexuality since 1800*, 2nd edn (London and New York: Longman).

Part IV
Ethics and Institutions

10
From Front Page to Front Stage: War Correspondents and Media Ethics in British Theatre

Christiane Schlote

Introduction

In 1927, *New York Times* critic Brooks Atkinson declared in his review of the so-called 'newspaper play' *Ink* that by 'an unwritten law, rarely violated, good plays cannot be written about the newspaper profession' (qtd. in Ehrlich, 2004, p. 27). Yet, according to Douglass Daniel, as 'a genre of television the newspaper drama is nearly as old as the entertainment medium itself', and by 1977, the year when CBS launched its top newspaper drama, *Lou Grant*, 23 newspaper dramas had been broadcast in the US since 1949 (1996, pp. 2–3). But while analyses of the representation of journalism in film and television have illustrated the processes by which 'journalism movies' and 'newspaper TV dramas' have contributed to making 'journalism matter in the popular consciousness' (Ehrlich, 2004, p. 15), the changing nature of conflicts and wars since 1990 has also influenced 'the modes of journalistic engagement' (Allan and Zelizer, 2004, p. 13), since, as Donald Matheson and Stuart Allan argue, 'the notion of journalists as neutral witnesses has become less tenable' in times of increased media management (2009, p. 179).

As Barbara Korte has shown in her study *Represented Reporters: Images of War Correspondents in Memoirs and Fiction* (2009), war correspondents garner particular cultural attention not only through the charisma of their profession, but also because of the very nature of war as their professional interest: 'War reporters are confronted with atrocities that arouse their feelings and stir their conscience while their professional ethos obliges them to do justice to the facts' (2009, p. 10). The ambiguity of their position arises from the complexity of their circumstances. Not only do they have to decide 'how far they can go when showing crimes against humanity', thus constantly negotiating between their professional obligation to report the facts and media ethics, but they further function as mediators between their audience's need for information and the attempts of those in power to control that information, and they are faced with the uncomfortable truth that 'despite all atrocities, a war may be profitable for them' and 'entail an exciting personal experience and opportunities for adventure' (pp. 10–11). In today's media, war journalists further 'function as actors in a double sense: they act in their specific professional field and [. . .] deliver the performance *of* a war correspondent for an audience', particularly when they 'report on television, as a visible, embodied presence – and via the camera – directly addressing an audience' (p. 13; emphasis original).

Although reflexivity and performative acts are of particular importance in war reporting, and media scholars argue that in regard to the coverage of news from the non-Western world 'visuals, drama and conflict are the only determinants of coverage' (Williams, 2011, p. 150), so far studies of the cultural representation of war journalists have mainly concentrated on film, fiction and memoirs. This chapter examines the representation of war correspondents and war photographers in three British plays, Stella Feehily's *O Go My Man* (2006), David Hare's *The Vertical Hour* (2008) and Vivienne Franzmann's *The Witness* (2012). Shifting the focus to the portrayal of war correspondents in drama, the chapter explores how British playwrights have responded to the nexus between the performativity of war reporting and drama, and how they address the motivations, practices and moral values of war correspondents and war photographers within the context of global media ethics.

Media ethics and the question of genre

Arguing that 'the internationalisation of ethical and moral duties places enormous pressure on journalists' (2006, p. 440), Howard Tumber analyses a series of questions which have long contributed to the public fascination with war reporting: 'How do correspondents handle the conditions of war and conflict? [. . .] How do they manage fear and danger? [. . .] What are their motivations for reporting conflict, given its strenuous demands on everything from health to personal and professional relationships?' (p. 440). Apart from the personal motivations and practices of individual war correspondents and photographers, since the 1970s there has also been a renewed interest in media ethics, partly prompted by the Watergate affair, resulting in the emergence of publications and journalist courses addressing applied ethics (Hickey, 2003, p. 44). The Society of Professional Journalists' current code of ethics 'expects journalists to "seek truth and report it", but also to "minimize harm", [. . .] to "act independently" and yet "be accountable"' (p. 51).[1] As Kevin Williams explains:

> In wartime journalism is faced with a number of ethical problems. Should graphic pictures of the dead be shown? Should the grief of families who have lost loved ones on the battlefield be intruded on? Should correspondents report from the enemy's side? Should report- ers accede to restrictions placed by the military on their movements in the war zone? [. . . A]t their heart is a basic ethical dilemma about the role of the journalist at times of armed conflict [. . .]. War exposes most starkly the gap between the rhetoric and reality that exists at the heart of the profession of journalism. (1992, pp. 154–5)

In their portrayal of war correspondents and photographers, numerous novels and more than 50 film and television productions (fictional and documentary) partly address these questions and ethical minefields.[2] While plays about war journalists and photographers are fewer, as in the case of film and fiction they also go back to the heyday of war reporting, 'the final decades of the 19th century, the so-called Golden Age of war corresponding' (Korte, 2009, p. 7). To the three British plays discussed in this essay may be added Richard Harding Davis's *The Galloper* (1906), Sophie Treadwell's *Gringo* (1922), Vincent Starrett and Gail Borden's unpublished *War Correspondent* (1929), Eugene O'Neill's *The Iceman Cometh* (1946), Martha Gellhorn and Virginia Cowles's *Love Goes to Press* (1946), Tom Stoppard's *Night and Day* (1978), Dennis Troute's *War Stories* (1979), Margaret Hollingsworth's *War Babies* (1987), Tanika Gupta's *Sanctuary* (2002), Nicholas Wright's *The Reporter* (2007), David Hay's *The Maddening Truth* (2008), Donald Margulies's *Time Stands Still* (2009), Roy Chatfield's *Tarbaby* (2010), Mari Lourey's *Bare Witness* (2010) and Helen Chadwick and Steven Hoggett's *War Correspondents* (2010).[3]

Within this list, three subgenres can be differentiated: 'biographical', 'testimonial' and 'metajournalistic' war correspondent plays. Biographical plays include Chatfield's *Tarbaby*, about the American photographer Lee Miller, who covered the Second World War for *Vogue*, Hay's dramatic portrayal of Martha Gellhorn in *The Maddening Truth* and Wright's *The Reporter*, tracing the last years of BBC correspondent James Mossman.[4] The multimedia performance *Bare Witness*, a joint presenta- tion of Melbourne's La Mama Theatre and fortyfivedownstairs based on stories Lourey gathered from photojournalists in Iraq, East Timor and the Balkans, and the song theatre performance *War Correspondents*, which features a mélange of songs, poems and extracts from interviews with war correspondents, can be categorized as testimonial plays. As Tumber has noted, for various reasons, 'foreign correspondents seem to produce the most books about themselves and their work' (2006, p. 440). In a similar vein, plays written by war correspondents about war correspondents may be termed 'metajournalistic'; they include Davis's *The Galloper*, Treadwell's *Gringo*, Starrett and Borden's *War Correspondent*, Gellhorn and Cowles's *Love Goes to Press*, Troute's *War Stories* and – in a doubly coded way – Stoppard's *Night and Day*.[5]

Neither *O Go My Man* nor *The Vertical Hour* or *The Witness* can be classified in any straightforward way as biographical, testimonial or meta-journalistic war correspondent plays. Yet each of the plays ran at the Royal Court Theatre and each has a war correspondent/photographer protagonist whose professional and private trials and tribulations provide the backbone of each play. According to former Artistic Director Ian Rickson, the Royal Court is 'not particularly interested in plays with wigs or plays set in drawing rooms. We want to put real life on stage in all its complexity' (qtd. in Roberts, 1999, p. xiv). But it is precisely this notion of 'real life' and its association with journalistic objectivity, which critics such as Stephen Ward no longer see as 'a viable ethical guide' (2004, p. 4), that is questioned in the plays. Feehily's second play, *O Go My Man*, which opened at the Royal Court on 12 January 2006 and inaugurated the Court's 50th anniversary year, shows the desperate attempts of the 45-year old Irish war correspondent Neil Devlin, who has just been covering the Darfur conflict, to try and sort out his private life.[6] *The Vertical Hour*, the first of Hare's plays to receive its world premiere on Broadway on 30 November 2006 at the Music Box Theatre in New York City, was directed by Sam Mendes. It prominently starred Julianne Moore as the thirty-something American foreign correspondent turned Professor of International Relations at Yale, Nadia Blye. Nadia joins her boyfriend, Philip Lucas (a physical therapist), for a trip to visit his father, Oliver (a nephrologist turned GP, played by Bill Nighy), in Shropshire, who, in a *Guess Who's Coming for a Discussion*-format, becomes her most challenging verbal sparring partner in a debate about the Iraq War.[7] The play's British premiere (with a different cast) was hosted by the Royal Court Theatre on 17 January 2008. The plot of Franzmann's *The Witness*, which premiered at the Royal Court Theatre on 1 June 2012, is also propelled by a verbal dispute, here between 'Joseph Potter, the most gifted photojournalist of his generation' (Franzmann, 2012, p. 73), and his adopted 19-year-old Rwandan daughter Alex, whom he saved on an assignment in Rwanda during the civil war and genocide (1990–93). The rescue of his daughter is ambiguously tied up with his award-winning photo – Alex's '[i]n that photo, I'm screaming for my dead mother on a pile of bloody corpses' (p. 24) is counterpointed by Joseph's 'I went in the church, I saw the bodies, I saw you and I took the shot. I heard the Interahamwe coming. I picked you up and ran' (p. 35).

O Go My Man and *The Vertical Hour* can be read as, respectively, postcolonial and gendered variations on the more conventional war correspondent play. Yet neither Neil's Irishness nor Nadia's gender are explicitly discussed, despite the fact that discourses such as 'the ethics of care', for example, examining the ways men and women frame and address ethical dilemmas (see Vanacker and Breslin, 2006), or the fact that women war correspondents still 'have difficult hurdles to overcome' (Tumber, 2006, p. 444), provide ample dramatic material. Notwithstanding the fact that, as Paul Cunningham explains, there are 'high-profile cases of media workers who've turned to alcohol and drugs' and that coming 'back to domestic life can be difficult [. . .], it can seem like you are leaving something "important" only to return to meaningless conversations about property, holidays and good schools' (qtd. in Feehily, 2006, p. 105), the portrayal of the war correspondent figure in each of the three plays seems to rely on the traditional (partly stereotypical) notions and images of war journalists as propagated in the media and/or fictional representations. These include being self-absorbed, extremely driven, traumatized, exploitative, promiscuous, unable to relate to others (especially to family and friends), suffering from an addiction (mainly alcoholism) and being on the edge, in general. In *O Go My Man*, Neil leaves his wife Zoë and their 15-year old daughter Maggie to live with Sarah, a floundering actress, who, in turn, has left her photographer partner Ian for Neil. Michael Billington (2006) finds this hard to believe, given that 'Neil seems too much of a self-lacerating shit to attract anyone' or, as Zoë puts it, 'I worried about you every night you were away. Northern Ireland. [. . .] Kosovo. Mogadishu [. . .]. I've put my whole life into you [. . .]. What have you ever done for me? [. . .] You make life shit for everyone' (Feehily, 2006, pp. 41–2). She also tells Sarah that Neil 'was finished when I met him. Booted from the Beeb for drinking and erratic behaviour. [. . .] I saved him' (p. 77).

Charles Spencer (2006) describes *O Go My Man* with its 'media folk in hip, tiger-economy Dublin' as 'a cross between Patrick Marber's *Closer* and a frothy piece of chick-lit' (apart from Neil, Zoë, Sarah, Ian and Maggie, there are various other characters from Ireland's media and art scenes).[8] In contrast, the war correspondent stories in *The Vertical*

Hour and *The Witness* are only played out between three main characters (with two additional minor student characters in the two short
lecture-like scenes, set in Nadia's office, which frame *The Vertical Hour*),
but the more intimate (and economical) cast does not necessarily result
in more complex war correspondent figures. Nadia, whom Ben Brantley
calls a 'former Christiane Amanpour-style television reporter' (2006),
is portrayed as an ambitious, single-minded careerist, who announces,
'I spend a lot of time in war zones – in Bosnia, in Serbia. In many ways
I can only say I prefer it there' (Hare, 2008, p. 11). Her pronouncements alternate between (partly trite) nostalgia, as when she recalls
her time in Sarajevo – 'Most nights I was looped, all of us were. [. . .]
Looped means drunk. [. . . Y]ou had relationships' (pp. 43–4) – and
vehement diatribes – 'Endless days [. . .] watching people die for no
purpose [. . .]. The first great war in Europe since 1945 and nobody's
able even to remember which country is which' (pp. 44–5).

War photography

Franzmann's acerbic portrayal of celebrated war photographer Joseph
is in no way inferior to the problematic dramatizations of Neil and
Nadia, but it is even heightened at times, whether regarding Joseph's
vices (whisky and drugs), his cynicism ('Bloody Belgians. It was all their
fault in the first place, wasn't it? [. . . C]olonising Rwanda and all that,
bloody bastards. Good chocolate though'; Franzmann, 2012, p. 51), the
way he abandoned his late wife Meg, or his despicable behaviour towards
his daughter and his ultimate moral failure as a witness of the Rwandan
atrocities. Similar to his assessment of Neil, Billington (2012) calls Joseph
an 'antihero' and 'cannot fault the performance of Danny Webb, who
does everything possible to humanise Joseph'. Not surprisingly, and
completing the prototypical sketch of the war correspondent character,
both Neil and Joseph suffer from nightmares. Neil is overheard shouting
'Kewa roota' ('blood rivers'; Feehily, 2006, p. 49) by his daughter and
caught screaming at his reflection in the mirror by Sarah with 'eyes wild
in [his] head' (p. 87). Finally, during his hostile-environment training,
his instructor tells him, 'You're cracking. You've cracked' (p. 94). Simon,
the mysterious third character in *The Witness* who arrives in the Potter
household like a Pinteresque outsider and claims to be Alex's brother,
who also survived the massacre in the Rwandan church, asks Joseph,
'[w]hen you sleep, what do you dream? [. . .] I hear you, shouting in
the night' (Franzmann, 2012, pp. 77–8).

According to Korte, 'role images [. . .] and ethical considerations [. . .]
preoccupied war journalists since the 19th century' (2009, p. 62), and

these aspects also dominate war journalists' memoirs, which are further marked by correspondents' own awareness of how their profession and its iconic figures (for example, Robert Capa) are represented in film and fiction. While war correspondents' perceptions of their profession and ethical dilemmas are addressed in all three plays under consideration, they are mainly contained within the private sphere, whereby the differentiation between public and private space(s) is acknowledged as blurry, but nonetheless still valid. The ethical dilemmas to be negotiated in the plays range from the privileged position of war journalists (Ian calls Neil an 'atrocity tourist'; Feehily, 2006, p. 47),[9] the debauched media world and war correspondents' public role and national loyalty (as somebody in favour of the 'invasion'/'liberation' of Iraq, Nadia is asked to brief the President; Hare, 2008, p. 30) to the thorny notions of witnessing and profit and publicity. As Spencer asks, are 'those who travel the world in search of shots of human misery [. . .] important witnesses to man's inhumanity to man, or are their methods and motivation more murky?' (2012).

According to Barbie Zelizer, when 'war is reduced to a photograph [. . .] journalism's images become a tool for interpreting the wars in ways consonant with long-standing understandings about how war is supposed to be waged' (2004, p. 115). But whereas Neil is shown flippantly discussing the editing of his Darfur film material ('we can go to the wide shot there – It's the burnt corpse of a child – but you can't tell what it is in the wide. Well yes – if you freeze-frame but even then it looks like a black blob – [. . .] it'll lose impact if we sanitise the thing completely [. . .]. Shots of massacred children are unacceptable but a few judicious cuts – sorted'; Feehily, 2006, pp. 27–8), Joseph's editing has tragic public and private repercussions and – as a gradually disclosed secret – functions as a structural device throughout *The Witness*, whose title is revealed as a *double entendre* in the following scene, when Alice asks Joseph why his award-winning photo of her rescue has been cropped:

Alex You left Simon to die and then you edited him out, cropped him like one of your fucking pictures. [. . .]

Simon He came into the church. [. . .] He saw our mother and you asleep by her side. He picked you up and he moved you from her. He waited for you to begin to cry [. . .]. He watched you crawl towards her body and when your hand reached hers, he took his photograph. [. . .]

Joseph I wanted people to take notice of it. [. . .] I've seen the worst side of humanity [. . .]. And ruined any hope of peace in my own mind so [. . .] I bore witness. [. . .] And I saved you. [. . .]

Simon   You saw me watching you. That is why you did not take me
as well. [. . . H]e saw the man he truly is. [. . . A]nd it was
unbearable for him.

(Franzmann, 2012, pp. 80, 88, 91–3)[10]

In both *O Go My Man* and *The Witness*, photos (and by extension the
figure of the photographer and exhibition spaces) are employed symbolically for the exploration of different functions of photography.
Apart from its association with realism – which all three plays adhere
to – photography is 'thought to work through a twinning of denota-
tive and connotative force, by which the ability to depict the world
as "it is" [. . .] is matched with a symbolic power [. . .] that helps us
recognize the image as consonant with broader understandings of the
world' (Zelizer, 2004, p. 117). Although in journalism denotation and
the 'truth value' of the photo are generally privileged over connotation
(p. 117), both forces are important, which is also reflected in the plays'
use of the medium. On the one hand, and within a private context,
photos are used to critically examine family and memory constructions and to link characters to a specific place, as in the case of Neil,
Zoë and Maggie's family photos, Ian's photos of Sarah and Joseph's
photos of weddings and Alex's rescue. On the other hand, and within
the war journalists' professional context, photos are allegedly used to
'break through the atrocity fatigue' (Feehily, 2006, p. 36), which is also
how Neil justifies his use of cruel images. Neil and Joseph both seem
to follow Susan Sontag's call for 'some kind of reaction' (qtd. in Korte,
2009, p. 141) which, especially in regard to Joseph's adoption of Alex,
clearly goes beyond mere witnessing. Yet in the case of Joseph and Ian
their use of photography is exposed as an unsavoury combination of
highly immoral, petty motives and their profession as despicably hypocritical. Joseph comes across as a ruthless 'manipulator of the historical
evidence' (Billington, 2012) who organizes a self-serving exhibition of
his work, while Ian publicly exhibits intimate photos of Sarah out of
revenge for her betrayal and without her permission.[11]

The private lives of war correspondents

In his analysis of *Troilus and Cressida*, Rolf Soellner observes that,

as if glimpses we get of the war action were not disillusioning enough
by themselves, we see Thersites scouting the battlefield like an ubiq-
uitous war correspondent, giving us sordid inside information not

intended for the homefront [. . .]. The war story is intertwined with the love plot, and the juxtaposition makes some ironic points about the congruity of the two most absorbing occupations of man. (1972, p. 207)

While *O Go My Man*, *The Vertical Hour* and *The Witness* also employ this same mix of genres, in contrast to one of the earliest war correspondents in British drama, the war correspondent and photographer protagonists in the three plays are hardly shown in action (apart from Feehily's very short opening scene showing Neil calling his editor from Sudan). The overall focus on their private life – poignantly captured in the title *O Go My Man*, 'an anagram of "Monogamy"' (Feehily, 2006, p. 27) – and the settings of the plays in Dublin, Shropshire and Hampstead Heath, respectively, preclude the war journalist characters from 'performing' their professional identities. According to Korte, '[t]elevision in particular encourages correspondents to playact' (2009, p. 24) and Martin Bell calls television news 'a theatrical medium' with a 'thespian character' (qtd. in Korte, 2009, p. 24). In turn, this affects the role of the audience who, when it is 'able to witness the act of witnessing as it takes place between characters', can 'become implicated [. . .] because it is receiving information about what takes place between the teller and the listener during the testimony encounter' (Malpede, 2000, p. 132). Since there is no direct witnessing scene in the three plays, however, 'the audience is let off the hook' and remain mere spectators (p. 132). Instead of a critique of war correspondents' 'basic cultural function of presenting and explaining war(s)' (Korte, 2009, p. 8) and their role as witnesses, the plays foreground the journalists' private problems, and the presumable subplots – including the dramatization of sexual politics in all three plays, the father–daughter relations in *O Go My Man* and *The Witness* and the father-son conflict in *The Vertical Hour* – assume centre stage. This not only obscures a wider perspective on global (media) ethics, but it also prevents a closer examination of war correspondents' professional values and coping mechanisms, as manifested in Tumber's questions above.

Neil's affair with actress Sarah most clearly illustrates the shift from public to private – 'We've both been postponing life', Sarah says, '[y]ou've had a front seat at other people's conflicts. Time to face your own' (Feehily, 2006, p. 88) – and from the world of war reporting and witnessing to the world of metatheatre, signalled by references to dramatic intertexts (for example, *Cymbeline*, *Henry V*, the Globe, *The Seagull*, *Woyzeck*, Kevin Spacey and Max Bygraves). The importance and critique of performance is emphasized through having an actress protagonist, Sarah, with her 'framed photograph of [herself] at Sarah Bernhardt's grave' (p. 52) and her pitiful descent from playing *Juno and the Paycock* at The Garrick to rapping as the Cheshire Cat in a furry cat costume in a hip-hop musical of *Alice in Wonderland* (the inset play in *O Go My Man*); through Nadia's describing her experiences in the White House as 'theatre' (Hare, 2008, p. 30); and through Philip's warning that his father's charm and sympathy is nothing more than 'an act. [. . . A] mask' (p. 59).

All three plays are firmly located in today's media- and celebrity-saturated culture, underscored by numerous references to high culture in *The Vertical Hour* (among them, William Blake, Sigmund Freud and William Shakespeare) and to high and popular culture and brand names in *O Go My Man* and *The Witness* (for example, the Wombles, *Born Free*, *Alice in Wonderland*, Sekonda watches, *Friends*, Hovis, Jon Snow, Stella McCartney, Hockney, Bang & Olufsen, *Blade Runner* and Mint Magnum), which, in the plays' war correspondents' view, exemplify the material and spiritual ills of our times. As Nadia recounts, 'fascination with handbags [. . .]. Kids with four-by-fours and private trust funds, coming in Gucci jeans and designer T-shirts saying, "Oh it's a matter of principle. I won't take class with Nadia Blye"' (Hare, 2008, pp. 45, 88). Together with the use of music and references to individual songs and artists (for example, Edith Piaf, Leonard Cohen, Celine Dion and Kanye West), these are also employed to delineate the gap between age groups and generations. But even Maggie and Alex do not function as redeeming characters leading the way into a brighter future; rather, they are portrayed as being as insensitive and spoilt as Nadia's ignorant Ivy League students.

Occasionally, passages can be read as referencing other war correspondent plays, yet there is no interrogation of the strategies and mechanisms of the dramatic representation of war reporting. The incorporation of popular songs and Ian's 'I couldn't live without my Hasselblad' (Feehily, 2006, p. 26) are reminiscent of Stoppard's use of music in *Night and Day* and its correspondents' constant gushing about their camera equipment. There are also formal borrowings. While *The Vertical Hour* and *The Witness* follow *Night and Day* in their more conventional two-act structure, the episodic *O Go My Man* (comprised of 20 scenes and thereby formally mirroring one of its main intertexts, *Alice's Adventures in Wonderland*) not only emulates Stoppard's comic take on three Western journalists in postcolonial Africa, but in its use of satire it also references one of the *ur*-texts of the fictional representation of war correspondents, Evelyn Waugh's *Scoop* (1938).

Billington (2012) has stressed Feehily's 'effortless mix of the real and the surreal', which is mainly created through a 'double Alice': the *Alice* musical-within-the-play and a character called Alice who, as a kind of 'immigrant everywoman' (in the roles of waitress, chambermaid, bag lady, patient and cleaner), interrupts the main characters' 'hedonistic craziness'. Spencer sees *O Go My Man*'s evocation of Darfur 'as a classic case of a dramatist bumming a lift on unimaginable suffering in order to lend a solipsistic play [. . .] a spurious significance' (2006). This critique may fall somewhat short, however, given Feehily's plays' inbuilt self-critique – which is also apparent in her interrogation of humanitarian aid workers in *Bang Bang Bang* (2011) – and her use of epic devices such as Alice as the commentator or the metaphotographic discourse in *Bang Bang Bang*. Within the group of self-obsessed characters in *The Witness*, Simon, like Alice, functions as the corrective moral voice. But, in contrast to Feehily's style, which Spencer has described as veering 'disconcertingly between bruising naturalism and flights of dotty surrealism' (2006), Franzmann draws on a similar mixture of styles and dramatic devices as Tanika Gupta in *Sanctuary* (2002), including the morality play, melodrama, the revenge play, symbolism and spatial metaphors.[12] While in *Sanctuary*, the pastoral image of an idyllic garden is gradually revealed to be the scene of revenge and brutal murder, in *The Witness*, the deceptive cosiness and sophisticated liberalism of Joseph and Alex's home in Hampstead Heath, which provides the claustrophobically foreboding setting throughout the play, is dismantled and turns into a site of betrayal, despair and moral hopelessness. Thompson has criticized Franzmann's use 'of the stock devices of melodrama – guilty secrets, the return of the past, an ambiguous stranger', on the grounds that these 'tricks need careful handling if not to appear mechanical or soapy. When yet another bitty short scene finishes on a climactic cliff-hanger and a blackout, without delving into the conflict just raised, it's clear that the soap-opera trap is one Franzmann hasn't avoided' (2012). Unlike *Sanctuary*'s dramatic finale, however, Franzmann avoids any neat closure of her problematization of the ethics of judgement. While, on the one hand, Joseph's story can evoke particular 'ethical attention' in the sense that Franzmann 'gives priority to the perception of particular people and situations over abstract rules' (Kearney and Williams, 1996, p. 31), on the other hand, Simon's counter-narrative can be seen serving an 'ethical-critical purpose' as an alternative story 'to the official story' that 'brush[es] history against the grain' (p. 40).

The plays decry Western liberalism's hypocritical self-righteousness and its decadent indifference, personified in the figure of the war correspondent and their followers and companions (editors, publishers, broadcasters and so on). But the dramatic exposure of the correspondents' professional ambiguity is coupled with a thematic and formal despair regarding the appropriate representation (in the theatre and in war reporting) of seemingly unsolvable global problems, such as endless wars, human trafficking, economic exploitation and ecological decline. These humanitarian disasters resist representation to the extent that, as Margot Norris has shown in connection with war literature, even 'in sincere and compassionate poetic and narrative strategies for representing mass killing, we find that omissions, repressions, disavowals, and displacements may inadvertently produce verbal or discursive violence to suffering populations' (2000, p. 5). Not surprisingly, neither Feehily's satirical treatment of geopolitics, which has been called a 'shambolic romcom' and an 'inchoate muddle' (Spencer, 2006), nor Franzmann's 'moral thriller' format (Spencer, 2012) – with Simon as the one character of integrity, 'every white liberal's dream of an educated young African', but nonetheless, 'with that CV [. . .] also a theatrical lead weight?' (Thompson, 2012) – seem to be sufficient responses to this ethical and representational deadlock.

As for Hare, who has not only worked as an occasional journalist himself, but whose oeuvre includes more than one journalism play – notably *A Map of the World* (1982) and *Pravda*, written with Howard Brenton (1985) – in *The Vertical Hour* he retreated to the verbal duel format (complete with a dark secret from Oliver's past) which can come across as polemical and didactic. Indeed, Brantley (2006) has referred to the play as a 'soggy consideration of the Anglo-American culture divide', embodied by Nadia's American 'can-do pragmatism' and Oliver's British 'detachment and indirection'. As Kara Reilly has argued, in comparison to Hare's 'more historiographical play *Stuff Happens*, [. . .] *The Vertical Hour* works on an intimate level to explore the personal as political' (2007, p. 673). This goes so far that, as soon as central ethical issues are at stake – as when Oliver says, 'I assume it wasn't you who said, [...] "Just bomb and hope for the best. [. . .] Sanction torture. [. . .] It doesn't matter if tens of thousands of people are killed"' (Hare, 2008, p. 90) – the personal takes over, involving at this point a clichéd representation of war reporters to boot. Thus Nadia recounts, 'I did have a relationship. [. . . A] hard-line reporter. [. . .] A professional. [. . .] Dodging bullets. [. . .] Heroic. [. . .] And in the evening ... he likes to get drunk' (p. 91).

In view of the observation that even war journalists' notion of 'a typical war correspondent has not only been shaped by the real role models [. . .] and their autobiographical texts, but also by fictional rep-resentations' (Korte, 2009, p. 65), their stereotypical representation in drama may not be surprising. To different degrees, all three plays thrive on Martin Bell's observation that '[w]ar reporting is like a habit and the more dangerous the war, the harder it is to break' (qtd. in Tumber, 2006, p. 439) without the aid of a reflection on – in the worst case lethal – risks involved, given that between 1995 and 2004, '341 journalists were killed while carrying out their work [. . .], only 68 journalists (20 per cent) died in crossfire, while 247 (72 per cent) were murdered, often in reprisal for their reporting' (Tumber, 2006, p. 441).

What is equally striking is the plays' privileging of ethical dilemmas engendered by the medium of photography, which may be accounted for by photography's 'specific attributes – its materiality, ease of access, frozen capture of time, an affective and often *gestalt*-driven view of the world that is thought to bypass the intellect and communicate directly with the emotions' (Zelizer, 2004, p. 117). The visual is foregrounded to the disadvantage of other pressing ethical concerns, including the 'qualified privilege of war correspondents not to be compelled to testify in war crimes proceedings' following *The Washington Post's* Jonathan Randal's challenging the subpoena 'to testify before the International Criminal Tribunal for the Former Yugoslavia' (Spellman, 2005, p. 123); the representation of non-Western people, including a discussion of the lack of images showing 'the effect of one's own war on civilians of the other side' (Zelizer, 2004, p. 116); the 'geographies of foreign correspond-ence' and 'journalism's unique productions of imperial vision' (Farish, 2001, p. 274), as addressed, for example, in *Night and Day*.

Even within the spectrum of controversial issues surrounding (war) photography, ethical concerns such as the neglect of 'conflicts that missed being seen almost totally – wars in East Timor, Sudan, Somalia, Liberia, and Zaire' (Zelizer, 2004, p. 116) or those where, as Allan Thompson has argued in connection with the Rwandan genocide, 'the lack of international media [. . .] contributed to the behaviour of the perpetrators [. . .] who were encouraged by the world's apathy and acted with impunity' (2007, p. 3), are disregarded in the three plays under examination (notwithstanding Neil's assignment in Darfur). In view of Kevin Williams's sobering conclusion entitled 'The Death of the Foreign Correspondent?', which shows that 'by and large the repre-sentation of world events [. . .] has remained constant in the post-war period, suiting the political and economic interests and aspirations of a small number of actors' despite 'the emergence of new media technol-ogy', that familiar 'stereotypes and a narrow geographical spread are found in the blogosphere' and that 'the internet still shows signs of being anchored to a national dimension' (2011, pp. 165–6), it may be preposterous to expect the plays' fictional war correspondents to report any differently. But perhaps future dramatizations of the world of war reporting might go beyond the private sphere of its actors and take to heart Nadia's impassioned speech about her professional calling – 'So much time spent reading [. . .] medieval literature, doing trigonometry, when meanwhile all the important things were being ignored. [. . . W]hy so many people live in such poverty. And so few live well. And what can we do about it? These huge facts, these enormous facts not up for study. Ignored. You'd think that to be alive would mean to want to find out' (Hare, 2008, p. 21).

Notes

1. For a history of journalism ethics see Ward (2004).
2. Films include *État de Siège* (Costa-Gavras, 1972), *Professione: reporter / The Passenger* (Michelangelo Antonioni, 1975), *Missing* (Costa-Gavras, 1982), *The Year of Living Dangerously* (Peter Weir, 1982), *Under Fire* (Roger Spottiswoode, 1983), *The Killing Fields* (Roland Joffé, 1984), *Salvador* (Oliver Stone, 1986), *War Photographer* (Christian Frei, 2001), *Live from Baghdad* (Mick Jackson, 2002), *Control Room* (Jehane Noujaim, 2004), *A Mighty Heart* (Michael Winterbottom, 2007), *The Hunting Party* (Richard Shephard, 2007) and *War and Truth* (Michael Samstag, 2007). For a compilation of movie and television clips, see Joe Saltzman and Lee Warner's two-DVD set *The Image of the War Correspondent in Movies and Television 1931–2007* (2008). See also Korte, 2009, pp. 175ff.
3. Thanks are due to Carl Forsman of New York's The Keen Company for putting me in touch with David Hay, and to David Hay himself for kindly sending me his unpublished play *The Maddening Truth*.
4. Apparently, a biopic of the late Marie Colvin is already in preparation (Child, 2012). For an analysis of 'KIA (Killed In Action) journalists', see Carlson (2006).
5. Although Stoppard did not work as a war correspondent, he did make a living as a journalist at Bristol's *Western Daily Press* and the *Bristol Evening World* in the 1950s and his ambition 'was to be lying on the floor of an African airport while machine-gun bullets zoomed over my typewriter' (Delaney, 1994, p. 1). Irish playwright William Denis Johnston temporarily worked as a war correspondent for the BBC; he recounted his experiences in his autobiography *Nine Rivers from Jordan* (1953) rather than in his dramatic work. The wartime experiences of the Russian dramatist and war correspondent Konstantin Mikhailovich Simonov influenced his fiction, plays and poetry. Emulating the real-life relationships of prominent war correspondent couples such as Cora and Stephen Crane, Martha Gellhorn and Ernest Hemingway, Gerda Taro and Robert Capa and Clare Hollingworth and Geoffrey Hoare, one variant of war journalist fiction written by war journalists links the genres of

war (correspondent) novel/memoir and romance (involving two war correspondents or a war journalist and a war photographer) and includes Wendell Steavenson's *Stories I Stole* (2004), Alan Furst's *The Foreign Correspondent* (2006), Tatjana Soli's *The Lotus Eaters* (2011) and Janine Di Giovanni's *Ghosts By Daylight: A Memoir of War and Love* (2012).

6. The playscript of *O Go My Man* includes an interview Feehily conducted with the Irish correspondent and presenter Paul Cunningham about his experiences in Darfur (Feehily, 2006, pp. 105–10).

7. Nadia provides a clue to the play's title when she notes, in 'combat medicine, there's this moment – after a disaster, after a shooting – there's this moment, the vertical hour, when you can actually be of some use' (Hare, 2008, p. 73).

8. Given the parallels between *O Go My Man* and *Closer*, Billington (2006) also advises 'imagin[ing] *Closer* and a touch of Lewis Carroll' in his review of *O Go My Man*.

9. As Cunningham explains, 'Journalists and aid workers are extremely privileged – if you don't like it, you can go home. Rattle a gin and tonic in a nice glass and drink your horror away [. . .]. [T]here is an impact, and [. . .] counselling is available on return. However, most correspondents don't usually want to talk to medical professionals afterwards. They just try to forget it' (qtd. in Feehily, 2006, p. 106). Gratifications also include 'a privileged view of history in the making' and 'the opportunity of extreme forms of travel' (Korte, 2009, p. 59).

10. According to Allan Thompson, a video by the British journalist Nick Hughes, who recorded the killing of two women in Kigali in April 1994 from a nearby building, is 'one of the only times a killing is recorded by the media' (2007, p. 1).

11. In this respect, Feehily's juxtaposition of Neil's Darfur photos and Sarah's reaction upon realizing that Ian has used their private photos allows her to reveal an almost obscene gap in perception: 'Fucking vulturism. [. . .] Pictures of me in my underwear? [. . .] What kind of sick pathetic sadso are you? [. . .] You don't have permission to expose me like this' (Feehily, 2006, p. 99).

12. Philip Gourevitch's *We Wish to Inform You That Tomorrow We Will Be Killed with Our Families: Stories from Rwanda* (2002) also appears as an intertext in both *The Witness* and *Sanctuary*.

Works cited

Allan, S. and B. Zelizer (eds) (2004) *Reporting War: Journalism in War Time* (London and New York: Routledge).

Billington, M. (2006) 'Review of *O Go My Man*', *Guardian*, 18 January, http://www.guardian.co.uk/stage/2006/jan/18/theatre (accessed 2 December 2012).

—— (2012) 'Review of *The Witness*', *Guardian*, 11 June, http://www.guardian.co.uk/stage/2012/jun/11/witness-review (accessed 1 December 2012).

Brantley, B. (2006) 'Battle Zones in Hare Country', *New York Times*, 1 December, http://theater.nytimes.com/2006/12/01/theater/reviews/01hour.html?pagewanted=all&_r=0 (accessed 2 December 2012).

Carlson, M. (2006) 'War Journalism and the "KIA Journalist": The Cases of David Bloom and Michael Kelly', *Critical Studies in Media Communication*, 23 (2), pp. 91–111.

Child, B. (2012) 'Charlize Theron in talks to play war reporter Marie Colvin', *Guardian*, 31 August, http://www.guardian.co.uk/film/2012/aug/31/charlize-theron-marie-colvin (accessed 3 January 2013).

Daniel, D.K. (1996) *Lou Grant: The Making of TV's Top Newspaper Drama* (Syracuse, NY: Syracuse University Press).

Delaney, P. (ed.) (1994) *Tom Stoppard in Conversation* (Ann Arbor: University of Michigan Press).

Ehrlich, M.C. (2004) *Journalism in the Movies* (Champaign: University of Illinois Press).

Farish, M. (2001) 'Modern Witnesses: Foreign Correspondents, Geopolitical Vision, and the First World War', *Transactions of the Institute of British Geographers*, 26 (3), pp. 273–87.

Feehily, S. (2006) *O Go My Man* (London: Nick Hern).

Franzmann, V. (2012) *The Witness* (London: Nick Hern).

Hare, D. (2008) *The Vertical Hour* (London: Faber and Faber).

Hickey, T.W. (2003) 'A Masochist's Teapot: Where to Put the Handle in Media Ethics', *Journal of Mass Media Ethics: Exploring Questions of Media Morality*, 18 (1), pp. 44–67.

Kearney, R. and J. Williams (1996) 'Narrative and Ethics', *Proceedings of the Aristotelian Society*, Supplementary Volume 70, pp. 29–45 and 47–61.

Korte, B. (2009) *Represented Reporters: Images of War Correspondents in Memoirs and Fiction* (Bielefeld: Transcript Verlag).

Malpede, K. (2000) 'Theatre of Witness: Passage into a New Millennium' in R. Mock (ed.) *Performing Processes: Creating Live Performance* (Bristol: Intellect), pp. 122–38.

Matheson, D. and S. Allan (2009) *Digital War Reporting* (Cambridge: Polity Press).

Norris, M. (2000) *Writing War in the Twentieth Century* (Charlottesville: University Press of Virginia).

Reilly, K. (2007) 'Review of *The Vertical Hour*', *Theatre Journal*, 59 (4), pp. 673–4.

Roberts, P. (1999) *The Royal Court Theatre and the Modern Stage* (Cambridge: Cambridge University Press).

Saltzman, J. and L. Warner (2008) *The Image of the War Correspondent in Movies and Television 1931–2007* (IJPC Associates).

Soellner, R. (1972) *Shakespeare's Patterns of Self-Knowledge* (Columbus: Ohio State University Press).

Spellman, R.L. (2005) 'Journalist or Witness? Reporters and War Crimes Tribunals', *Gazette: The International Journal for Communication Studies*, 67 (2), pp. 123–39.

Spencer, C. (2006) 'Casualties of Love and War', *Telegraph*, 19 January, http://www.telegraph.co.uk/culture/theatre/drama/3649467/Casualties-of-love-and-war.html (accessed 2 December 2012).

—— (2012) 'Review of *The Witness*', *Telegraph*, 11 June, http://www.telegraph.co.uk/culture/theatre/theatre-reviews/9324908/The-Witness-Royal-Court-Theatre-Upstairs-review.html (accessed 2 December 2012).

Stoppard, T. (1999) *Plays Five (Arcadia, The Real Thing, Night and Day, Indian Ink, Hapgood)* (London: Faber).

Thompson, A. (ed.) (2007) *The Media and the Rwanda Genocide* (London: Pluto Press).

Thompson, W. (2012) 'Leigh Party Explodes, Genocide Girl Drops Out: UK Stage', *Bloomberg.com*, 18 June, http://www.bloomberg.com/news/2012-06-17/leigh-party-explodes-genocide-girl-drops-out-u-k-stage.html (accessed 1 December 2012).

Tumber, H. (2006) 'The Fear of Living Dangerously: Journalists Who Report on Conflict', *International Relations*, 20 (4), pp. 439–51.

Vanacker, B. and J. Breslin (2006) 'Ethics of Care: More than Just Another Tool to Bash the Media?', *Journal of Mass Media Ethics: Exploring Questions of Media Morality*, 21 (2–3), pp. 196–214.

Ward, S.J.A. (2004) *The Invention of Journalism Ethics: The Path to Objectivity and Beyond* (Montreal: McGill-Queen's University Press).

Williams, K. (1992) 'Something More Important than the Truth: Ethical Issues in War Reporting' in A. Belsey and R.F. Chadwick (eds) *Ethical Issues in Journalism and the Media* (London: Routledge), pp. 154–70.

—— (2011) *International Journalism* (London: Sage).

Zelizer, B. (2004) 'When War Is Reduced to a Photograph' in S. Allan and B. Zelizer (eds) *Reporting War: Journalism in Wartime* (London and New York: Routledge), pp. 115–35.

11
Kicking Tots and Revolutionary Trots: The English Stage Company Young People's Theatre Scheme 1969–70

Graham Saunders

The Royal Court and the 1968 generation

Long-established theatres like to accrue mythologies about themselves that can in time become a set of ethics that are consciously subscribed to. Ever since its first season in 1956, the English Stage Company (ESC) has considered itself to be a radical theatre on the basis of its promotion of work that broke away from existing norms as well as, in a wider context, its presenting itself as a theatre of social conscience, with a crusading and oppositional stance. George Devine, its first artistic director, put ethics at the forefront of the theatre's identity in an often-quoted piece of advice:

> You should choose your theatre like you choose a religion. Make sure you don't get into the wrong temple. For me the theatre is really a religion or way of life. You must decide what you feel the world is about and what you want to say about it, so that everything in the theatre you work in is saying the same thing. [. . .] A theatre must have a recognizable attitude. (qtd. in Browne, 1975, p. 10)

This comparison to a religious creed defined the early years of the theatre through a series of commandments laid down by Devine that have endured to this day, where phrases such as 'a writer's theatre' and 'the right to fail' have almost become enshrined as lore. From its staging of oppositional voices starting with John Osborne's *Look Back in Anger* (1956), to the active stance it took against theatre censorship in the 1960s by producing Edward Bond's *Saved* (1965) and *Early Morning* (1968), to its resistance against the effects of Thatcherism in work such as Caryl Churchill's *Top Girls* (1982) and Louise Page's *Falkland Sound/Voces de Malvinas* (1983), the ESC pursued and continues to see itself as a theatre aligned to ethical principles of conduct.

Periodically, however, this ethical reputation has been questioned. John McGrath, for example, contends in *A Good Night Out* that the Royal Court has long been a bourgeois theatre masquerading as a radical one (1981, pp. 7–15), while more recently fellow playwright David Greig notes the same masquerade played out in the building's look after refurbishment in 2000. To Greig, the 'distressed, unfinished look' of exposed brickwork, and presumably also the appearance of bullet holes in the theatre's logo situated in the downstairs bar, are nothing more than a stylish but deceptive façade, giving the impression of a theatre in the midst of a revolution when in fact 'deep down everything is the same' (2008, p. 212). This appearance of radicalism masking a more conservative set of artistic values has in fact been a long-running criticism of the ESC, going back as early as its tenth-anniversary year. Indeed, in 1966, Hilary Spurling the critic of *The Spectator*, wrote a stinging article entitled 'Angry Middle Age' in which she lambasted the theatre for being 'touchy, lugubrious, embattled, inflexible [and] middle aged in outlook if not in years' (qtd. in Roberts, 1999, p. 114). While one can debate the fairness of Spurling's criticisms, in one area at least the ESC's social conservatism came to the fore – namely the defensive way in which the company responded to a generation of new writers and practitioners who were about to come of age at this time.

By 1968, the whole theatre and performance landscape was rapidly undergoing change. This included the proliferation of Arts Labs promoting interdisciplinary and multimedia work, the formation of pub and lunchtime theatres in major cities producing plays by new writers, as well as the creation of new touring companies such as Portable Theatre and General Will. While on the surface this new generation seemed to broadly share the same social and political ethics that underpinned the ESC's artistic policy, Howard Brenton talks of 'a generational and professional dust up between us and them, with them saying you are not going to get your hands on our theatre' (qtd. in Rees, 1992, p. 204). The reason for this came down to a clash based around the key ethical issue of the political and social function of art. While both parties saw theatre as an initiator of change, the means by which this could be achieved became the source of contention. The ESC was and remains to this day a playwright's theatre, and while Brenton, together with David Edgar and David Hare, belonged to this tradition, many of their contemporaries' work was collaborative and often non-text based. More significant even was their ethos of using performance to address specific communities directly, whether it was the working-class audiences that touring groups such as Portable and Red Ladder targeted, or the inner-city communities that Ed Berman's Interaction worked with. Many of these groups deliberately set out to establish contact with these communities directly; by contrast, the ESC was building based, metropolitan and, unlike Joan Littlewood's neighbouring Stratford East Theatre, showed no interest in wanting to build up relationships with its immediate local community. In the late 1960s, the ESC gave the impression of haughty detachment from both the excitement and turbulence of the times. With the notable exception of William Gaskill's attempt to acknowledge and welcome alternative theatre culture into the building for the 1970 Come Together Festival, between 1969 and 1972 an entire generation was effectively sidelined or excluded from a theatre that logically should have been their natural home.[1]

The Young People's Theatre Scheme

However, in one area, namely the ESC's work for young people, practitioners from the counterculture managed to surreptitiously gain a foothold within the theatre's hierarchy and introduce some of these new ideas. From the late 1960s to the mid-1980s it is arguable that the ESC's work with young people best demonstrated Devine's original ethical conception for the theatre. While this work subjected the ESC to widespread hostility in the media and brought the theatre into conflict with its major funder, the Arts Council of Great Britain, it provided a salutary reminder of the theatre's founding principles. This chapter concentrates on three examples of work that took place between 1969 and 1970 which saw these new ethical principles put into action: the workshops entitled 'Violence in the Theatre' that formed part of the ESC's 1969 Edward Bond season, the student-devised 'Revolution' season that same year, and an updated revival in 1970 of Ann Jellicoe's *The Sport of My Mad Mother* (1958).

The ESC's involvement with young people began in 1960 as an informal arrangement initiated by George Devine. In 1966, under his successor William Gaskill, a Young People's Theatre Scheme (YPTS) was reestablished on a firmer basis and funded by a small supplementary grant of £5000 by the Arts Council (Browne, 1975, p. 86). Gaskill's appointment of Jane Howell to run the Young People's Theatre was to be a significant decision. Howell, one of the ESC's associate directors at the time, represented a break from the generation associated with the 'golden age' of the Royal Court. Howell's assistant, Pam Brighton, who took over at the beginning of 1970, was even more directly involved in the new theatre counterculture through her previous association with the theatre collective Brighton Combination, whose work involved a number of community initiatives. Together, Howell and Brighton revitalized the Schools Scheme, not only producing revivals of landmark Royal Court plays such as *Roots* (1959) and *Look Back in Anger*, but inviting visiting companies such as the Bread and Puppet Theatre from New York. Many of these productions were preceded by lectures and workshops; other innovations included the introduction of free student cards that enabled tickets to be bought at the special price of 5 shillings a seat. Some of the material degree of Howell's success can be assessed in Terry Browne's history of the ESC, which cites a figure of 11,000 students attending productions two years after the inauguration of the Schools Scheme (1975, p. 86).[2]

The 'Violence in the Theatre' workshops

January 1969 saw the ESC's Edward Bond season. This was an important commemorative event to mark the role the company had played in ending the Lord Chamberlain's powers as theatre censor and finally allowing audiences the opportunity to see *Saved*, *Early Morning* and *Narrow Road to the Deep North* (1968) in full productions. Schools also attended special matinee performances on 20, 24 and 27 March that included a series of workshops for the students. These took place in the morning and were entitled 'Violence in the Theatre'. The workshops involved cast members from the Bond plays and director William Gaskill in a series of scenes from *Agamemnon*, *Macbeth* (c.1603), *Julius Caesar* (c.1599), *Suddenly Last Summer* (1958) and *Entertaining Mr Sloane* (1964), as well as Bond's *Early Morning* and *Saved*.

In a letter to teachers, Howell pointed out that the Bond plays contained violent scenes more suited to older students, but justified their inclusion by pointing out that 'in none of them is violence glamourised nor the morality facile – which is not true of the daily television serials to which [the children] are continually subjected' (1969a). However, when Mary Gordon, a school inspector, attended one of the workshops her reaction was somewhat different. In her report, Gordon mentions that in excerpts from *Early Morning* and *Entertaining Mr Sloane* students witnessed a man 'kicked in the groin, until he died', after which the actors issued an invitation 'for two boys to go on stage where they were shown the secrets of kicking each other in the groin and simulating pain' (1969). For Gordon, 'much of the dialogue and action [. . . in the Edward Bond extracts was] not only coarse and profane but thoroughly degrading' (1969). Her concluding paragraph not only rejects any claims to educational merit, but clearly aligns itself with the values of the recently ousted Lord Chamberlain:

> It seems to me that whether or not Edward Bond may be considered a good or great dramatist is a matter of opinion. It is a fact that two of these plays of his now being shown to the schools were banned by the Lord Chamberlain before he was abolished. Surely it is open to question whether it is good or even morally defensible to present living theatre in this form to adolescent pupils, and whether it is right for the Department [of Education] to support the Royal Court Theatre in this policy. (1969)

Gordon's report reached her superior, John Allen, at the Department of Education, who in turn passed on her criticisms to the Arts Council's Drama Department. In the financial year of 1969–70, the Schools Scheme had been granted a supplement of £3,690 in addition to the annual £89,000 grant to the ESC. With this financial support came a responsibility to investigate complaints over work by companies or artists it supported. In a letter to Arts Council Drama Officer Jean Bullwinkle, despite unchivalrously calling his colleague Mary Gordon 'tiresome and unreliable', Allen concedes 'what [Gordon] says is at least something we should be aware of' (1969). At this point no further action was taken, but in the following year events would take a course that made the Arts Council's direct intervention into the affairs of the ESC inevitable. Less than one month after Gordon's report, Howell started a summer project for schools. While the Royal Court had been visited by over twenty thousand students since the Schools Scheme had started (Howell, 1969b), she wanted to go beyond merely facilitating trips. As she explained in a draft proposal to the Arts Council in support of the project, it would 'encourage an appreciation and development of understanding of theatre' (qtd. in Capon, 1969), an aim that shares close affinities with Aristotelian ethics, which Nicholas Ridout defines as geared towards 'the improvement of your character and the fulfilment of its potential' (2009, p. 3).

'Revolution'

Howell took inspiration from an earlier project she had undertaken with the Young People's Theatre Scheme in 1967, where together with fellow director Philip Hedley a production had been staged of Jellicoe's *The Rising Generation* (1967), a play about the Girl Scout movement, paired with *Dance of the Teletape* (1967) by Charles Hayward. Both plays had involved six professional actors and one hundred and twenty children. The new project was to be called 'Revolution'. Howell wrote to two and a half thousand participating schools in London asking interested students to devise a series of short scenes based on what they understood by the term over the course of two weeks. The project attracted twelve groups of one hundred and forty children drawn from eleven schools in London and Hertfordshire. Once the work was underway, Howell visited work in progress to advise and encourage.

While Howell wrote that 'Revolution' was, 'concerned in developing [. . .] individual points of view [. . .] however right wing this may be!' (1969b), the choice of visits and invited speakers arranged to add stimulus to the children's improvisatory work seemed perversely designed to antagonize. Trips included visits to Harrods department store and to an exhibition on the Biafran famine in Nigeria, while speakers included representatives from the National Front Party to the Squatters' Association. The choice of topic, while undeniably current, might also have been seen as inadvisable given how it might be perceived by others. In the Britain of 1969 talk of revolution was much in the air – in 1967 three hundred students from Albert Hunt's Bradford College group had staged the 1917 Russian Revolution on the streets of Bradford, only to be overtaken by the real *événements* in Paris during May the following year; at the same time, London had witnessed mass demonstrations against the war in Vietnam, university campuses were occupied by student protestors and there were fears held in some quarters that organizations such as trades unions and schools were being infiltrated by Marxist fifth columnists.

Moral Panics and *The Sport of My Mad Mother*

'Revolution' was performed in July 1969 and passed off without incident. However, the following May both this production and the 'Violence in the Theatre' workshops back in January became the subject of a visit by two conservative MPs, Brian Batsford and Dame Irene Ward, to the Arts Council's Chairman Lord Goodman. The timing of the visit is puzzling when one bears in mind the considerable lapse of time since the two productions had been performed. Arts Council files seem to give credence to the fact that these performances were not the real reason for the meeting: in fact, the more likely cause was another current YPTS production, a rewritten version of Jellicoe's *The Sport of My Mad Mother*. Despite Jellicoe's play not being mentioned in any of the correspondence resulting from the meeting, other evidence makes it seem likely that concerns raised over these earlier productions were being used as a stalking horse by a group of Conservative MPs to undermine the whole YPTS. Following the visit, Goodman's memo to Nelson Linklater, the Arts Council's Drama Director, is worth quoting in full, for it not only clearly illustrates Goodman's own prejudices, but demonstrates all too well the mechanisms by which moral panics can be generated:

> If what they told me was true – and I could hardly believe the evidence of my ancient ears – lunatics have seized power. Apparently groups of children are invited to the Theatre to see demonstrations of violence. Appropriate children are invited on the stage to be taught how to kick each other. I have loved and admired [the Royal Court] for 100 years as a means of imparting the loftiest of thoughts of humanity clothed in the most grandiloquent language. How my conception squares with instructions in kicking I need to have explained to me in some detail by the mental defectives engaged in these activities. I was told that the children, not satisfied with kicking each other, were regaled with excerpts from *Saved* and taught to hurl a handy stone at any adjacent baby. I was also told that they were instructed in revolutionary techniques – how to provoke revolution. Now, both Mr B[latsford] and the Dame are Tories and on the right, but they are both honourable and decent folk and cannot have made all this up. If public money is really being used for these purposes something urgent – and violent and revolutionary – needs to be done and it is not only the children who should take instruction in kicking. (1970a)

Stanley Cohen was amongst the first to identify and analyse the processes behind the creation of moral panics in relation to disturbances between Mods and Rockers that originally broke out on Easter Bank Holiday in 1964 at the seaside resort of Clacton, but remained a source of widespread concern until 1967. One of the key features Cohen identifies is the use of exaggeration and distortion (1972, pp. 31–8), and it is revealing, in this light, to see how the two separate events – the 'Violence in the Theatre' workshops and the production of 'Revolution' – become conflated in Goodman's apoplectic memo. Goodman's outburst also reflects his adherence to the Aristotelian notion of the ethical function of theatre as shaping the moral development of character, yet whereas

Howell and Gaskill clearly saw 'Revolution' as helping to enable the moral development of the young, Goodman saw their work as embodying the very corruption of this ethic. Not surprisingly, Goodman's memo prompted an immediate investigation whose outcomes are interesting. Looking at 'Revolution' first, the Arts Council's Drama Officer Jean Bullwinkle concludes in her report that the 'students were not "instructed" in revolutionary techniques, but instead studied how revolution comes about, and various different aspects of revolution in its widest terms' (1970a).

In fact, 'Revolution' had been a notable success, with extra performances organized at the larger Roundhouse during August. While Browne states that 'the final product didn't interest many critics to any great extent' (1975, p. 86), this is contradicted by the amount of attention 'Revolution' attracted in the national press. Further, in the context of the two MPs' complaints, it is instructive to bear in mind the number of positive reports from several of the more conservative newspapers. While no doubt originally prompted by similar motives to that of Batsford and Ward, journalists seemed pleasantly confounded by what they actually experienced. Peter Lewis, writing in the *Daily Mail* after attending the Sunday night production at the Roundhouse, was impressed by just how sceptical the one hundred and forty performing students were about the ideals of the counterculture. Here, 'neither hippies nor demonstrating students cut much ice with them' (1969). Lewis quoted one boy from a group who, after their improvisation about sexual revolution, commented, '[w]hat we're trying to get across is that though we live in a permissive society we're not necessarily affected by it' (1969). Writing in the *Telegraph*, John Barber, who saw the production at the Royal Court, described the general tone of the students' work as 'mostly vaguely Leftish' but noted one scene where 'revolutionaries who deposed a bowler hatted government turned out themselves to be incapable of ruling – owing to their lack of education' (1969), and saw this as indicative of the students' innate suspicions towards political revolution from the Left. In contrast to Goodman's hysterical memo, both journalists considered 'Revolution' a worthwhile exercise and were left feeling 'how adult, how shrewd and how sceptical a generation they are' (Lewis, 1969) and that 'for such a release of dramatic and idealistic energy the Royal Court's enterprise and unsinkable patience was wholly justified' (Barber, 1969). The journalists had also instinctively understood the ethical nature of the 'Revolution' project, where the short scenes presented not only demonstrated the young people's understanding of the term but also allowed, through performance, a public forum to question actively these same responses.

Likewise, the Edward Bond workshops became another kind of forum that provided an opportunity for young people to explore ethical questions related to *Saved*, a play that in itself was a deliberate series of ethical problems put before an audience, without the consolation of the playwright providing the audience with firm moral guidance. The workshops enabled an *a priori* opportunity for young people to explore the ethical problems posed by *Saved* through a careful build-up of the circumstances immediately before the scene in which Pam's baby is stoned to death by the gang of youths. A more balanced picture of what took place during the 'Violence in the Theatre' workshops also emerged once the Arts Council began its investigations. Jean Bullwinkle's report points out that the stoning scene was deliberately excluded from the workshop and draws attention to the fact that even in Mary Gordon's otherwise critical report, care was taken to make mention of this. While Bullwinkle adds that the actors' demonstration of performing a stage kick was perhaps inadvisable within an educational framework, she was satisfied that it was far from being the melee of kicking that Goodman imagines took place (1970a).

As mentioned earlier, the two MPs' visit to see Lord Goodman seems odd given most politicians' concerns with issues of the moment, and it is instructive to find in the Arts Council's files a letter to Lord Goodman from another Conservative MP, Patrick Jenkin, less than a week after the visit from Batsford and Ward to voice concerns on behalf of a constituent over a current YPTS revival of Jellicoe's *The Sport of My Mad Mother* at the Royal Court Theatre Upstairs:

> The complaint is that both the set and the dialogue embody the frequent use of obscene language with such words as 'fuck', 'cunt', 'bollocks' and 'piss'. These words appear as graffiti on the walls of the stage set and, as I said, are repeated frequently throughout the dialogue. [. . . My constituent] himself has a daughter aged 13 and would be quite horrified if her school were to take her to see the play. (1970)

Jenkin also outlines his constituent's concerns over the suitability of the play for audiences in the chosen age range of thirteen to fifteen, and the lack of notification given about the bad language used in the play. Jenkin then asks Goodman what steps the Arts Council, in its capacity as a funding body, can take 'to see that its money is not spent on aiming obscene artistic productions at the young?' (1970).

For maximum effect, Jenkin also sent a copy of the letter to Jennie Lee, then Labour Minister of State for Education. As Stanley Cohen points out, moral panics cannot be created artificially; to take root successfully, they must exploit already existing, albeit latent, public disquiet on an issue (1972, pp. 31–8). Bringing together the sensitive subject of education of the young with latent anxieties over the permissive society had all the necessary combustive ingredients to potentially detonate a national moral panic. The Education Minister's Private Secretary, J.H. Eden, evidently thought so too: in his letter to the Arts Council's Drama Director, he writes that while the Minister would not wish 'to interfere with the artistic policies of individual theatres and that the question of grants to the Royal Court and to other theatres is one for the Arts Council alone', yet also points out that, '[n]evertheless – and especially as there is an "educational" element involved here – we should be grateful for your comments' (1970). The clear inference here is that when the education of the young is at stake, combined with the risk of a moral panic breaking out, normal considerations given to the Arts Council's often cited 'arm's length policy' no longer apply. The letter must also have been of concern to Lord Goodman, particularly considering the close personal and working relationship he had established with Jennie Lee, who in her former position as the first ever Minister for the Arts had responsibility for renewing the Arts Council's charter in 1967 and has often been seen as presiding over its 'Golden Age' of expansion in the mid-1960s.

Jenkin also must have known this, and the visit to Goodman from Batsford and Ward a week earlier, followed swiftly by Jenkin's letter, more than suggests that the ESC's work with young people was part of a carefully targeted attack by a group of opposition Conservative MPs in an election year. Even though Harold Wilson did not announce the 1970 election until 18 May, a week after Jenkin's letter, it was widely expected that it would take place in either the summer or autumn of 1970. In January, the Conservative Shadow Cabinet had met at Selsdon Park Hotel in Surrey to discuss policy for the forthcoming election. The meeting was seen at the time as marking an important ideological shift in thinking for the Party (Sandbrook, 2006, p. 760), and one of the main proposals – an emphasis on law and order – might speculatively have been one of the reasons for the scrutiny given to the ESC's work with young people.

More direct clues that Jenkin and his colleagues' thoughts were focused more on the forthcoming election than the moral welfare of the young can also be found in a report made for the ESC on *The Sport of My Mad Mother* by Geoffrey Hodson, who at the time was Senior

Inspector for Drama with the Inner London Education Authority (ILEA) and London County Councils (LCC). In it, he describes the graffiti that so enraged Jenkin's constituent as 'sexual references, colour and race prejudices' and notably 'impolite suggestions for the Pope and Mr Heath. [. . .] There were no diagrams' (Hodson, 1970). Whereas today the racist language would most likely give the greatest cause for concern, what really seemed to galvanize the MPs' sense of moral outrage were suspicions that the ESC were promulgating political bias to impressionable young people who in all likelihood would be voting in the next election.

The collective action by the three MPs also bears many features associated with the creation of moral panics. One of these is the involvement of what Erich Goode and Nachman Ben-Yehuda call 'activists'; these include the general public, the media and what they describe as 'political elites' (1994, p. 20), who seek to initiate and stir up widespread national disquiet targeted at a particular issue or social group. Yet *The Sport of My Mad Mother* seemed an unlikely catalyst for provoking such disquiet. Written in response to the early rise of an identifiable youth culture in the late 1950s, the play is more of an experiment in ritual than an example of social realism. The bad language referred to is absent in the original text; it is part of a number of changes that Pam Brighton made as director, including the decision to substitute the Teddy Boys of the original for skinheads, who now replaced Mods as the latest national folk-devils. Following two weeks of open rehearsal where school groups had been invited to watch and later participate in a series of short workshops and discussions, *The Sport of My Mad Mother* opened for a week's run at the Theatre Upstairs on 4 May. This was successful enough to be extended by a further week for matinee performances on 2 and 4 June.

The Royal Court and the cultural stereotyping of youth

Jean Bullwinkle was once again charged with investigating this new complaint. In her report, she not only mentions the bad language, but one other change associated with updating the play, namely when the character of Steve 'rolls and smokes a reefer' in the opening scene (1970b). This incident seems to have gone unnoticed by Jenkin's constituent, and if performed today it would be the production's attitude to smoking and the tobacco industry – the theatre programme thanks Dunhill and Players Cigarettes and Ronson for the donation of a lighter – that would create the moral panic.[3] Bullwinkle concluded that the use of bad language was appropriate within the context of the play. Yet the standards by which she comes to this conclusion are interesting:

> When I saw this production, it was attended by an audience of very tough young people, many from poor parts of London, the majority of whom had never been to a theatre before. I spoke to some of their teachers and lecturers afterwards, who said that these children would not normally think of going to the London theatre, partly because they were not attracted by what it had to offer them. But they were most enthusiastic about *The Sport of my Mad Mother*, which they said was right 'on' the wavelength of those particular children. (1970b)

This targeting of the play at a very specific socioeconomic group is also apparent in Pam Brighton's letter to schools earlier in the year publicizing the YPTS's season of work; here she describes her hope that Jellicoe's play 'will appeal to non-academic kids – hopefully the kids the play was written about' (1970). The same sentiments are also found in Hodson's report, in which he describes the production as 'an early theatre experience for the skin-head types' (1970), who together with their teachers had not been offended by the bad language. However, Hodson also reports speaking to a group of pupils and teachers from a Peckham girls' school who had been studying the published text of *The Sport of My Mad Mother*: far from it being on their 'wavelength', as Bullwinkle put it, Hodson reports that the party 'came out of the Royal Court production completely shattered; the teachers angry [while the] girls thought the acting very poor, and resented being played down to' (1970).

This raises the question of whether the YPTS, either consciously or unconsciously, were guilty of crude cultural stereotyping by offering a play about a violent London gang because it was all these 'non-academic, tough kids' – as Geoffrey Hodson calls them (1970) – would ever appreciate. This was certainly Lord Goodman's response to the Drama Director's report, which he dismisses as an unconvincing liberal defence of the ESC's work with young people:

> The argument appears to be that if they are young people who come from a rough area, then there is no harm in using words, on the footing that the worse their environment the less necessary it is for us to redeem them from it. This argument I do not find particularly attractive. [. . .] If they have had the misfortune to hear the words before from an irresponsible or uninstructed adult, those self-same

words should not have the seal of authority vested upon them by state subsidised theatres. (1970b)

Goodman's view accords with playwright Gregory Motton's recent excoriating attack on the culture of the Royal Court in his book *Helping Themselves: The Left-Wing Middle Classes in Theatre and the Arts*, which points out that, despite coming from wealthy upper middle-class backgrounds, Jellicoe and other playwrights from her generation at the ESC created their own vision of the working class in plays such as *The Sport of My Mad Mother* or John Arden's *Live Like Pigs* (1958). Motton calls such creations 'the ideologically working class' (2009, p. 105) and claims it was imposed as a cultural imprimatur through a set of perceived behavioural codes that frequently depicted these characters as violent, materialistic and ignorant. For Motton, those who genuinely came from this class were seen 'like animals in a zoo [. . .] need[ing] to be better fed' (p. 115). This argument also lay at the nub of objections from the group of pupils and teachers from Peckham that Hodson mentions in his report. While they had come to the Royal Court in search of what Goodman calls 'more elevated and edifying performances' (1970b), instead they felt condescended to and offered the kind of fare that it was assumed people from their background would most readily respond to.

Despite the YPTS being largely vindicated in Bullwinkle's report, Lord Goodman was clearly not satisfied, and in an unusual move representatives from the Arts Council's three major Panels – Literature, Drama and Music – together with the Secretary General and a representative from the Department of Education who held an interest in children's theatre were called by Goodman to a special meeting to discuss the matter (Goodman, 1970b). Although the outcome is not recorded in the files, it made the Arts Council take unprecedented action. Writing to William Gaskill on 27 May, the Secretary General not only expressed concern over recent work by the YPTS, but more surprisingly added 'that [the Arts Council] could not contemplate complete provision of subsidy for further performances of this sort' (Linklater, 1970). While the Arts Council had used the same threat to the ESC the previous year in a row over critic Hilary Spurling being denied free tickets by the theatre,[4] the decision to consider withdrawal of subsidy because of artistic policy directly contravened the Arts Council's 'arm's length policy' to those in receipt of funds. Fortunately, at a meeting of its Young People's Theatre Panel on 5 June it was declared 'that the Arts Council should avoid any action of censorship in young people's theatre work' (Linklater, 1970), and no further action was taken.

When taken together, these three case studies raise ethical concerns relating to British cultural life that still remain to this day. For example, Mary Gordon's bringing together of the terms 'morality' and 'education' in her original concerns over the ESC's 'Violence in the Theatre' workshops – or more accurately, the media's coalescence of them – produced an irrationalism associated with moral panics. In relation to this, Cohen identifies a process he terms the Disaster Analogy, where reactions to or preparations for the outbreak, or even the threat of a major public outcry, often mirror the actions taken in the event of a natural disaster. Two of these features, overreaction and an institutionalization of the perceived threat (Cohen, 1972, pp. 144–8) are exactly what took place over the ESC's work with young people. Here, documentary evidence supports the argument that the ESC's Young People's Theatre Scheme became the target of direct political intervention by the Conservative MPs Batsford, Jenkin and Ward, set out to create a moral panic in election year by discrediting the YPTS through association with the wider 'permissive society' that included Labour's recent social reforms on the abolition of theatre censorship and the legalization of abortion and homosexuality. In turn, the MPs' attack against the ESC also succeeded in panicking a normally liberal body like the Arts Council to actively consider censorship through denial of funding to one of the country's most significant new writing theatres.

Yet the moral panic that the YPTS scheme caused also had some positive outcomes. For instance, it raised the question of who should hold ultimate responsibility for safeguarding the interests of young people when theatre and education come together. Bullwinkle's investigation into the ESC's activities includes an extract from a report on the Bond workshops by Susanna Capon, who was also a member of the Arts Council's recently inaugurated Young People's Theatre Panel. Written originally as a response to John Allen's letter to Bullwinkle over Mary Gordon's concerns, while positive about the overall merit of young people seeing Edward Bond's work, Capon was dubious about the educational merit of the morning workshops, commenting that 'the linking material was completely over the audiences' heads [and] the discussion groups afterwards too fell straight into the trap of non-qualified people dealing with large moral issues' (1969). While Lord Goodman questions Capon's endorsement of children seeing extracts from the work of Bond, he is in agreement with her views on theatre practitioners taking it upon themselves to assume the role of educators: 'It is quite terrible for the Arts Council as a body to agree with forcing down the throats of young children the jejune views of the socially inexperienced who happen to have control of institutions where children forgather' (1970b). Capon's background in theatre education actually endorses Mary Gordon's original concerns over ESC staff being unqualified as formally recognized teachers, yet setting themselves up by proxy to both enact and discuss sensitive material with young people.

Conclusion

People such as Jean Howell and Pam Brighton had a radical and re-energizing effect on the ESC's work, which restored a sense of its founding ethics to the theatre at a time when it was being criticized as irrelevant and out of touch. In this way, 1969–70 could be seen as the period when the Royal Court, in at least one area of its work, followed in the spirit of Ed Berman's Interaction group in London and Bill Harpe's St George's Project in Liverpool, who both saw theatre as integral to developing young people's social and intellectual wellbeing. That someone like Brighton had managed to infiltrate an institution such as the Royal Court, notwithstanding the opposition of politicians and even the Chairman of the Arts Council, all of whom were clearly rather hostile to the ideals of alternative theatre, is a notable achievement; yet it also serves to demonstrate how peripheral the Schools Scheme was seen to be at the time in relation to the Court's other activities – in Philip Roberts's opinion, its existence can be entirely attributed to the persistence of William Gaskill as one of the theatre's Artistic Directors, together with Howell and Brighton (Roberts, 1986, p. 58).

At the same time, it is all too easy to concentrate solely on the radicalism of people like Howell and Brighton without also showing just how responsive they were to existing historical traditions. Whereas their pioneering work always attempted to make theatre directly relevant to the lives of young people, their programmes always drew attention to the main repertoire of the ESC. In an age that has come full circle, whereby the concerns of young people sometimes seem to be the *only thing* worth exploring dramatically, it would be remarkable nowadays to see, as Brighton did in April 1970, praise for Michael Blakemore's production of George Bernard Shaw's *Widowers' Houses* (1892) that was playing on the main stage and prefacing the event by saying, '[a]s you no doubt know, this is Shaw's first play completed in 1892 when he was 36 years old' (Brighton, 1970). Not only does this refreshingly assume a prior historical knowledge, but a belief in the value of young people's exposure to unfamiliar work, whether it be from the classical canon or Howard Barker's *No One Was Saved* (1970), written especially for the YPTS. This refusal to patronize, together with an openness to address both contemporary and classical work, stands in contrast with much Theatre in Education work today, which seems to be concerned with producing narrow and imaginatively restrictive issue-led projects on topics such as drugs, bullying or self-harm rather than providing the opportunities for young people to experience the sheer diversity of drama. Far from being dangerous radicals, figures such as Howell and Brighton not only showed a genuine respect for the Royal Court's past but also introduced a far-reaching schematic to how its future could be envisaged.

Notes

1. For accounts of this exclusion, see Roberts (1986, pp. 123–38) and Doty and Harbin (1990, pp. 99–102).
2. There is some contradiction in figures here, with Howell's draft outline for the scheme to the Arts Council citing a total of 20,000 schoolchildren attending performances since 1966 (Howell, 1969b).
3. Programme notes for the Royal Court Schools Scheme, *The Sport of My Mad Mother*, Undated, Arts Council of Great Britain archive 34/41.
4. For accounts of the row, see Roberts (1999, pp. 132–5) and Saunders (2011, pp. 1–17).

Works cited

Allen, J. (1969) 'Letter to Jean Bullwinkle', 6 May, Arts Council of Great Britain archive 34/41.

Barber, J. (1969) '140 Children act out "Revolution" Theme', *Telegraph*, 28 August.

Brighton, P. (1970) 'Letter to Schools', 10 April, Arts Council of Great Britain archive 34/41.

Browne, T.W. (1975) *Playwright's Theatre: The English Stage Company at the Royal Court* (London: Pitman Publishing).

Bullwinkle, Jean (1970a) 'Memo to Lord Goodman, The English Stage Company', 14 May, Arts Council of Great Britain archive 34/41.

—— (1970b) 'Memo to Nelson V. Linklater, English Stage Company', 19 May, Arts Council of Great Britain archive 34/41.

—— (1970c) 'Memo to Mr Linklater, English Stage Company', 1 June, Arts Council of Great Britain archive 34/41.

Capon, S. (1969) 'Extract from Miss Susanna Capon's Report on the English Stage Company', 24 August, Arts Council of Great Britain archive 34/41.

Cohen, S. (1972) *Folk Devils and Moral Panics: The Creation of Mods and Rockers* (London: MacGibbon and Kee).

Doty, G.A. and B.J. Harbin (eds) (1990) *Inside the Royal Court Theatre 1956–1981* (Baton Rouge: Louisiana State University Press).

Eden, J.H. (1970) 'Letter to Nelson V. Linklater', 15 May, Arts Council of Great Britain archive 34/41.

Goode, E. and N. Ben-Yehuda (1994) *Moral Panics: The Social Construction of Deviance* (Oxford: Blackwell).

Gordon, M.I. (1969) 'Visit to the Royal Court Theatre 27 April 1969', Arts Council of Great Britain archive 34/41.

Greig, D. (2008) 'Rough Theatre' in R. D'Monté and G. Saunders (eds) *Cool Britannia: British Political Drama in the 1990s* (Basingstoke and New York: Palgrave Macmillan), pp. 208–21.

Hodson, G. (1970) 'Report of a Visit, Tuesday 2 June 1970, to Royal Court Theatre's The Theatre Upstairs, *The Sport of My Mad Mother*', Arts Council of Great Britain archive 34/41.

Howell, J. (1969a) 'Letter to Participating Schools on the Edward Bond Season', 28 January, Arts Council of Great Britain archive 34/41.

—— (1969b) 'For the Consideration of the Drama and Young People's Theatre Panel', 29 May, Arts Council of Great Britain archive 34/41.

Jenkin, P. (1970) 'Letter to Lord Goodman', 11 May, Arts Council of Great Britain archive 34/41.

Lewis, P. (1969) 'Astonishing this Insight into What Your Children Think', *Daily Mail*, 18 August.

Linklater, N.V. (1970) 'Memo to the Chairman, English Stage Company', 14 September, Arts Council of Great Britain archive 34/41.

Lord Goodman (1970a) 'Memo to Nelson V. Linklater', 5 May, Arts Council of Great Britain archive 34/41.

—— (1970b) 'Memo from Chairman to Drama Director, Royal Court Schools Productions', 2 June, Arts Council of Great Britain archive 34/41.

McGrath, J. (1981) *A Good Night Out – Popular Theatre: Audience, Class and Form* (London: Methuen).

Motton, G. (2009) *Helping Themselves: The Left-Wing Middle Classes in Theatre and the Arts* (Deal: Leveller's Press).

Rees, R. (1992) *Fringe First: Pioneers of Fringe Theatre on Record* (London: Oberon).

Ridout, N. (2009) *Theatre & Ethics* (Basingstoke and New York: Palgrave Macmillan).

Roberts, P. (1986) *The Royal Court Theatre: 1965–72* (London: Routledge).

—— (1999) *The Royal Court and the Modern Stage* (Cambridge: Cambridge University Press).

Sandbrook, D. (2006) *White Heat: A History of Britain in the Swinging Sixties* (London: Little, Brown).

Saunders, G. (2011) 'Tickets, Critics and Censorship: The Royal Court, the Arts Council and *The Spectator* 1969–1970', *Theatre Notebook*, 64 (2), pp. 1–17.

Index

Printed and bound in the United States of America